A WESSEX NATIVITY

A WESSEX NATIVITY

Celebrating Midwinter in Somerset, Dorset and Wiltshire

COMPILED BY

JOHN CHANDLER

First published in the United Kingdom in 2010
by The Hobnob Press, PO Box 1838, East Knoyle, Salisbury, SP3 6FA
www.hobnobpress.co.uk

Some material included in this publication was previously published in *A Wiltshire Christmas* (Alan Sutton 1991), *A Somerset Christmas* (Alan Sutton 1994), *Thomas Hardy's Chistmas* (Alan Sutton 1997) and *A Country House Christmas* (Sutton Publishing 1999)

British Library Cataloguing in Publication Data
A catalogue record for this book is available from the British Library

ISBN 978-1906978-22-8
Typeset in Minion Pro 12/16pt. Typesetting and origination by John Chandler
Printed by Lightning Source

The illustration used on the cover and title page is 'Christmas', an etching by Robin Tanner published in 1929, and reproduced by kind permission of the University for the Creative Arts, Farnham.

Contents

Acknowledgements

THIS BOOK, WHICH includes material collected intermittently over twenty years, owes an enormous debt to the staff, past and present, of libraries and record offices in the Wessex region. These include Bath Reference Library; University of the West of England Library, Bristol; University of Bristol Library; Wiltshire & Swindon History Centre, Chippenham; Wiltshire Heritage Museum Library, Devizes; Dorset History Centre, Dorchester; Dorchester Reference Library; Dorset County Museum, Dorchester; Exeter Central Library; Westcountry Studies Library, Exeter; University of Exeter Library; Salisbury Reference Library; Swindon Central Library; Somerset Archives, Taunton; Somerset Studies Library, Taunton; Somerset Archaeological & Natural History

Society, Taunton; Weston Super Mare Library; Yeovil Reference Library.

Authorship and source, including copyright acknowledgement where appropriate, of all extracts are given in the text and footnotes. I have written the unattributed pieces. The vignette illustrations have been drawn from various out-of-copyright sources and are included for decoration only. I owe formal thanks to the Dorset, Somerset, and Wiltshire & Swindon archive services for permitting me to publish manuscript sources in their care: in the footnotes documentary sources are abbreviated DHC, SRO and WSA respectively.

In the four anthologies from which some of the material included here derives (see Introduction for details) I offered my thanks to the many individuals who helped me during their compilation in the 1990s. My principal new debt is to my wife Ruth, for her constant support and encouragement to finish it at last. It will solve our Christmas present problem this year, and we hope that it will solve yours.

JHC
November 2010

Introduction

OME YEARS AGO (books about Christmas tend to hark back to an undefined past) I was commissioned by a publisher to compile an anthology of writing about Christmas in Wiltshire. Somerset followed, and then two more, so that by the time I tackled Dorset a pattern was emerging and themes recurred.[1] Those books are long out of print, but I occasionally hear of carol services that have rifled them, and I continue to be bemused by everyone's annual submission to the tyrant 'Christmas spirit'. A potent magic indeed, as the Christmas phenomenon (and its anthologist) sweeps up history, literature, religion and folklore, laced with rose-tinted nostalgia. We are encouraged to enjoy it, and to behave in extraordinary and out-of-character ways – and most of us do, even if we are not quite sure why.

I feel freer about it now. Most of my own family imperatives to toe the Christmas line have passed, and now as my own publisher my editorial constraints have gone too.[2] So this is a different book from its predecessors. It remains a celebration of Christmas, in a way, and it includes a good deal of what I collected before. But I have read more, discovered more and thought more about the knot of traditions entangled in the modern Christmas, so there are a great many additions and revisions. It is a much longer book, too, since in

---

1 *A Wiltshire Christmas* (1991); *A Somerset Christmas* (1994); *Thomas Hardy's Christmas* (1997); *A Country House Christmas* (1999); all published by Alan Sutton / Sutton Publishing.

2 In 2001 I restarted Hobnob Press, publisher of this volume.

effect it combines three separate county treatments into one. I hope that, as a sampler for dipping into it will entertain, and also that it will provide a resource for those who find Christmas intriguing, or who need inspiration when planning a seasonal entertainment.

The Wessex of my title embodies the historic southern English counties of Dorset, Somerset and Wiltshire, the land that I know best. There is a common misapprehension that Thomas Hardy reinvented the name of the Saxon kingdom of Wessex as the setting for his novels. He seems to have believed so himself, and he was certainly responsible for popularising the term, and for spawning its widespread current use for business and tourism. But William Barnes had written of people appreciating his dialect 'beyond the bounds of Wessex' in 1868, six years earlier than its first appearance in Hardy's *Far from the madding crowd*. Hardy's Wessex went further, but the dialect of Barnes (according to Hardy himself) was restricted to Dorset and the areas to the north and north-west.[1] So I think that I may impose some homogeneity on my three counties, for the purpose of this book, even if the Wessex landscapes encountered between Swindon and Lyme, Bournemouth, Minehead and Bath, display great variety.

Medieval saint's day festivals were often regarded as three-day events – the eve (the day before), the mass (the day itself) and the morrow (the day after). This book loosely reflects the sequence, beginning with the build-up and preparations, then taking us through Christmas day, and winding down into New Year. Within this arrangement is a hybrid text, partly anthology, partly my own writing. I have linked and introduced the anthology pieces with short passages in italics, but I have also written more extended essays about, for instance, the first Christmas card, the Glastonbury thorn and misrule. Without making things too serious I have tried to approach Christmas as a historian interested in the culture, traditions and

1   See Hearl, T W, 'The origin of Hardy's "Wessex"', *Somerset & Dorset Notes & Queries*, xxix (1969), 63-4; Chedzoy, A, 'A note on "Wessex"', *Somerset & Dorset Notes & Queries*, xxxvi (2008), 265-6.

social dynamics of our most significant annual festival; and I have tried to reflect the idiosyncratic ways in which it has been celebrated in Wessex, and the contribution of Wessex people and traditions to the universal Christmas.

The history of Christmas has been long studied and written about, and it may be helpful at the outset to put the whole strange phenomenon into context.[1] Many cultures and religions have evolved midwinter festivals, to mark the turning point in the sun's annual cycle. The vast Roman empire, out of which Christianity grew, had several such traditions inherited from the peoples it conquered. When, three centuries after its founder's death, Christianity became accepted as the state religion, it absorbed elements of the pagan midwinter, and began to identify the birth of Jesus with the rebirth of the sun at the winter solstice. The claim now posted annually outside churches that 'Christmas is Christ's Birthday', has absolutely no biblical authority, and seems in fact to be contradicted by the birth narrative in Luke's gospel – shepherds did not 'abide' in fields during the cold Palestine winter. But Christmas has stuck at 25 December.

It has been the custom – and remains a useful shorthand – to divide the history of the English Christmas into three periods, changing at around 1600 and 1850. The changes were gradual, and the dates are very approximate. By 1600 the Christmas celebrated in England, just as the language spoken, reflected the two great cultural traditions which underpin Englishness. One, inherited from southern Europe, included the pagan Roman celebrations of feasting, holidays extending over several days, present-giving and misrule – or topsy-turvydom – into which were incorporated Christian festivals.

---

1   Particularly valuable are Hutton, R, *The stations of the sun* (Oxford UP, 1996), 1-123; Pimlott, J A R, *The Englishman's Christmas: a social history* (Hassocks: Harvester Press, 1978); Golby, J M, and Purdue, A W, *The making of the modern Christmas* (Batsford, 1986); Miller, D, *Unwrapping Christmas* (Oxford 1993). The following paragraphs rely on these works, and on arguments developed later in this book.

These centred on the birth, circumcision and baptism of Jesus Christ, and the feasts of a cluster of saints – Nicholas, Stephen, Thomas and others – which fell around this time. The medieval church crystallized all this into the twelve days of Christmas, established patterns of religious services, and introduced familiar elements, such as the crib, the nativity play and the carol.

The other tradition arrived from northern Europe, brought by successive migrations of Celtic, Anglo-Saxon and Viking peoples, and their contribution is more obscure and diverse. Grouped under the obscure name 'Yule', their contribution to midwinter celebration seems to have included decoration with greenery (including holly, ivy and mistletoe); dressing up in disguise and begging (guising, mumming, hoggling); fire rituals, including candles, yule logs or brands and ashen faggots; and blessing animals and crops (the wassail). And just as the Latin and Teutonic elements melded into the English language, so the Mediterranean and Norse traditions became confused and combined into the English Christmas.

After about 1600 the traditional Christmas, along with other reminders of the pagan and Catholic past, came under attack from religious zealots and, to a lesser extent, mainstream protestants. Outlawed but never extinguished during the 17th century, Christmas survived, but in a watered-down strain. Shifts in society loosened the bonds of local hospitality, communal holidays and rural traditions. By 1800 the calendar customs linked to the agricultural year were becoming irrelevant to many in an industrialised, urban world; and Christianity, where it was observed at all, took many different forms. Christmas day remained a holiday, and Christmas itself a nostalgic, if irrelevant ideal; but it was treated with indifference, in much the same way as most people today enjoy a bank holiday at Whitsun with little interest in its religious or cultural significance.

Christmas was rescued during the 1840s, it might be said, as a form of social engineering. Already writers, such as Washington Irving and the young Charles Dickens, were trying to reconstruct a traditional 'baronial' style Christmas, replete with medieval traditions, as part of a harking-back to a golden age before the industrial revolution. In 1843 Dickens wrote *A Christmas Carol*, which preached consideration by the rich for the poor, the centrality of the loving family, and kindness to children. At a stroke Christmas was revitalised, as a tool for reconciling the widening gulf between the new working and middle classes, and it was embraced with enthusiasm by the latter, fearful of where such a gulf might lead. One thing led to another. Rapidly old customs were re-invented, such as the carol, which now reflected Victorian piety; or refined, such as the tree, which came to symbolize the united family; or relocated, such as gifts (formerly given at new year), which now focussed on toys and sweets for children, and charitable giving to the deserving poor. And new customs emerged, including the sending of greetings cards (1840s), filling of stockings (1850s), and performance of pantomimes (1860s). An old character from the mumming plays, the eponymous Sir Christmas or Father Christmas, became identified with a fictional American character, Santa Claus, based on St Nicholas (rampant by the 1880s), and was ruthlessly exploited for commercial gain thereafter. New 'traditions' and motifs arrived – robins, reindeer, crackers, bells – sometimes from nowhere; the King broadcast to the empire (1930s); and turkey and plum pudding became the standard Christmas fare. The Victorian middle-class Christmas filtered eventually to every corner of society, fuelling nostalgia, indigestion and marital disharmony.

It is against so variegated a background that this book has been compiled. Time and again its contributors (myself included) dive into the first age of Christmas, either to try to understand it, or to bring it back, or to regret its passing, or to use it to make sense of what is going on around us. Sometimes we dip into the bran tub of Christmas to find a meaning quite different from the conventional Christian message, about human nature, the supernatural, rustic humour or simply surviving the winter.

Superficially Christmas is a time of jollity, fellowship and excess. Scratch the surface and we find also nostalgia, bitterness – tragedy even. Go deeper still and we discover that a society's response to Christmas reflects society itself. I hope that my multi-layered approach to a fascinating subject, which so profoundly affects everyone every year, will appeal to Wessex people interested in their history, and to Christmas enthusiasts generally.

John Chandler
East Knoyle

1
Wassailing and Other Folk Customs

HIS EVENING I went down to Bath to stay with Thersie at 13 Raby Place till Saturday. A stormy morning and one is all the more glad that the wedding morning yesterday was so gloriously lovely. John Cozens carried my carpet bag to the station and entertained me on the way with reminiscences of the time when he was the chief singer in Langley Burrell and the head of the Wassailers. When the old 'Wassailing Set' broke up John took possession of the ancient 'Wassailing Bowl' which he uses now to feed his fowls with. He promised it to me and he also promised to dictate to me some day from memory the old Langley Wassailing Song which they used to sing and also their Langley Christmas Carol.

John said in regard to that he thought this Christmas Carol was as good as any of the hymns sung in Church if it were sung in any form. But it depended on the form it was sung in.

The Langley Burrell Wassailers he said were famous for being the best in all the country round. No one could beat them or come anight them. They used to go to both the Langleys, both the Tythertons, Draycot, Chippenham, etc. John says the singing in Langley Burrell Church was never very good. 'It was a sort of humbling job.'[1]

---

1   Plomer, W (ed.) *Kilvert's Diary* (1960 ed.), ii, 303-4.

So wrote the Revd Francis Kilvert in his diary on 2 January 1873, comparing carol singing with the performances of an alternative ritual, by then discontinued.[1] *'Wassail' derives from Old English* wes-hāl, *meaning 'good health', and once this passed out of the vernacular its participants smoothed the name into their dialect, or tried to make sense of it. Later in January 1873 Kilvert recorded the words of the Langley wassail, which began 'We'll sail and we'll sail all over the town . . .' – an ingenious derivation recorded also just over the Gloucestershire border in 1969.*[2] *But 'good health' remained the sentiment, as a midwinter blessing for the coming year – to people, to farm animals and to crops. In Wessex, as elsewhere, these three classes of beneficiary have all been wassailed, either separately or in combination, and the ritual has at times been merged into other seasonal celebrations.*

Although widespread across England, wassailing customs varied between regions. In the cider country of Somerset and Dorset, and spilling over into Devon, it was the apple-orchards that most needed blessing. In the dairying claylands of north Wiltshire and the Upper Thames it was the cattle. Wherever the tradition was maintained it seems to have involved drinking (the wassailing cup or bowl), singing and – more often than not – begging, all in the name of good fellowship.

The Victorian and later folklore collectors, such as Alfred Williams and Walter Raymond, were keen to observe the wassail and record its variations, because they sensed (to some extent correctly) that it was of high antiquity. Enthused by Sir James Frazer's The Golden Bough *(1890), which brought together folk customs from around the world and wove them into a plausible ancient system, they sought and found parallels in other cultures, and so postulated for the wassail a prehistoric origin.*

1 Discussed by Hultin, N C, 'The songs and ballads of R F Kilvert', *Folklore*, xcii (1981), 174-89.

2 Plomer, W (ed.) *Kilvert's Diary* (1960 ed.), ii, 315; cf Cawte, E C, *Ritual animal disguise* (1978), 145-6.

Williams, desperately short of money, was paid a guinea by a local newspaper for the following contribution in 1926 (he repeated most of it for a rival paper two years later).[1] He had served in India during the First World War, and was keen to bring his oriental experience to bear on the subject.

The Wiltshire Wassail
Alfred Williams

HE CUSTOM OF wassailing was popular all over England, but the manner of its observance differed widely in almost every county or area. It is not an easy matter to give reasons for the many forms in which it occurs here and there. Some have thought that it was identical with the 'waes-hael' of the Saxons. It was usual for the ancient itinerant minstrels to bear a bowl of spiced wine to the houses of the well-to-do at Christmas time, and to drink 'wassail' to them, hoping, of course, to receive a larger entertainment in return. This explanation is as plausible as any, touching the more modern idea of the wassail; but there are so many other features connected with it that it is well-nigh impossible to explain them all to our satisfaction.

I speak of the Wiltshire wassail, but I have never found that it had any special or distinctive feature of its own. It seems to me, from what I can gather, that there was one general wassail custom pertaining to north Wiltshire and South Gloucestershire. This custom may have had a wider observance; but if it did I have never met with any evidence of it. Except on the line of the Thames, and round about Malmesbury, I know nothing about it. At Appleton, Cumnor and Eynsham, near Oxford, the wassail was observed. This I was told by

1   Clark, L, *Alfred Williams: his life and work* (1945), 177. The following passage was published in *Wiltshire Gazette*, 2 Dec. 1926, and another version (from which a few sentences have been added) appeared in *North Wilts Herald*, 21 Dec. 1928.

aged people of that district living before the war; but I could obtain no particulars, nor any version of the song. Away from the Thames line, either in Wiltshire or Berkshire, I have not heard anything about it. No doubt it was observed; but the observance lingered longer in some quarters than it did in others.

I always considered that I was fortunate to have undertaken my search for folk songs just when I did, i.e. in 1914, before the war came and altered the face of everything. At Cricklade, that famous old Thames-side town, noted for every kind of sport and miscellaneous activity, I found the last living member of the company of local wassailers. The old man, who was ninety years old at the time that I knew him, as well as being a wassailer – he was known to the locality as 'Wassail' Harvey – was a rare singer of folk songs. In my collection of *Upper Thames Folk Songs* there are many good pieces of his rendering; he knew several hundreds of folk songs, besides a large mass of folklore. It also fell to his lot to act in a rustic play, 'The Shepherd and the Maiden', that was produced every year at Bark Harvest at the Cricklade tanyards. This too is in the book mentioned above; and though it is not a brilliant piece, it is certainly readable, and interesting as a folklore relic. From him I learned full details of the local wassail as it was practised in his day; it had been discontinued for about half a century.

There was a recognised company of wassailers at Cricklade, trained to conduct the ceremony. They had an effigy of an ox, made of a withy frame with a cured skin stretched over it. The head, horns and tail were intact. The breast and foreparts were stuffed with straw, and they fitted two small red lamps into the eye-sockets. Herein we have a clue to the exact significance of the wassail, which was not merely a drinking of healths, but a ceremony performed in order to obtain fertility of crops, and the prosperity of flocks and herds. It was only an effigy that figured in the rite in later years; but earlier it was a live animal. In this we may see the gradual decay of the ceremony. The change from the live beast to the effigy was the first step – faith in the efficacy of the rite had waned, and the husbandman no longer lent his ox to walk in the procession. But popular enthusiasm kept the custom going for a time, until, we may suppose, the cool reception given to the wassailers quenched their ardour. If no gifts were forthcoming, and if the bowl were not filled, there would be no procession, and no song. The fact is that wassailing, as a popular custom, had become unprofitable.

At Christmas time, while the mummers and carol singers were going their rounds, the wassailers paraded in procession. Two of the sturdiest crept inside the framework of the effigy and carried it along on their backs, imitating the swaying motion of the beast. When the spectators pressed too near the ox was made to swish its tail. This kept a clear space for the wassailers, and provided amusement for the crowd. The chief wassailer walked before, carrying the wooden bowl, that was decorated with ribbons and mistletoe. The remainder of the company followed behind, dressed in fancy costumes ornamented with coloured ribbons. At every farmhouse, or dwelling of the better class people, they sang their merry song; and the mistress of the house, or the maid, brought out warmed spiced ale, or hot punch, with toast and roasted apples, and replenished the bowl. They also pinned new ribbons to the dresses of the wassailers, which were treasured as trophies. Old 'Wassail' Harvey told me that there used to be many other things connected with the Cricklade practice in the time of his father and grandfather, but they had fallen into disuse.

The Cricklade wassail song is worth reading; and one has only to compare it with the Yorkshire version to see that it is the better of the two, and more suggestive of vigorous, healthy local life.

WILTSHIRE WASSAIL SONG
Wassail, wassail all over the town,
Our toast is white, and our ale is brown;
Our bowl it is made of a sycamore tree,
And so is good beer of the best barley.

Here's to the ox, and to his long horn,
May God send our maester a good crap [crop] o' corn!
A good crap o' corn, and another o' hay,
To pass the cold wintry winds away.

Here's to the ox, and to his right ear,
May God send our maester a happy New Year!
A happy New Year, as we all may see,
With our wassailing bowl we will drink unto thee.

Come pretty maidens, I suppose there are some,
Never let us poor men stand on the cold stone;
The stones they are cold, and our shoes they are thin,
The fairest maid in the house, let us come in;
Let us come in, and see how you do.
MAID: Yes, if you will, and welcome, too.

Here's to the maid, and the rosemary tree,
The ribbons are wanted, and that you can see:
The ribbons are wanted, and that you can see:
With our wassailing bowl we will drunk unto thee.

Now, boteler, come, fill us a bowl o' the best,
And we hope that thy soul in heaven may rest;
But if you do bring us a bowl o' the small,
Then down shall go boteler, bowl and all,
Then down shall go boteler, bowl, and all.

Now maester and mistress, if you are within,
Send down some of your merry, merry men
That we may eat and drink before the clock strikes ten;
Our jolly wassail,
When joy comes unto our jolly wassail.

Village people in Yorkshire, in celebrating the wassail at Christmas, carried with them 'Advent Images', i.e. images of the Virgin and the Child. The images were borne in a box containing evergreens and whatever flowers could be obtained at that season of the year. The occupiers of the house at which the children sang the song, if they gave anything, were entitled to choose any flower or leaf they desired from the box. This was solemnly preserved, in the belief that it would cure the toothache. This observance is seen to be partly of a religious origin; but the true wassail custom is undoubtedly much older than the Christian era.

In Herefordshire, also two elements, the Christian and the pagan, were present in the wassail. The Christian element is recognised in the first part of the ceremony; and this was common to several parts of the country. On Wassail Eve, beyond the Severn, the farmer and his servants walked out into a field of young wheat, and there they kindled thirteen fires, twelve small in a circle, and a larger one in the middle. Having done this, and pledged each other with a cup of old cider, they returned to the house. The thirteen fires represented the Christ and the Twelve Apostles.

At the farm a supper was provided by the mistress and maids, at which figured a large flat cake with a hole in the centre. After supper the company, including the bailiff, or herdsman, proceeded to the cattle-stall, carrying the cake, and a bowl of strong ale. There the farmer pledged the first ox, with a draught of ale, and all the others followed on, toasting the oxen, according to their respective degrees, and calling them by name, trace of which appears in the Cricklade custom. Following this, the farmer took the cake and hung it on the horn of the finest ox. The ox was then tickled to make it toss the cake. If the ox threw the cake forward into the crib it was claimed by the bailiff; and if it was thrown behind it was taken by the mistress. The remainder of the evening was spent in mirth and merriment.

In Devonshire the wassail took a different form. Here it was the apple trees that were toasted; but the underlying idea was the same, i.e. the wish for rural prosperity and increase. We gather that in Devonshire the farmer and his work-people at evening went into the orchard bearing a bowl of old cider, with roasted apples in it. There, standing round one of the most fertile trees, they drank of the cider and toasted the tree with this, or a similar rhyme:

> Here's to thee, good apple tree,
> Well to bear – pocket-fuls, hat-fuls,
> Peck-fuls, bushel bag-fuls.

Then they drank more cider, and threw the remainder, with the roasted apples, over the tree.

My own opinion is that the true origin of the Wiltshire wassail was in the ox, either as the symbol of fertility, or as representing the idea of tillage, and, consequently, of general prosperity. It is not impossible that the ox incorporated both these ideas. In any case, the Cricklade practice appears to have been consistent with the original tradition. This tradition was Aryan, and it was carried to this country by Aryan settlers, probably by the founders of the early Celtic group.

This particular homage to the ox is observed all over India at the present time, as everyone knows who has been there. Accordingly, the sacred ox roams wherever it pleases, feeds at will upon the farmer's crops, or the Brahman's meal in the bazaars. It walks about the streets of the stateliest city, enters the temple and lies down, and no one thinks of molesting it. In the old English May Day festivals the ox was led in solemn procession, covered with gay trappings, and adorned with garlands of flowers; and I have seen exactly the same thing during the festivals at the holy city of Hardwar, in North India. So the ox in procession, in the Wiltshire wassail, is quite in keeping with the older custom, both here and in the east.

Wassailing the trees, as was the rule in Devonshire, was, without doubt, Eastern in its origin; how much of our folklore has come to us across the wild wastes and deserts of South-West Asia and Europe? Tree-worship is common today all over India, and I have often witnessed it round about Roorkee, in the Punjaub. There women go into the orchards with milk, flowers and sweetmeats, and, after winding threads round the trunk, place their offerings at the base, or throw the milk (or water) over the tree and depart. Fertility is the root idea in this, as it was in the Devonshire custom. It is to be noted that all the customs were observed primarily by village people, farmers and husbandmen. The more enlightened dwellers in towns and cities took no share in them, and were not directly concerned. The connection was between contemporary and primitive occupations, and as such it has a certain historical interest as pointing not only to our ethnical, but also to our geographical origin.

A few years earlier, prompted by Cecil Sharp's publication and comments on a wassail song from Bratton, near Minehead, a devotee of Frazer's comparative approach to folklore had taken the origins of the Somerset wassail to remarkable and improbable lengths.

Wassailing the Orchards
W O Beament

 N THE NOTE on [Sharp's wassailing song] the ceremony as practised at Bratton is described, which adds to the accounts given by previous correspondents the ceremonies of dancing round the tree while singing, and of stamping upon the ground at the conclusion of the dance. However the writer of that note and correspondents . . . would assign the ritual to the cult of an earth spirit or possibly the Magna Mater. That is to post-date the whole of the survival which, it seems impossible to doubt, has come down mutilated but uncontaminated from the awakening of the religious sense among the 'pre Aryan' peoples of Western Europe. There are five points in the survival which deserve mention: (i) The Tree, (ii) The Song and Dance, (iii) The Libation, (iv) The Noise and (v) The Toast placed in the Branches.

(i) The Tree is a living sacred Pillar (i.e. a phallic object) and is thus the localization of the spirit in *mana* which causes all generation, so the fruitfulness which is sought is not merely that of apples but of all crops, of herds and of men. This spirit or *Daimon* as he is better described reappears in folk lore as the *Dying Youth* whose death and resurrection synchronize with the fall and spring of the year. We are taken back to a shadowy age where matter and spirit – man and god were undistinguished and undefined: all that can really be grasped is the idea of *mana* – power or energy – which can flow from and to all being material and immaterial.

(ii) The Ritual Song whose actions have become erased and of whose original words little trace remains once described and represented an act of generation, birth or fructification. Words and pantomime alike are as species of 'sympathetic magic' – they induce *mana* rather than form an act of worship.

(iii) The Libation of cyder, poured, according to Mr Phillpotts, on the roots, but originally over the tree (cf. Jacob pouring wine on the Pillar of Bethel – 'the house of God,' i.e., the localization of Yahweh's divinity) is not so much a drink for a spirit – as a carrying forward from one year to the next of the life juice of the Tree. That cyder last year was the juice of a living and bearing tree – it has much *mana* which by the pouring out is brought into contact with the 'dead' tree.

(iv) The Sacred Dance has imitated the desired result; the Song has said in words what the Dance has done in act; the Life of the Old has been brought into contact with the New. We now see a later stratum of cult, in which the 'Life Force' has been realized as a more or less anthropomorphic Spirit, 'who must be awakened' from the sleep of death. Hence the shouts, stamping and gun-firing.

(v) In nearly all representations of Sacred Trees we find birds also shewn. Everyone will remember the doves of Aphrodite and that goddess's connection with Adonis who is only a Syrian personification of the Vegetation-Daimon. Hence the offering of toast for the birds, which is a still later accretion to the original ceremony, marking the era of development of the full blown god and goddess.[1]

Before the advent of this 'scientific' (or pseudo-scientific nonsense) approach to folklore emerged, there was a gentler, less complicated appreciation of the dying tradition. Walter Raymond, a native of Yeovil, devoted much of his life to the study of Somerset folklore and traditions, and during the 1890s published several novels of country life, in the genre set by Thomas Hardy. Here, from Tryphena in Love, *which appeared in 1895, we find ourselves in the middle of a jittery romantic scene between hero and heroine – when there is a kerfuffle outside.*

Catching the Words
Walter Raymond

ISS MERVIN SEEMED to take a great fancy to you, John,' she said, suddenly looking up from the burning logs.

The words startled him. He could not hide his agitation sufficiently to answer her.

But happily, to his relief, at that moment came the sound of voices by the porch.

'The Wassailers!' he cried eagerly. 'Now I must get the words. Find some paper to write them down. Do, Tryphena! There's a dear.'

The singing began at once.

The black dog o' Langport have a-burned off his tail,
An' this is the night of our jolly Wassail.
Vor 'tes our Wassail,

---

1   *Somerset & Dorset Notes & Queries*, xvi (1919), 139-40.

An' 'tes your Wassail,
An' joy be to you, vor 'tes our Wassail.

'Quick, Tryphena; have you got it? Quick.'

Wassail! Wassail! all roun' about town,
The cup it is white, the ale it is brown;
Vor 'tes our Wassail,
An' 'tes your Wassail,
An' joy be to you, vor 'tes our Wassail.

The cup is a-made o' the merry ashen tree;
The beer is a-brewed o' the best barley,
Vor 'tes our Wassail,
An' 'tes your Wassail,
An' joy be to you, vor 'tes our Wassail.

'You will have to do it when they come in, Tryphena. I would
not miss getting the words for anything,' he said, his voice trembling
with anxiety.

Missus an' Measter a-zitten by the vire,
An' we poor travellers a-traipsen drough the mire,
Vor 'tes our Wassail,
An' 'tes your Wassail,
An' joy be to you, vor 'tes our Wassail.

Missus an' Measter be you zo well a-pleased
To zet 'pon your table-board the white loaf an' cheese,
Vor 'tes our Wassail,
An' 'tes your Wassail,
An' joy be to you, vor 'tes our Wassail.

Maid, perty maid, wi' the little zilver tag
Now do ee urn to door an' show your perty lag,
Vor 'tes our Wassail,
An' 'tes your Wassail,
An' joy be to you, vor 'tes our Wassail.

'Nip down to door, Tryphena. I suppose they mus' come in. They'll be ill-pleased else,' cried Mrs Pettigrew from the foot of the stairs in an unwilling tone of discontent. She regarded such songs and rites as obsolete, but it was bad judgement to offend the labouring folk. John, thinking only of the verses, wistfully watched the girl depart.

Maid, perty maid, wi' the perty zilver lace
Now do ee come to door an' show your perty face,
Vor 'tes our Wassail,
An' 'tes your Wassail,
An' joy be to you, vor 'tes our Wassail.

'I won't have 'em go upstairs, Tryphena,' added Mrs Pettigrew sharply. 'They'll bring in all too much dirt as 'tes.'

Maid, perty maid, wi' the little silver pin,
Then do ee ope the door an' let us all in,
Vor 'tes our Wassail,
An' 'tes your Wassail,
An' joy be to you, vor 'tes our Wassail.

He heard the door open and the clatter of their hob-nailed boots upon the kitchen floor. Then he waited, listening intently to catch Tryphena's voice inquiring about the words. But he could hear nothing clearly above the noise and din of the whole company. And at last, before departing, they sang again:

Missus an' Measter, now we mus' be a-gwain,
But do ee ope the door when we do come again,
Vor 'tes our Wassail,
An' 'tes your Wassail,
An' joy be to you, vor 'tes our Wassail.

Some little time elapsed before Tryphena returned and quietly resumed her seat. 'I've got most of it,' she said, 'and old Abe is coming in tomorrow.'

'You dear,' he cried enthusiastically.

But Tryphena did not respond as formerly, and for a while she was silent. Then gazing into the fire, she began to build her castle in the air. 'Miss Mervin told me what a lot she thought of your saying the poetry, John,' she began . . .[1]

It is easy to see why Walter Raymond was regarded by some as a Somerset Hardy, and for a while he enjoyed considerable popularity – his collected works were reissued in a uniform memorial edition after his death. Twelve years Hardy's junior, he outlived him by three years, dying in 1931. But he was a genial optimist, and his plots do not contain the harshness and depth of the master. He had a good ear for dialect, as the passages included in this collection demonstrate, picked up – it is said – by eavesdropping the gossip in country pubs, such as the Royal Oak in Withypool on Exmoor, where he lived for a time.[2]

Raymond was not the only Somerset author to interweave custom and dialect. Here, from the Blackdown Hills in 1923, the writer has thickened the dialogue to the point where the 'vurriner' may have some difficulty.

1   Raymond, W, *Tryphena in love* (1912 ed.), 110-13.
2   Clark, E V, *Walter Raymond: the man, his work and letters* (1933), 43-4.

The Wassailing Party
F W Mathews

HE BIG SETTLE was pushed back from its usual place near the fire, and a sturdy long stool or 'vertu' was placed nearly end-to-end with it, alongside a table, on which reposed several large jugs, with their smaller accompaniments of mugs, one-handled and two-handled, and nearby a jar of tobacco. Beneath the table stretched several pairs of corduroy covered legs, some lanky, some short, some bandy or bowed, and all presenting a solid array of hob-nailed soles facing the warmth of the ashen 'facket' [faggot] that blazed on the broad hearth-stone.

The occasion was the wassailing of the apple-trees, but the purpose of this preliminary meeting was to warm up the inner and outer person before going out into the 'Home Orchet' for the observance of the old custom.

'Wull, maester, us be a comed wance moar to wish th' ole Zummerzet tree gude luck. I kin mind thik ole tree zince a was but zoo high,' said an old weazened man, indicating with his sinewy hands and knotted fingers the height of the tree in its younger days.

'Ees, Dan, wance more, and I be sa glad to zee ee all here, looking sa viddy,' replied the old 'maester', his round face beaming under the influence of good fellowship, pleasant memories, a warm fire – and good 'zider'. 'Now, veel up, me gude vullers, gie a rale gude swig, and let's 'ave a zong or two vore we goes out in the cold. Yu kin gie us wan, cahn'ee, Jan – thik ole lidden about the vuzz-taps.'

'I du most vergit en, maester, but ah'll try what I can du.'

'Yur, yur,' 'That's raight,' 'Goo on, Jan' – from various corners.

'Wull, then, wan leedle drap – yurr goos,' and in a lusty voice he trolled forth the following:

Oh the vuzz he be a blessing ver us all,
He'm a shelter ver the purty burds to rest;
And his taps du make a sparkling vire in Vall,
Oh the vuzz o'bushes all's the vurry best.

Now the vuzz is all a bloomine on the hill,
And the vuzz-bush is a gude ole vriend to I;
Vor e drows his blossoms wi a rare gude will,
If the saison be a lapprey wan or dry.

Oh the vuzz du keep a glowin vaace and bright,
And never lookies dull the whole year droo;
The vuzz-bank's gold's a glorious cheery zight.
He smiles the Old Year out and welcomes Noo.

He du layve off bloomin' so zum voakes du tell,
When luv and kissin's out o' vashion turned;
But I've never know'd layve off – never shall!
Ef du – may all noo-vashioned voak be burned.

Uproarious applause greeted this warm sentiment, and proved the spirit of Marian days not dead, while many an arch approving glance was cast over shoulders at the cheerycheeked maids who stood behind, alert to attend where the jug or cup seemed to need replenishing.

'Now, Tom, thee cast gie us a zong tu, cassen?' quoth Maester.

'Doan know's I caan, zur, but Aw'll tell 'ee a yarn, of yu be a-minded.'

'Awright, goo vore.'

'Wull, I went to Tant'n, zom time agone, and when I was in to Vower Alls [the Four Alls], a chap there told I bout ole – no I ont tell his name – ow 'e comed home wan night bit later'n usual, and that wadden very airly nayther.

'His ole dumman [woman] ad gone to baid and leff the back door unbolted, so he went in pantry and looked round ver summat tu ait, ver the walk 'ome 'ad made en a bit pickish. Wull, in pantry he found a main gude bowl-vull o' custard and a big spune handy by. He took em in by the vire – there was a bit left in grate – and he zot down and tucked into it, and ait the lot. And he enjoyed it, too. Then he zot a bit longer and smoked a pipe, and valled asleep in chair. Next morning 'e went out and done up the hoss and comed in to breakus. Zoon' he clapped his haid inzide door, his wife said, "Purty goins on agin last night. 'Ave 'ee zeed thik basin I put in cubberd in pantry?"

'"Ees, I 'ave sure, and clained en all up. 'Twas mortal gude custard, too."

'"Custard, yu gurt fule," her scraimed, "custard! Why that was starch, yu drunken toad, and *there was dree yards o' lace ver my petticoat in it.*" '

'Ho, ho, ho! Haw, haw, haw!' roared the company at the conclusion of the tale, the initial volley of laughter tailing off into spasmodic bursts and shrieks from one and another as various aspects of the scene tickled the risibilities of the hearers.

'Where du er live tu, dist zay, Tom?' queried one.

'Didden zay at all, and baine gwain to tell,' quoth Tom, 'but I doos a gude laff to mezell every time I passes thik owze when I goes to Tanton market.'

'Thy turn next, Beel, gie us wan of then ole zongs thee grandfather larned thee.'

'Ees, zur, ow'll theaze du – "The Ole Varmer and the Pixy-men".'

'Fuss-raet; toon up an' less 'ave thikky-wan.'

With a throat-clearing sip of the 'zider', and a preliminary adjustment of the unaccustomed collar, Bill gave his song, which though rather long, was listened to with great attention by the company, to whom time was of less moment than a tale, and the making out of a good long evening the recognised procedure for such an event as the celebration of Old Twelfth Eve.

'That's a gude un, Beel,' said Maester, 'and a purty long un, too. However dist mind en all? Time's gittin on, I zee,' glancing over at the 'long-sleever' in the corner. 'Come on, boys, light up the lanterns,' and out trooped all the company of men and lads to the orchard.

'Now then, round in a ring,' and they grouped themselves round the oldest tree in the orchard.

The first part of the ceremonial of wassailing was to take a piece of toasted bread and dip it in a mug of cider, then put it up in the fork of the tree. The one who had placed the bread stood back, the oldest member of the company came forward, pointed an old blunderbuss up into the branches and blazed away, while all the others shouted, 'Hip, hip, hooray!' 'Good luck to thee!' and such other appropriate remarks as occurred to them.

Then, the older members of the company leading with the solemnity befitting such a sober ritual, came the old wassail song:

Wassail, wassail, all round our town,
Our cup it is white and our ale it is brown;
Our bowl is made of the good old ash tree,

So now, my brave fellows, let's drink unto thee.
Hatfuls, capfuls, dreebushel bagfuls,
And a gurt heap under the stairs.
Hip, hip, hurrah (shouted *ad lib.*)

There was an old man who had an old cow,
And how for to keep her he didn't know how;
So he built up a barn for to keep his cow warm,
And a little more cider won't do us no harm.
Harm, me boys, harm; harm, me boys, harm;
A little more cider won't do us no harm.

Down in an old lane there lived an old fox,
And all the day long he sat mopping his chops;
Shall we go and catch him, oh, yes, if we can,
Ten thousand to one if we catch the old man.
Harm, me boys, harm; harm, me boys, harm;
A little more cider won't do us no harm.

A poor little robin sits up in a tree,
And all the day long so merry sings he;
A widdlin and twiddlin to keep himself warm
And a little more cider won't do us no harm.
Harm, me boys, harm; harm, me boys, harm;
A little more cider won't do us no harm.

A lady comes round with her silver pin,
Pray open the door, and let us all in;
For this is our 'sail, our jolly Wassail,
And jolly go we to our jolly Wassail.
Harm, me boys, harm; harm, me boys, harm;
A little more cider won't do us no harm.
Hurrah, Hurrah (again *ad lib.*)

The music was as quaint as the words, and the tune was somewhat like the old barrel organ's tune that I once heard played to a hymn in one of the old country churches, in that it fitted the words sometimes.

'Zing up boys! A little more zider ont du us no harm,' chimed in old Dan, at the conclusion of the song, a remark which of course evoked much laughter, and the production of the required beverage, brought out piping hot by the thoughtful maids. Sipped to the accompaniment of interjected, 'Good luck, ole apple tree,' it proved very comforting.

A final tipple indoors, with a 'mouthful' of bread and cheese, and the ancient ceremony was over, but for the time-honoured concluding song of old Dan, without which none of the assembly would have considered the evening properly brought to a close.

'Now then, Dan'l, "The Juniper Tree" vore us goes home,' and Dan'l, nothing loth, gave the well-known old song, *The Juniper Tree*.

> On the first day of Christmas my true love gave to me
> A part of a juniper tree;
> On the second day of Christmas my true love gave to me
> Two turtle doves and a part of a juniper tree.

And so it went, each verse the longer by one line, and all the other lines repeated, till the last time there came the formidable list of:

> Twelve bulls a-blaring,
> 'leven lords a-leaping,
> Ten ladies a-dancing,
> Nine bears a-biting,
> Eight hares a-running,
> Seven swans a-swimming,
> Six geese a-laying,
> Five golden rings,

Four collie birds,
Three French hens,
Two turtle doves,
And part of a juniper tree.

This memory-taxing catalogue finished, 'Goodnight, Maester; goodnight, Missus,' was the leave-taking, and in the clear night air could be heard for some time, as the various small groups dispersed, the refrain of the old song in different parts of the parish: 'And part of a juniper tree.'[1]

While Raymond and Mathews clearly saw themselves as continuing participants in enjoyable proceedings, others watched from the sideline and tried to analyse what was going on before it died out. Stourton stands near where our three counties meet, on the edge of Blackmore Vale, Hardy's 'land of the little dairies', so it is understandable that, as around Cricklade, the cattle should be blessed by the wassailers. But by 1908, when the custom was reported in The Antiquary, *this significance was forgotten, having died out elsewhere in the neighbourhood.*

A Softer Generation
E E Balch

UITE DISTINCT FROM the mummers, though also coming on Christmas Eve, was the Christmas bull. The head of a bull with great bottle eyes, large horns, and lolling tongue, was manipulated by a man stooping inside a body composed of a broomstick, a hide of sacking and a rope tail.

---

1   Mathews, F W, *Tales of the Blackdown borderland* (Somerset Folk Series 13, 1923), 118-29.

The bull knocked at the door with its horns, and, if allowed to enter, chased the young people round the house, with fearsome curvets and bellowings. Even in the surrounding parishes the Christmas bull is unknown, and I have never heard of the custom being practised in other parts of the country. The man in whose possession the bull was until quite recently, knows that it has been in his family for over one hundred years. It was used till about ten years ago.

On Old Christmas Eve came the wassailers with their traditional song:

Wassail, wassail
All round the town!
Your cup is so white,
And your beer is so brown.

Missus and master,
Now we are come here,
Give us a cup
Of your best Christmas beer.

CHORUS
For it's our wassail,
And a jolly wassail,
And joy be to you,
For it's our wassail.

Pretty little maiden,
With your silver lace,
Open wide your hall-doors
And show us your face.

Pretty little maiden,
With your silver pin,

Open wide your hall-doors
And let us all in.

Missus and master,
A-sitting by the fire,
And we poor sinners
A-dabbing in the mire.

Missus and master,
If you be so willing,
Send out your youngest son
With the round shilling.

Missus and master,
We must be gone,
God bless you all
Till we come again!

The wassailing serves as a link between the jollities connected with Christmas and those which cluster round the agricultural festivals; though the custom of wassailing the apple-trees, which, I believe, survives in Devonshire, has disappeared here. Hardy, rough, and hearty were the men who used to sing such songs as these. A softer generation may well listen to the stories they can tell before they altogether sink into silence.[1]

In fact Somerset wassailing has not sunk into silence, as anyone visiting the Butcher's Arms *at Carhampton on the appropriate evening (Old Twelfth Night) will discover.[2] But our author is correct to link wassailing with other Christmas festivities. Walter Raymond had done this in*

1   *Antiquary* xliv (1908), 381-82.
2   Hutton, R, *The stations of the sun* (1996), 48, describes this and another revival.

Young Sam and Sabina, a novel published more than a decade earlier, in 1894. The hero and heroine engage in a little unnoticed flirtation in the apple orchard, but their wassail is only the sequel to another custom, the ashen faggot, a Wessex variation on the yule log or brand.

A Peculiar Witchery
Walter Raymond

HERE THEY ALL were. Happy souls! of the days before hospitality went away by rail.

'Come on! Zit down! Now then, Missus, where's thik bit o' supper?' cried the farmer, in a voice boisterous enough to raise the roof.

A singular angularity of elbows and knees, which marks the earliest period of a rural festivity, vanishes under the genial influence of good cheer. A roast turkey invites contemplation and affords food for thought. A ham, well cured, is an inspiration, particularly if there still lingers in the mind a recollection of the pig to which it once belonged; and cousin John Priddle had known that pig from its earliest infancy. It puts a man at ease to sit down with an old acquaintance. Every tongue was loosened; every heart was gay; and when supper was finished they drew around for the great carousal.

'Come on! All draw up! Now then, Missus, make haste wi' the cup.'

"Tes a wonderful girt fakket, sure enough,' chirped Christopher.

'Ay, ay! Wi' a extra bind to please Widow Sharman.'

'He'll make the women-volk hop more 'an once, I'll warrant un!' cried cousin John Priddle, rubbing his hands.

'Zo he will. Now then, Missus, dap down the cup 'pon the settle close handy like. Put back the chimbley-crooks. Move out, Sabina. Now then, soce, let's heave un on!'

So the great ashen faggot was lifted upon the hearth, and the eager flames leapt up around it, licking with their red tongues the hazel binds.

Now the glory of the ashen faggot was this. When a bind burst, sometimes with a mighty crack, casting bright sparks and splinters out into the room, and the women shrieked and pushed back their chairs, and the men threw back their heads and laughed, – then, and not until then, the cup was handed round, and everybody drank his best without loss of time, so that it might be drained and filled again before the next explosion.

'I never didn' zee a better fakket, not in all my life,' exulted Christopher.

'I think the vire have a-got hold o' un now,' shouted the farmer, taking up the cup, and resting it upon his knee in readiness.

'Look out! Look out!' cried cousin John Priddle, and Widow Sharman nervously raised her apron to cover her face.

It was a false alarm. The faggot went on burning without any sense of responsibility, just as if the discomfort of thirst and the blessing of cider had ceased to exist.

'Put the cup down avore the vire, Zam. Else he'll get cold,' nervously suggested Mrs Grinter.

'I never didn' zee a fakket hold together so long in all my life,' suggested cousin John Priddle, in considerable anxiety.

'I sim myself, 'tes a funny thing,' agreed Christopher, stroking his bald head to promote thought.

"Tes,' said the widow.

'Zo 'tes,' chimed in Mrs Grinter, with an unusually anxious expression on her little sharp face. 'An' eet o' cou'se, it can't be another. Pick up the cup, Zam. He'll get so hot else we shan't be able to hold un to our lips.'

'I'll be lolled if I shan't want bastin' soon. I be so dry as chips,' moaned Christopher.

'Here, push out measter's little voot-stool, Sabina. Dap down the cup 'pon he. Little bit closer. No, not too close. Zo.'

Farmer Grinter drew the back of his hand across his forehead. 'Do make I puff an' blow,' he said, and sighed at the delay.

'I'll be daazed,' whispered cousin John Priddle, 'if I don't think they bands be witched.'

A fearful solemnity fell upon that party, as if everyone were afraid to speak; and, although the flames were now rushing high up the chimney-back, all stared into the glowing mass and quite forgot their thirst. One by one the binds melted away like wax. As Christopher afterwards protested with suspicious emphasis, they were all 'to a miz-maze like,' and he broke out all over into a most terrible sweat.

The startled voice of Sabina first broke the silence. 'Massy 'pon us! Why, there be chains in the vire.'

'What?' yelled old Sam Grinter, leaping to his feet, making not only the women hop, but Christopher and cousin John Priddle as well. 'Then, so sure's the light, somebody have a-got at my fakket. Dash my wig and burn my feathers! if they didn' chain thik there poor fakket up under they halsen withes so as he couldn' bust. An' we all a-zot round like jackass-wools. That's gwaine beyon' a joke. I don't zee no joke in that.'

'I do call it ignorance,' said cousin John Priddle.

''Tes.' 'Zo 'tes.' 'An' that 'tes,' chorused the ladies.

Just a glimmer of mischief, or was it only a fancy of the firelight, flickered upon Christopher's little round face, and then he said quite quickly, extending his hand for the cup.

'But if they thought to keep Sophia from drinking, they'll be main-well a-sucked in.'

That was the way they always joked Sophia, but she only took the cup, and smiled, and sipped.

The moon was well up and joviality completely restored by the time they were ready to wassail the apple-trees.

'Come on, then! Come on! Have 'ee got your guns?' cried the farmer, as, still clutching the cup, he led the way across the mow-barton, weird with mysterious shadows from the stacks, and into the little dark orchard behind the homestead.

The women-folk had thrown shawls over their heads, and on they all went, laughing, stumbling over the leaning trunks in the uncertain light, and sometimes running into the boughs, on their way to the old Jack Horner tree in the corner.

The ceremony was simple, but impressive. The farmer had brought the sodden toasts from the evening's carousals, and now placed them in the 'vork' of the tree. Then the company repeated the ancient formula:

> Apple-tree, apple-tree
> I do wassail thee
> To blow an' to bear
> Cap-vulls an' hat-vulls an' dree bushel-bag-vulls
> An' my pockets vull, too.

Then they cheered and fired their guns, with such infinite success that even Christopher's old flintlock went off – after a brief interval. And thus, please God, was an admirable crop ensured, and the proceedings came to an end.

Yet not quite to an end. There is a peculiar witchery about the moonlight glancing between apple-trees. It seems to dance and sparkle upon the branches, and yet in the shadow the ground is as black as night. It has a confusing effect upon the brain. A feeling of fantastic unreality as of a ubiquitous will-o'-the-wisp creeps over the imagination, and even Solomon in all his glory might easily lose his way.

They all lost their ways.

The unanimity of Middleney suffered a slight shock on the question of the situation of Church Farm, for Mrs Grinter saw the orchard gate, distinctly and with considerable asperity, in two opposite directions.

Sabina knew she was right, and said so with a self-reliance which carried conviction – at least as far as Ashford was concerned.

So they found themselves apart.

'Look there, Mr Ashford!'

'What is it? Where?'

The girl's arm was raised, pointing to a branch overhanging their heads upon which grew a thick mass glistening in the moonlight.

He stood staring with all his might; but, before he could recognize the mistletoe, with a burst of laughter she had flitted away among the trees.[1]

What is Hoggling?

CHURCHWARDENS' ACCOUNTS, THE yearly tallies of income and expenditure connected with running church and parish, are a rich seam of social history. Rarely do they survive before about 1700, but a few extend back into the middle ages, to offer tantalising glimpses of the local

1   Raymond, W, *Young Sam and Sabina* (1912 ed.), 150-5.

impact of great events. One of the earliest volumes to be published by the Somerset Record Society, in 1890, was devoted to the early churchwardens' accounts of six parishes, from the Black Death to Queen Elizabeth, and its editor was Edmund Hobhouse, a former bishop in New Zealand, who having retired to Wells had helped to found the society.[1]

In the course of his work Hobhouse repeatedly ran up against references to 'hogglers', and so included in an appendix the following observations, which (as it turned out) were to lead to a grand confusion.

> The existence of this class of men, of their name and of the share assigned to them in the life of the parish is so novel to me, and to all whom I confer with, that I deem it expedient to put on record all I know about them, in hope that their place and function in the Village Church community may be cleared up fully hereafter. I offer the following helps:
>
> There were Hogglers and Hoggling lights maintained in the church at Templecombe, at Pilton, Yatton and Morebath [Devon]. At Croscombe they were a guild with wardens, bringing their surplus, after guild-expenses paid, to the churchwarden's audit, like the other guilds.
>
> At Banwell they made a much more important contribution, under the name of 'le Hogeling', apparently by taking charge of common lands and cattle running on them, and bringing the profits to the parish audit.
>
> At Banwell, the Hogglers continued to bring their subsidy in Elizabeth's reign. At Cheddar, Hogeling money is found an item of receipt up to 1630, but whence it accrued, is unexplained.

---

1   Edmund Hobhouse 1817-1904, entry by K W Orr in online *Dictionary of New Zealand Biography* (accessed 8 Sept 2009).

The class was the lowest order of labourer with spade or pick, in tillage or in minerals. The word still survives in the Mendip villages, though not a class-name, as it was in the days of Hannah More. When her sister Patty, 1795, addressed a Provident Club thus: 'Let the men of Shipham and Rowberrow become honest and good graziers and Hoglers. They are placed on this spot by Almighty God . . . An honest Hogler is as good in the Almighty's eyes as an honest squire . . .'

The word has now fallen in use to describe not the lowest class of workman but the lowest class of work and workmanship. 'You might hoggle them potatoes, but you can't dig them, i.e. properly,' was said in scorn to a young inexpert girl in 1889 in Churchill. 'A hoggling job'; 'He has been and hoggled my potatoes', are current expressions in Cheddar and Priddy, used to discredit the manner of work.

For our purpose the sense of the now-dying-out word is clear enough, and the social and other facts we gain from the records are important. The lowest class of hand-worker in our villages, whether in field or in minery was called by the name of Hoggler. It was the lowest in the social rank and in means. It must have included the serf, and yet it was allowed to take its place amongst other classes in organized aid to the church ; and poor as it was, it was willing to bring its continual contribution if not in money to the Church Wardens' coffer, at least to the maintenance of a light, one of the continuous devotions of the sanctuary. Moreover its acceptance as an organized Guild implies an acknowledgment of its being in matters spiritual on an even level with the rest, and the effect of acting in a Guild must have been to elevate its members in capacity for orderly management and control, and also in self-respect.[1]

1   Hobhouse, E (ed.) *Churchwarden's accounts . . . 1349-1560* (Somerset Record Society 4, 1890), 251-2.

All this was good enough for the compilers of the *Oxford English Dictionary* who, after labelling the word, 'of uncertain origin and meaning', added references from Hobhouse's edition, and his definition: 'a field labourer of the lowest class'.[1] Scholars sent Hobhouse notes from time to time of new occurrences, which he kept, and long after his death they were published in 1930. Meanwhile in Surrey, Sussex and Kent a similar word, 'hognel' began to turn up in churchwardens' accounts, and the debate was reopened.[2] Was there a connection with the Scottish hogmanay ('hognel-money' perhaps); or with *hogenhyne*, an Old English word for a domestic servant; or with hogget, a two-year old sheep? And did the hogglers look after and rent out sheep, scrabble for iron ore, form a respectable guild; or were they the churchwardens' assistants, or merely clumsy beggars? Opinion was as diverse as the apparently multi-tasking hogglers and hognellers themselves.

Clearly what Somerset scholarship needed was for someone to examine all the surviving early churchwardens' accounts and to list every reference to hogglers. That someone was a professor of English at an American university, Dr James Stokes, who was working for a Canadian project to catalogue, county by county, the records of early English drama. And in an appendix – running to over sixty pages – to the Somerset volumes, he did just that, and also published his conclusions in a journal article in 1990.[3]

Professor Stokes had made an important discovery in a court deposition concerning the large parish of Keynsham, between Bath

---

1   This remains the definition in the online *Oxford English Dictionary* (accessed 9 Sept 2009).

2   Lambert, U, 'Hognel money and hogglers', *Surrey Arch. Collections* xxx (1917), 54-60; note in *Somerset & Dorset Notes & Queries* xx (1930), 62-3, no.58.

3   Stokes, J (ed.), *Records of Early English Drama: Somerset*, 2 vols (Toronto, 1996), 641-708; Stokes, J, 'The Hogglers: evidences of an entertainment tradition in eleven Somerset parishes', *Somerset & Dorset Notes & Queries* xxxii (1990), 807-17 (no.359).

and Bristol, during the troubled period of controversy between Puritans and Laudians over religious observance. A local farmer was summoned as a court witness in 1630, and explained that:

> The manner of hoglinge heretofore hath byn that the churchwardens of the parishe of Kainsham for the tyme being with some others with them have usuallie on St Steevens & St Johns day [26 and 27 Dec.] yeerelie gon to Whitchurch & Charleton [outlying districts within Keynsham parish] to the Inhabitants thereof & soe collected thire benevolence towards the reparacon of the Church of Kainsham aforesaid. And sayeth that heretofore in such theire hogling they have used to singe songes & bee very merrie & have good entertaynement att such howses they went to: but now of late yeeres they have not used soe mutch to sing as they weare wont to doe . . . William Heyward gave entertainment . . . to those of Kainsham that came a hoglinge to him, & afforeded them good cheere & beere.[1]

This sounds very similar to the activities of some of the wassailers, mummers and carol singers who populate this book, and by examining all the Somerset references Professor Stokes was able to draw some more conclusions. Hoggling generally happened around Christmas, although it could also take place at Easter or at other times, particularly when fund-raising was needed for the church. Far from a begging activity by the lowest class of society, its purpose was to solicit money for the parish accounts (in some cases it was the major source of income), and as such the participants included the leading members of village society, men, women and children. At Blagdon it was so well organised that the hogglers included a bag carrier (for the donations) and a writer (who presumably noted down payments

1   Ibid, 808.

and IOUs). As a custom it was medieval, occurring as early as 1428 in Glastonbury and 1444 in Tintinhull, and in some cases the hogglers formed a processional guild. By 1630 it was dying out, as the extract quoted above seems to suggest – or rather, the singing, drinking and fund-raising carried on, but were transferred to other sets of customs.

So to return to Bishop Hobhouse and his followers, the sheep seem to have been a red herring (in a manner of speaking). The similarity of name misled them into finding a connection, which was simply that a farmer turns up in the records hoggling one day, and organising sheep on another. The derogatory senses of hoggle, grubbing around for items of little value, is presumably a re-use, or folk interpretation of the older word, linking it with porcine characteristics. In this connection it is worth noting that the Oxford English Dictionary defines the verb 'piggle' as: 'to uproot; to pick or scrape at'; and as a noun as: 'a long-handled, many-pronged hook for digging or mixing.' Piggling, unlike hoggling, is quite straightforward.

2
Carols and Carolling

HE ZEST OF these bygone instrumentalists must have been keen and staying to take them, as it did, on foot every Sunday after a toilsome week, through all weathers, to the church, which often lay at a distance from their homes. They usually received so little in payment for their performances that their efforts were really a labour of love. In the parish I had in my mind when writing the present tale, the gratuities received yearly by the musicians at Christmas were somewhat as follows: from the manor-house ten shillings and a supper; from the vicar ten shillings; from the farmers five shillings each; from each cottage-household one shilling; amounting altogether to not more than ten shillings a head annually – just enough, as an old executant told me, to pay for their fiddle-strings, rosin [resin], and music-paper (which they mostly ruled themselves). Their music in those days was all in their own manuscript, copied in the evenings after work, and their music-books were home-bound.

It was customary to inscribe a few jigs, reels, hornpipes, and ballads in the same book, by beginning it at the other end, the insertions being continued from front and back till sacred and secular met together in the middle, often with bizarre effect, the words of some of the songs exhibiting that ancient and broad humour which our grandfathers, and possibly grandmothers, took delight in, and is in these days unquotable.

The aforesaid fiddle-strings, rosin, and music-paper were supplied by a pedlar, who travelled exclusively in such wares from choir to choir, coming to each village about every six months. Tales are told of the consternation once caused among the church fiddlers when, on the occasion of their producing a new Christmas anthem, he did not come to time, owing to being snowed up on the downs, and the straits they were in through having to make shift with whipcord and twine for strings. He was generally a musician himself, and sometimes a composer in a small way, bringing his own new tunes, and tempting each choir to adopt them for a consideration. Some of these compositions which now lie before me, with their repetitions of lines, half-lines, and half-words, their fugues and their intermediate symphonies, are good singing still, though they would hardly be admitted into such hymn-books as are popular in the churches of fashionable society at the present time.[1]

So wrote Thomas Hardy in August 1896 to introduce a new edition of what had become, in the two decades since it was first published, the classic story of country carol-singers, Under the Greenwood Tree. *By now Hardy had forsaken novels and turned to poetry, but I have always felt this passage to be a masterpiece of prose, conveying precisely everything it was necessary to know, and a whole world besides – a world that was vanishing into history.*

Carols from Dorset

 HE RUSTIC SINGERS of Hardy's novels and short stories – whose adventures we shall hear about shortly – were modelled on his own grandfather and the village ancients of his childhood. Hardy preserved their song books, and in other Dorset parishes they were kept too, so that some

1 Hardy, T, *Under the Greenwood Tree* (1974 ed.), 27-8.

have survived to the present. Christopher Wordsworth, rector of the now deserted village of Tyneham on Purbeck from 1889-97, was a noted scholar, son of a bishop and great-nephew of the poet. His parish clerk gave him three such singers' books from nearby Combe Keynes. One, a small handwritten volume, contained 55 carols and the national anthem, one per page, and mostly of four stanzas. It had been written out by someone of the name of Lake, but the cover (which may originally have belonged to another book) was inscribed 'Joseph Willcoxs Book, Coombe Keynes, Dorset, 1839.' The other end of the book had the date 1823, but the contents 'Long may Victoria rein' was written against 'God save our gracious Queen', which dates it to 1837 or later. This Dorset version of the national anthem includes the lines:

> Confound their politics
> Flusterate their navish tricks
> On hir our hopes we Fix.
>   God save us all.

The carols, apart from 'While shepherds watchd their flocks by night', are not those of the modern hymn book – not quite, though the phraseology of the first lines (listed by Wordsworth) is similar. Words such as 'hark', 'awake', 'behold', 'arise', 'rejoice', and 'glorious' recur very often, and – as befits a rural Dorset collection, there are plenty of shepherds, sheep and stars.

The second book contained the tunes for all these carols, and three others. Wordsworth reiterated the description of another collection, that the tunes were 'extremely simple, and bear evident marks of unskilled hands'. Interleaved in the book was a copy of, 'A Feu Lins Printed by the Request of Henery Bishop', with a warning that his untimely death might be a warning to those who carry on the unlawful practice of smuggling. It probably commemorated a fatal event in 1832.[1]

---

1   *Somerset & Dorset Notes & Queries*, iv (1897), 194-8.

Another Dorset clergyman, Canon Charles Mayo, from another part of Dorset, Long Burton near Sherborne, was also busy rescuing carols, in this case from a worn and soiled manuscript in possession of one of the singers.

> Behold the day is come,
>   And heavenly hosts appear,
> Angels to shepherds testify
>   The King of Glory near
>
> Arise, Rejoice and Sing
>   With hymns of sacred mirth,
> For Christ, the Lord, this day is born,
>   So celebrate his birth.
>
> Behold, He comes with peace
>   To us and all mankind;
> In Bethlehem City there was born
>   The Saviour of mankind.
>
> Glory to God on High,
>   And heavenly peace on earth,
> Good-will to men, to angels joy,
>   At our Redeemer's Birth.[1]

Canon Mayo followed this with several others from the same parish, Long Burton, although the first was claimed to have been introduced by a man who came hay-trussing from Upwey near Weymouth.

> Awake and join the cheerful choir
>   Upon this joyful morn,

---

1   *Somerset & Dorset Notes & Queries*, iii (1895), 63-5.

And glad hosanna loudly sing,
 For joy a Saviour's born.

Let all the Choirs in earth below
 Their voices loudly raise;
And sweetly join the cheerful Band
 With Angels in the skies.

The shining Host, in bright array,
 Descend from heaven to earth;
And all with gentle hearts and voice
 Proclaim a Saviour's Birth.[1]

The Long Burton carols are mostly simple, formulaic productions, such as this:

Behold, what glorious news arrives,
 From Heav'n this blessed morn,
Hark! Angels shouting thro' the skies
 To us a Saviour's born

To tell the news the heavenly host
 Appeared in the air,
And humble shepherds in the field
 Those joyful songs did hear.

Wise men from far beheld the star
 Which was their faithful guide,
And when it pointed forth a way
 Then God they glorified.[2]

1   *Somerset & Dorset Notes & Queries*, iii (1895), 113-15.
2   *Somerset & Dorset Notes & Queries*, iv (1897), 72-3.

. . . Or this:

> Rejoice, rejoice, ye earthly tribes,
> > And hail this happy morn,
> This is the day, the blessed day,
> > Our Saviour Christ is born.
>
> Rise, every human vocal voice,
> > And touch each warbling string;
> In gladness let our hearts rejoice,
> > Sing praises to our King.
>
> The praises of our new-born king
> > Will through the land resound,
> In lofty hymns to Him we'll sing
> > And wake the nations round.[1]

One of the set, however, displays more sophistication, both in its metre and its vocabulary:

> While shepherds were feeding their flocks in the field,
> The birth of a Saviour to them was reveal'd;
> And angels assembling in clouds did appear,
> While shepherds lay trembling and smitten with fear.
>
> Forbear to be fearful, ye have reason to sing.
> Rejoice and be cheerful, glad tidings we bring,
> For born in the City of David therefore,
> A Saviour of pity, to whom we adore.

---

1   *Somerset & Dorset Notes & Queries*, iii (1895), 180-1.

He came to redeem us from guilt and from sin,
In love he would have us new lives to begin,
In love each believer shall gladly adore,
For ever and ever, when time is no more.[1]

Hardy wrote of the pedlars, composers in a small way, who wrote some of these hymns. Llewelyn Powys drew an affectionate portrait of one of the more accomplished of them, Thomas Shoel of Montacute, near Yeovil; and this is followed by an example of Shoel's work, an allegorical piece, never straying far from the story of the Nativity, nor from Shoel's own rough experience of life.

Thomas Shoel
Llewelyn Powys

HOMAS SHOEL WAS born in the year 1759. His father and mother died when he was still young. He first attempted to earn his living as a weaver, but his health giving way in that employment, he eventually became a farm-labourer and village carrier. He married a woman named Phyllis Bool when he

1   *Somerset & Dorset Notes & Queries,* iii (1895), 134-5.

was twenty-three years old. They appeared to have been passionately attached to each other and to the children of their marriage, but hopeless poverty wore them down and brought death to all but Shoel himself and one boy, who was afterwards drowned at sea. Shoel's mind never recovered from the shock of these pitiful years, and much of his poetry is made up of reiterated lamentations.

In 1797 he was married a second time by the Vicar of Montacute, William Langdon, to a woman named Mary Taunton. By her he had three daughters – Mara, Miriam, and Julia. He died in 1823, but even then disaster continued to pursue his family. His daughter Mara inherited his exceptional sensitiveness of nature and after his death became obsessed by religious emotions. As late as her fiftieth year she gave birth to twins, and this exceptional occurrence may have accentuated her weak nervous condition. In any case, she took her own life. Shoel's second daughter, Miriam, died young, living as an invalid for the last few years of her life at Norton-sub-Hamdon, from which village her corpse was borne through sandy bye-lanes to the Nonconformist burial-plot at Five Ashes. It is in this same Puritan graveyard that Thomas Shoel himself lies. The acre is romantically situated in the middle of an arable field on the top of the long wind-swept ridge that lies between Odcombe and Ham Hill, far from any human habitation. The cemetery is surrounded by a high stone wall as a precaution against possible body-snatching, and has for an entrance a single narrow aperture fitted with an iron gate, the rusty bars of which only reluctantly clank admittance to a traveller. The place is said to have been first used for burying some of Cromwell's soldiers killed in a local engagement at the time of the Civil War. Shoel's youngest daughter Julia alone of his children lived to a great age, and was still alive in the year 1886 when my father became Vicar of Montacute. Indeed, one old woman remembers seeing my father hurry along after Julia Burt in order to carry for her a bucket of water that she was bringing to her cottage from the fountain at the Cross. There are still living in Montacute two of Julia Burt's grandchildren. Mrs Ellen

Greenham, one of these great-grandchildren of the poet, has allowed me to see a family Bible given by Thomas Shoel to Mara and the old book still contains the poet's careful calligraphy and the date 1819.

Thomas Shoel published three books of sacred music: *Ode for Christmas Day*, *The Chearful Psalmodist*, and *Peace*; also innumerable Psalm tunes, hymn tunes, and 'Easy Anthems'. The best known of all his religious tunes is perhaps his 'Joy to the World', which when I was a boy was regularly sung by the carol singers at Christmas. There used at that time to live at Montacute an old man named Samuel Geard, a lusty member of the church choir. The family of Geard had seen better days. Samuel Geard's own father had been a prosperous sailcloth manufacturer. He, however, had been content to earn his bread without cark or care as an under-gardener at Montacute House. On a certain Christmas midnight when the Borough, as the village square at Montacute is called, was white with a fine nativity snow, and a bitter wintry wind was huffling against the sloping roofs from the north-east, Geard heard the carol singers begin to strike up with the 'old tunes'. In a moment he was out of bed, and opening wide the casement window, stood in his nightgown exposed to the shrewd 'draughts', joining with his magnificent bass voice in the 'Shepherd's music' as heartily as the best of the carol singers. His friends called up to him not to risk his life in such a foolish manner. 'I can't bide in bed when you be out singing Wold Tom Shayell,' came back the obstinate answer. (The local pronunciation of the name Shoel was Shayell and not Shoel.) In those days they used to make a great deal of carol singing, the orchestra that accompanied consisting of clarinet, flute, fiddles, and bass viol, and I have been told it was the custom of the cellist to go to the churchyard and tune his strings to the tone of one of the six bells – perhaps to the one which has, 'He that heareth me to sound, Let him alwaies praies the Lord,' engraved about its wide rim.[1]

---

1   Powys, L, *Somerset essays* (1937), 132-5.

Cold was the air, the wind blew strong,
And darkling grew the evening sky;
When pass'd a beggar-man along
And wish'd a friendly shelter nigh.

His coat was rent, his feet were bare,
And slow he crippled o'er the stones;
Through his torn hat high stared his hair,
And shrivell'd skin disclos'd his bones.

With hands benum'd and stiff with cold,
Close folded on his troubled breast;
The weather-beaten wretch behold!
And let your sorrows guess the rest.

Ah! has he left his native plain
To seek employment far abroad,
But work unable to obtain,
Is toiling back his homeward road?

Behold him pass the Public door,
And cast in vain a wistful eye,
For Inns do not receive the poor,
Whose pockets can't their wants supply.

Now to a stall behold him lie,
Glad with the ox a bed to share;
But poorly cover'd from the sky
And shiver'd by the piercing air.

Good natur'd hind! o don't deny
A shelter in your master's shed;

O grant some straw that he may lie,
A little warm for such a bed.

Come gentle sleep, and let thy hand
Find out the beggar where he lies;
O let thy care-deceiving wand,
Seal for a while the sufferers' eyes.

In vain I wish – the downy power
Flies from the thorny bed of care,
Indignant at misfortune's hour,
And frighted far by stern despair.

His haggard eyes he fain would close,
But ah! his dear distressful train
Rush on his thoughts with all their woes,
And near to frenzy drive his brain.[1]

*By contrast to Shoel, whose work was published in his lifetime, and the
anonymous carollers of Long Burton, whose work their vicar was allowed*

1   Shoel, T, *Poems by Thomas Shoel* (1821), 109-11.

to transcribe, some traditional village carols were jealously guarded by their performers. In 1930 the Wiltshire author and local literary celebrity, Edith Olivier, compiled for the Women's Institute movement little books of traditional recipes and folklore, from contributions sent in by institute members. This extract is from a village near Wilton.

Carol Singing at Berwick St James
Mrs D Cook

 ROM FAR BACK beyond living memory, the men of Berwick have gone out carol-singing in the earliest hours of Christmas morning. The carols are not written, but handed down from generation to generation. There are recitative passages, too; and they end with:

> We wish you a merry Christmas,
> We wish you a merry Christmas,
> We wish you a merry Christmas
> And a Happy New Year!

It is a thrilling thing to be awakened in the dark or the moonlight of a Christmas morning, at about two o'clock, perhaps, by the powerful men's voices.

When we came here first we did not understand, and crept shivering out of bed to hurl down money and thanks (not perhaps of the heartiest). But it was explained to us afterwards that nothing is expected at that hour, but that the listeners shall stay snug in bed and realise that it is Christmas morning.

The carol singers come again in the evening of Christmas Day, and then is the time for thanks and shillings.

The words of the carols are more or less secret. One may write them down as one hears them, I suppose, but that, somehow, is not easy. Mr Kitley, of this village, who is 78 and who sang the carols for most of his lifetime, tried to get me a written record of them. 'I asked Tom Blanchard, and he wouldn't say as what he would and he wouldn't say as what he wouldn't.' Mr Blanchard seems to have special rights in the carols, because 70 years ago or more his great uncle, Isachar Blanchard, was leader both of the carol-singing and of the Berwick Band.

Isachar was 'a noted man with the violin'. He used to take his violin and accompany the carols with it. (I should like to note, in passing, that about 100 years ago the church music in Berwick used to be two violins and a bass viol.)

This year the words of the carols were written down for the use of some lads going out for the first time. But these were told to let no-one else see them.

Years ago, the singers used to practice on Christmas Eve in a house – now pulled down – that stood somewhere opposite the present Reading Room. At midnight they started out. In those days they did not go to Winterbourne Stoke. During the last dozen years or so the old customs have begun to break up. Nowadays the singers go to Winterbourne Stoke on Christmas Eve and have already sung there before they begin their singing in Berwick on Christmas morning.[1]

This secrecy surrounding the homespun local carols has meant that many have been lost. When Alfred Williams in 1927 contributed an article on 'The Folk Carol in Wiltshire' to the Wiltshire Gazette *he could only give the words of two complete carols, and one of those came from Poulton, a Wiltshire village transferred to Gloucestershire in 1844; his other example is from Castle Eaton near Cricklade.[2] In 1890 Geoffrey Hill, the vicar of Harnham on the outskirts of Salisbury, published a collection of Wiltshire folk songs and carols, in which he included two*

1   Olivier, E (ed), *Moonrakings* (1930).
2   Williams, A, 'The folk carol in Wiltshire', *Wiltshire Gazette*, 29 Dec 1927.

short carols which he had heard sung at Britford nearby.[1] *And in 1942 an early nineteenth-century carol, possibly from Clyffe Pypard near Wootton Bassett, was published alongside other miscellaneous folklore.*

Wiltshire Carols

From Poulton

> God sent for us the Sunday,
> All with His holy hand,
> He made the sun fair, and the moon,
> The water and dry land.
>
> There are six good days in the week,
> All for a labouring man,
> The seventh day to serve the Lord,
> The Father and the Son.
>
> For the saving of your soul, dear man,
> Christ died upon the cross;
> For the saving of your soul, dear man,
> Christ's precious blood was lost.
>
> Three drops of our sweet Saviour's blood
> Were freely spilt for me;
> We shall never do for our sweet Saviour
> As he has done for we.
>
> My song is done, we must be gone,
> We stay no longer here;

1   Hill, G, *Wiltshire folk songs and carols* (1890).

So I wish you all a Merry, Merry Christmas,
And a Happy New Year!

From Castle Eaton

Come, all you merry gentlemen, let nothing you dismay,
Remember Christ the Saviour was born on Christmas Day
To save poor souls from Satan's path long time been gone astray,
That brings tidings of comfort and joy.

When the shepherds heard those tidings it much rejoiced their
    minds,
They left their flocks a-feeding in tempest, storm and wind,
Straightway they came to Bethlehem and sang of God so kind,
That brings tidings of comfort and joy.

God bless the rulers of this house and all that dwell within,
God bless you and your children, I hope you heaven will win;
God bless you and your children that live both far and near!
And, good Lord, send us a joyful New Year!

From Britford

Rejoice, the promised Saviour's come,
And shall the blind behold;
The deaf shall hear, and by the dumb
    His wondrous works be told.

Light from the sacred shore shall spread,
O'er all the world shall beam,
In pastures fair shall all be led,
    And drink of comfort's stream.

The weary nations shall have rest,
The rage of war shall cease,
The earth with innocence be blest,
  And plenty dwell with peace.

Also from Britford

Awake and join the cheerful choir,
Upon this joyful morn.
And glad Hosanna loudly sing
For joy a Saviour's born.

Let all the choirs on earth below
Their voices loudly raise;
And sweetly join the cheerful band
Of Angels in the skies.

The shining host in bright array,
Descend from heaven to earth;
And all the gentle heart and voice
Proclaim a Saviour's birth.

Perhaps from Clyffe Pypard

The first great joy our Mary had
It was the joy of one,
To see the blessed babe
Sucking at her breast bone,
Sucking at her breast bone good babe,
And blessed may she be,
With Father, Son and Holy Ghost
And all the blessed Three.

The next great joy our Mary had
It was the joy of two,
To see the blessed Jesus
Making the lame to go,
Making the lame to go, good man,
And blessed may he be,
With Father, Son and Holy Ghost
And all the blessed Three.

The next great joy our Mary had
It was the joy of Three,
To see the blessed Jesus
Making the blind to see,
Making the blind to see, good man,
Etc., etc.

The next, etc., the joy of four [forgotten].

The next great joy our Mary had
It was the joy of five,
To see the blessed Jesus
Making the dead alive,
Making the dead alive, good man,
Etc., etc.

The 6th. 7th and 8th joys forgotten

The next great joy our Mary had
It was the joy of nine,
To see the blessed Jesus
Turn water into wine,

Turn water into wine, good man,

Etc., etc.[1]

This last half-remembered carol is a variant of 'The Seven Joys of Mary', which had been collected and published in 1871.[2] It is one of a number of counting or cumulative Christmas songs and carols, of which 'The Twelve Days of Christmas' and 'Green grow the rushes O', are the best known. In a story published in 1891 in a popular magazine the blind Exmoor author Alice King provided the setting for their performance, a test of memory, sobriety and stamina.

Songs Ancient and Curious

MONG THE ELDER folk there is much handing round of cobler's punch', a West-Country mixture of cider and gin, and much singing of songs. These songs are many of them very quaint as to words; the two most characteristic, perhaps, are a song, the chorus of which imitates all the noises made by the different animals on a farm, the whole party going into the performance when the chorus comes round with right good heart and will; and a song which glorifies the good qualities and useful properties of the horned Exmoor sheep. The songs are interspersed with Christmas carols, some of which are very ancient and curious, and the music of which has never probably been printed, but lives in the minds and hearts of the people alone, re-echoing on from Christmas to Christmas, backward and backward, until, as we strain

---

1   *Wiltshire Arch. & Nat. Hist. Mag.*, l (1942), 36-7.

2   Bramley, H R, and Stainer, J, *Christmas carols new and old*, 1st series (1871), no.12; see discussion of this carol in *New Oxford Book of Carols*, 462-3.

our ears to catch the sounds, they are at length lost in the murmur of the waves of time.[1]

The song which Alice King probably had in mind, in which the chorus imitates farmyard animals, was described in a local newspaper in 1922.

The following simple composition, made up on similar lines to 'The House that Jack Built', is known to have been chanted with great gusto at many of these old-fashioned parties. Like that of the man with a tin whistle along a street kerb, the music consisted of 'variations', and just followed the inspirations of the party, whilst, where necessary, the natural cries of the birds and animals were interpreted in the best possible spirit by old and young.

 I bought a cock and the cock pleased me, I set my cock all under a tree, my cock went cock-a-doodleloo, and joy to all the neighbours' cocks, and well done my cock, too.

 I bought a hen and the hen pleased me, I set my hen all under a tree, the hen went chit-a-chaff, chit-a-chaff, the cock went cock-a-doodleloo, and joy to all the neighbours' cocks, and well done my cock, too.

 I bought a duck and the duck pleased me, I set my duck all under a tree, the duck went quit-a-quaff, quit-a-quaff, the hen went chit-a-chaff, the cock went cock-a-doodleloo, and joy to all the neighbours' cocks, and well done my cock, too.

 Then follow in a similar manner, the additions of a goose, with her toosee-toosee; a cat, meow-meow; dog, bow-wow; sheep, baa-baa; horse, neigh-neigh; cow, moo-moo; turkey, gobble-gobble; donkey hee-haw, hee-haw; and the bird, sweet-sweet.

 By the time the bird begins to sing probably several members of the company have failing memories of the order of the purchases,

1 King, A, 'A withered rose', *Home Chimes*, Dec 1891 (offprint in SANHS Library).

which generally results in a hilarious jumble up of the various calls of the creatures concerned, and the switching off to some other Christmas game and amusement. [1]

And here is an old Christmas carol from Frome, preserved on a fading sheet of paper in the Somerset Record Office. It is of the 'Green Grow the Rushes' construction.

> What shall us sing?
> Sing all over one.
> What was one?
> One was God, the righteous man.
> Save our souls, the next, Amen.

> What shall us sing?
> Sing all over two.
> What was two?
> Two was the Jewry,
> One was God, the righteous man.
> Save our souls, Amen.

> etc. introducing the following in turn:

> Three was the Trinity. . .
> Four was our Lady's bow'r [?I . . .
> Five was the dead-alive. . .
> Six was the crucifix. . .
> Seven was the lump of leaven. . .
> Eight was the crooked-straight. . .
> Nine was the water-wine. . .
> Ten was the golden pen. . .

1   *Somerset County Herald*, 22 Dec. 1922.

Eleven was the gate of heaven. . .
Twelve was the ring of bells. . .[1]

A very similar version of this carol was published in 1902 by the rector of Horsington, near Frome,[2] which prompted several learned responses from antiquaries. J B Medley reported a variant from nearby Lullington.

I not only heard this carol repeated but sung by an old woman who lived and died at Lullington, Somerset. She was born at Upton Noble, but had married the clerk of Lullington, and was a source of amusement and instruction to me all the time she lived. I always took the 'Golden Pen' either as the Inspired Pen of the Gospels, or the Pen or Fold of the Sheep, without finding out what it meant in the singer's mind. She pronounced 'Twelve' as 'Twell,' I suppose to make it rhyme with Bell. The following is her version of the Carol.

Sing all over One. What was One?
One was God, the Righteous Man,
To save our souls in rest, Amen.
       etc. etc. etc.
Two was the Jewry.
Three was the Trinity.
Four was the Lady bore.
Five was the Man alive.
Six was the Crucifix.
Seven was the Star of Heaven.
Eight was the Crooked Straight.
Nine was the Water-wine.
Ten was the Golden Pen.

1   SRO DD/SAS C/2401/32.
2   *Somerset & Dorset Notes & Queries*, viii (1902), 174-5.

Eleven was the Gate of Heaven.
Twell was the Holy Bell.[1]

The fumblings of folklorists and musicologists to make sense of these arcane incantations was at its height after 1900, and the turning point to understanding them is often reckoned to have taken place in September 1903 in the vicarage garden at Hambridge near Bridgwater. There Cecil Sharp, a lawyer turned music master who was staying with his friend the Revd Charles Marson, heard the gardener, John England, singing a folk-song, 'The seeds of love'. From this encounter, as his biographer wrote, Sharp, 'felt that a new world of music had been opened to him. From now on his course was set and he never turned back.'[2] Between 1903 and 1909 he collected and published five series of 'Folk Songs from Somerset', and in the last of these included and discussed Somerset carols.

Compared with other parts of England, Somerset is not, perhaps, especially rich in folk-carols. Carol singing at Christmas time is, however, customary in many parts of the county, and several villages have special carols of their own, which are not found elsewhere, and of which they regard themselves as the sole owners. But these, unlike 'The Ten Joys of Mary' and 'A Christmas Carol' ['Come all you worthy gentlemen'] are not genuine folk-carols. They date, I believe, from the eighteenth century and are, patently, the compositions of cultivated or semi-cultivated musicians. They may, perhaps, have been written by some of those stringed or wind-instrument players who accompanied the services in the village churches before the introduction of harmoniums and organs. These rustic musicians could play from note and had acquired quite enough elementary

1 *Somerset & Dorset Notes & Queries*, viii (1902), 218; see also ibid, 356-7.
2 Karpeles, M, *Cecil Sharp: his life and work* (1967), 31-3.

musical knowledge to invent simple harmonized tunes. A few of these 'composed' carols are printed, but most of them are in manuscript; while some are now preserved, in a more or less corrupt state, by oral tradition only. To the musical historian these are not without interest, even if their artistic value is not very great. In any case, they could not properly be included in a collection of traditional folk-songs.[1]

Sharp was distinguishing, therefore, between the local, home-made carols that were performed by village bands in the eighteenth and nineteenth centuries, and an older folk tradition, which included the strange counting carols embracing secular and pagan imagery, and which existed in the middle ages. Then they were not restricted to Christmas, or even to religious themes. A curious local survival is found on a small piece of parchment among the Bridgwater borough archives. It is a deed, and concerns the lease of property in west Wales in 1471; but soon after it was created (to judge by the handwriting) someone jotted down on the back the words of two carols, one for Doomsday and the other for Christmas. They are in English, with a few words in Latin. The word laetabundus *is significant, because this links the carol to an influential Latin chant believed to have been composed by St Bernard of Clairvaux, and several times translated into English. The Bridgwater carol, however, is not itself a direct translation, and it neatly combines the sacred sentiment with hints of a pagan past – 'holy' and 'yffy' are of course the holly and the ivy, symbolizing the union between man (holly) and woman (ivy), and the subject underlying one or more very ancient folk-carols.[2]*

1   Sharp, C, *Folk songs from Somerset*, 5th series (1909), ix-x; see also Sharp, C and Karpeles, M, *English folk song: some conclusions* (4th ed, 1965), 124-5.

2   Original is SRO D/B/bw 123; see Greene, *The early English carols* (1935), pp.lxxviii-lxxxiii, xcviii-xcix, 10-11 (no.14a), 244 (no.362); Dunning, R W, and Tremlett, T D (eds.), *Bridgwater Borough Archives*, v (Somerset Record Soc 70, 1971), 6-7. An example of a 'Holly and Ivy' carol from Somerset is in Tongue, R L, *Somerset folklore* (1965), 209-10.

Hay hay take good hede wat you say
a doumsday we schull y see
Fader & sone in trinite
w't grete power and magisti
and angelys in grete aray

An angele w't a trumpat shall blow
that all the worlde schall yt yknow
they that beyne an yyrth soo low
they schull a ryse all off the clay

They that byne in [yrth] soo deppe
they schall to thys trumpat take heed
And a ryse and full sorre wyppe
that ever they wer to yenst to say

God hymselffe suner hyt ys
that schall ene the dome I wys
And therfore owys hym th't hath I do amys
Fore they they schull rehersse here pay

Holy holy holy holy holy yffy yffy

Letabundus exultet fidelys chorus alleluia
[Let the joyful chorus of believers rejoice, alleluia]

gaudeamus [let us rejoice]
now well may we myrthys make
For Jhu mankynd hath take
Of a mayden w'toutyn make [husband]

res miranda [a thing of wonder]
A kyng of kyngs now forth ys browgth

Off a maydyn th't synnyd nowght
Nether in ded nether in thowgth

sol de stella [a sun of a star]
An angell of counsell now ys bor'
Off a mayde as y sayd be fore
To saw all th't was for lore

semper clara [ever shining]
that sonne hath never downe goyng
And thys lyght no tyme lesyng
This ster' ys evermore scheyinyng

para forma [of the same nature]
Ryght as the stere browght forght a beme
Oute of the wych comyyth a marvelose streme
So dud th't mayde w'towtyn weme'

Holy holy & yffy yffy holy yffy Holi

With a few exceptions most of the Christmas carols familiar to us today fall into neither of Cecil Sharp's categories: the folk-carol of venerable antiquity; nor the homespun creation of local musicians. Today's repertoire is largely the work of Victorian and later clergymen and would-be poets and hymnographers. These two are unlikely to feature in today's carol services.

Christmas Carol for the Year 1780
Michael Burrough

The author was mayor of Salisbury, whose attempts at verse remained unpublished.

The pure the holy spotless Lamb, on this auspicious day
From heaven's glorious mansions come, to take our sins away.

This was amazing tenderness, this was stupendous love
Shown to a wretched sinful race, by God that reigns above.

For this with joy the earth it rings, with men's loud song of praise
To God the mighty king of kings, and angels joyn the joys –

Yet oh, our praises are too weak, our tongues too feeble are
Such grace, such wondrous love to speak, such goodness to declare.

But oh, th' eternal gratitude, that we are bound to pay
Commands our praises shold be shew'd, commands our thanks this day.

Hosanah to the Father be, hosanah to the Son,
Hosanah to the holy three, the blessed three in one.

Glory honour praise and power to the new God for ever
Jesus Christ is our redeemer, Halalujah praise the Lord.[1]

An Xmas Carol
W W Butler

This effort was penned in 1901 by a master at Brynmelyn School, Weston super Mare, for the school magazine. It is headed 'An Xmas Carol'. (Surely a schoolmaster should have known better.)

The Earth has donned her garb of Winter's white;
Two weary Bards tramp slowly o'er the snow;
Though cold the wind, and chill the frosty night,
They sing this cheerful Carol as they go –

Give me the home where the Yule log burns
Heaped high on its ample hearth;
The home to which the wanderer turns
By many a varied path.

The home where friends meet once again,
Whose friendships never tire;
Where tales are told whose ghosts remain
Around the Christmas fire.

While pealing bells proclaim to all,
As merrily they chime,

1   WSA 473/381.

The happy days our minds recall,
A good old Christmas time.

Give me the hearth where the Yule logs burn,
Piled blazing side by side;
The hearth to which our hearts must turn
To keep the Christmastide.[1]

The shepherds sing; and shall I silent be?
George Herbert

This is not really a carol, but a Christmas poem by a poet who wrote several of our best-loved hymns. George Herbert was the aristocratic but saintly rector of Bemerton, near Salisbury, who died and was buried there in 1633. The volume of devotional poetry for which he is famous, The Temple, *was published in the following year.*

All after pleasures as I rid one day,
 My horse and I, both tir'd, body and mind,
 With full cry of affections, quite astray;
I took up in the next inn I could find.
There when I came, whom found I but my dear,
 My dearest Lord, expecting till the grief
 Of pleasures brought me to him, ready there
To be all passengers' most sweet relief?
Oh Thou, whose glorious, yet contracted light,
 Wrapt in night's mantle, stole into a manger;
 Since my dark soul and brutish is thy right,

---

1 Handwritten school magazine, *The Eagle*, i, 9 Dec 1901, 10-11, in North Somerset Studies Library, Weston super Mare.

To Man of all beasts be not thou a stranger:
    Furnish and deck my soul, that thou mayst have
    A better lodging, than a rack, or grave.

The shepherds sing; and shall I silent be?
    My God, no hymn for thee?
My soul's a shepherd too; a flock it feeds
    Of thoughts, and words, and deeds.
The pasture is thy word: the streams, thy grace
    Enriching all the place.
Shepherd and flock shall sing, and all my powers
    Out-sing the daylight hours.
Then we will chide the sun for letting night
    Take up his place and right:
We sing one common Lord; wherefore he should
    Himself the candle hold.
I will go searching, till I find a sun
    Shall stay, till we have done;
A willing shiner, that shall shine as gladly,
    As frost-nipt suns look sadly.
Then we will sing, and shine all our own day,
    And one another pay:
His beams shall cheer my breast, and both so twine,
Till ev'n his beams sing, and my music shine.[1]

Were it not for the interest shown by churchmen and folklorists during the later nineteenth century, the tradition of carol-singing at Christmas, like many others, might have died out. The waits, the urban equivalent of Hardy's village musicians, who had maintained the tradition of singing carols, became regarded as a nuisance, and their 'performance'

1   Herbert, G, *The complete English works* (Pasternak, ed., 1995), 78.

condemned as, 'easily mistaken for a howling cat'. [1] Hardy himself, though so devoted to the traditional country ways, must have sensed this unease, and in a short story published in 1894 even went so far as to point the finger of blame on a cheating performer.

Old Andrey's Experience as a Musician
Thomas Hardy

WAS ONE OF the quire-boys at that time, and we and the players were to appear at the manor-house as usual that Christmas week, to play and sing in the hall to the squire's people and visitors (among 'em being the archdeacon, Lord and Lady Baxby, and I don't know who); afterwards going, as we always did, to have a good supper in the servants' hall. Andrew knew this was the custom, and meeting us when we were starting to go, he said to us: "Lord, how I should like to join in that meal of beef, and turkey, and plum-pudding, and ale, that you happy ones be going to just now! One more or less will make no difference to the squire. I am too old to pass as a singing boy, and too bearded to pass as a singing girl; can ye lend me a fiddle, neighbours, that I may come with ye as a bandsman? "

'Well, we didn't like to be hard upon him, and lent him an old one, though Andrew knew no more of music than the Giant o' Cernel [Cerne Abbas giant]; and armed with the instrument he walked up to the squire's house with the others of us at the time appointed, and went in boldly, his fiddle under his arm. He made himself as natural as he could in opening the music-books and moving the candles to the best points for throwing light upon the notes; and all went well till we had played and sung "While shepherds watch," and "Star, arise," and "Hark the glad sound." Then the squire's mother, a tall gruff old lady,

---

1   Pimlott, J A R, *The Englishman's Christmas* (1978), 108-9, 141-2.

who was much interested in church-music, said quite unexpectedly to Andrew: "My man, I see you don't play your instrument with the rest. How is that?"

'Every one of the quire was ready to sink into the earth with concern at the fix Andrew was in. We could see that he had fallen into a cold sweat, and how he would get out of it we did not know.

"'I've had a misfortune, mem," he says, bowing as meek as a child. "Coming along the road I fell down and broke my bow."

"'O, I am sorry to hear that," says she. "Can't it be mended?"

"'O no, mem," says Andrew. "Twas broke all to splinters."

"'I'll see what I can do for you," says she.

'And then it seemed all over, and we played "Rejoice, ye drowsy mortals all," in D and two sharps. But no sooner had we got through it than she says to Andrew,

"'I've sent up into the attic, where we have some old musical instruments, and found a bow for you." And she hands the bow to poor wretched Andrew, who didn't even know which end to take hold of. "Now we shall have the full accompaniment," says she.

'Andrew's face looked as if it were made of rotten apple as he stood in the circle of players in front of his book; for if there was one person in the parish that everybody was afraid of, 'twas this hook-nosed old lady. However, by keeping a little behind the next man he managed to make pretence of beginning, sawing away with his bow without letting it touch the strings, so that it looked as if he were driving into the tune with heart and soul. 'Tis a question if he wouldn't have got through all right if one of the squire's visitors (no other than the archdeacon) hadn't noticed that he held the fiddle upside down, the nut under his chin, and the tail-piece in his hand; and they began to crowd round him, thinking 'twas some new way of performing.

'This revealed everything; the squire's mother had Andrew turned out of the house as a vile impostor, and there was great interruption to the harmony of the proceedings, the squire declaring he should have notice to leave his cottage that day fortnight. However, when we got to the servants' hall there sat Andrew, who had been let in at the back door by the orders of the squire's wife, after being turned out at the front by the orders of the squire, and nothing more was heard about his leaving his cottage. But Andrew never performed in public as a musician after that night; and now he's dead and gone, poor man, as we all shall be![1]

1   Hardy, T, *Life's Little Ironies and a Changed Man* (1977 ed.), 171-3.

3
The Mummers

N ADDITION TO the out-door sports, there were the indoor amusements, and most notable of all among these were the Mummers, which, forty or fifty years ago, were to be met with in every town and village in North Wilts, during the winter months, up to Christmas Eve. These Mummers, who used to go about from house to house, and more particularly to the public-houses, during the winter evenings, performing a rude kind of play founded on the legend of St George and the Dragon, consisted of six or eight men, who used to wear various kinds of disguises, and who during the season would throw the money they got for their performances into a common fund, which they would distribute at the close of the season *pro ratio* among themselves.

Sometimes the company would aspire to nothing more than a recitation set down for each character, but occasionally there would be found a company numbering some ten or twelve persons, including a fiddler, a comic singer, and a dancer, and then the performance would be of a more elaborate character, and the services of the company could only be obtained by a previous engagement, for their 'rounds' were so formed as to include a visit to all the principal residences and farm houses in the neighbourhood. The words of the play performed by these Mummers were partly traditional, and partly local, and were handed down by word of mouth from generation to generation.

The plot of the Mummers' play, as I recollect it, was very simple, and quite orthodox. It opened with a general challenge to any knight in Christendom to come forth and dispute some point which was elaborately set forth. The challenge having been accepted, a deadly conflict with swords followed. Fabulous sums of money and everlasting fame were then offered to anyone who should restore the dead knight to life again, which had the effect of bringing forth some wonderful doctor who had a magic pill, one of which being thrust into the mouth of the prostrate body restored animation and the state *in quo ante* [it was in before], which consummation was duly celebrated by singing, dancing, and what other forms of rejoicing the company was capable of.

As my father was at this time the only bookseller in business in Swindon, I well recollect that every year, just before winter set in, there would be no end of applications for 'Mummer's books'. But these we could never supply, for the simple reason that they were not in existence; and there was therefore no help for it but for those who would play the Mummer's part to get some old Mummer to repeat the words of the several parts over and over again until the learner had got them by heart. Of course, this mode of transmission from the old 'un to the young 'un had its disadvantages. But it had its advantages also, for it admitted of such addition to the dialogue as wit, or fancy, or the circumstances of the times dictated.[1]

More than most places, Swindon and the surrounding area were transformed during the nineteenth century; and in 1885 the local newspaper proprietor, William Morris, set down his reminiscences of the town before the railway came. Thomas Hardy, too, was in reminiscing mood when he was interviewed in 1901 for an American magazine.

1   Morris, W, *Swindon fifty years ago (more or less): reminiscences, notes and relics of ye old Wiltshire towne* (1885), 141-9.

The Odd Sort of Thrill
Thomas Hardy

H: THEN AGAIN, the Christmas Mummers flourished well into my recollection – indeed, they have not so long died out . . . Our mummers hereabouts gave a regular performance, 'The Play of St George' it was called. It contained quite a number of traditional characters: the Valiant Soldier, the Turkish Knight, St George himself, the Saracen, Father Christmas, the Fair Sabra, and so on. Rude as it was, the thing used to impress me very much – I can clearly recall the odd sort of thrill it would give. The performers used to carry a long staff in one hand and a wooden sword in the other, and pace monotonously round, intoning their parts on one note, and punctuating them by nicking the sword against the staff – something like this: 'Here comes I, the Valiant Soldier (nick), Slasher is my name (nick).'

Interviewer: The pacing and rhythmic sing-song suggest kinship with the Chinese acting I have seen in San Francisco and New York. And what was the action of the play?

TH: I really don't know, except that it ended in a series of mortal combats in which all the characters but St George were killed. And then the curious thing was that they were invariably brought to life again. A personage was introduced for the purpose – the Doctor of Physic, wearing a cloak and a broad-brimmed beaver.

Interviewer: How many actors would there be in a company?

TH: Twelve to fifteen, I should think. Sometimes a large village would furnish forth two sets of mummers. They would go to the farmhouses round, between Christmas and Twelfth Night, doing some four or five performances each evening, and getting ale and money at every house. Sometimes the mummers of one village would encroach on the traditional 'sphere of influence' of another village, and then there would be a battle in good earnest.

Interviewer: Did women take part in the performances?

TH: I think not – the Fair Sabra was always played by a boy. But the character was often omitted.

Interviewer: And when did the mumming go out?

TH: It went on in some neighbourhoods till 1880, or thereabouts. I have heard of a parson here and there trying to revive it; but of course that isn't at all the same thing – the spontaneity is gone.[1]

1   Archer, W, 'Real conversations: conversation 1: with Mr Thomas Hardy', *The Critic* (New York), 1901, reprinted 1979.

In asking about women mummers, Hardy's interviewer showed no sign of recalling that the novelist had drawn on these memories in The Return of the Native, *when Eustacia Vye disguised herself as a boy in order to play the part of the Turkish Knight, and join in the Egdon mummers' performance at Mrs Yeobright's Christmas party.*

Before the play of 'St George' could be performed there had to be a practice, and this took place in Captain Vye's fuel-house.

Eustacia's Adventure
Thomas Hardy

N A LEDGE in the fuel-house stood three tall rush-lights, and by the light of them seven or eight lads were marching about, haranguing, and confusing each other, in endeavours to perfect themselves in the play. Humphrey and Sam, the furze and turf cutters, were there looking on, so also was Timothy Fairway, who leant against the wall and prompted the boys from memory, interspersing among the set words remarks and anecdotes of the superior days when he and others were the Egdon mummers-elect that these lads were now.

'Well, ye be as well up to it as ever ye will be,' he said. 'Not that such mumming would have passed in our time. Harry as the Saracen should strut a bit more, and John needn't holler his inside out. Beyond that perhaps you'll do . . .'

The mummers, including Eustacia in disguise, arrived at Mrs Yeobright's house at the appointed hour, to find the party in full swing. But they were stuck outside.

'Is there no passage inside the door, then?' asked Eustacia, as they stood within the porch.

'No,' said the lad who played the Saracen. 'The door opens right upon the front sitting-room, where the spree's going on.'

'So that we cannot open the door without stopping the dance.'

'That's it. Here we must bide till they have done, for they always bolt the back door after dark.'

'They won't be much longer,' said Father Christmas.

This assertion, however, was hardly borne out by the event. Again the instruments ended the tune; again they recommenced with as much fire and pathos as if it were the first strain. The air was now that one without any particular beginning, middle, or end, which perhaps, among all the dances which throng an inspired fiddler's fancy, best conveys the idea of the interminable – the celebrated 'Devil's Dream'. The fury of personal movement that was kindled by the fury of the notes could be approximately imagined by these outsiders under the moon, from the occasional kicks of toes and heels against the door, whenever the whirl round had been of more than customary velocity.

The first five minutes of listening was interesting enough to the mummers. The five minutes extended to ten minutes, and these to a quarter of an hour; but no signs of ceasing were audible in the lively Dream. The bumping against the door, the laughter, the stamping, were all as vigorous as ever, and the pleasure in being outside lessened considerably.

Another ten minutes passed, while the mummers debated whether or not to open the door.

At this moment the fiddles finished off with a screech, and the serpent emitted a last note that nearly lifted the roof. When, from the comparative quiet within, the mummers judged that the dancers had taken their seats, Father Christmas advanced, lifted the latch, and put his head inside the door.

'Ah, the mummers, the mummers!' cried several guests at once. 'Clear a space for the mummers.'

Hump-backed Father Christmas then made a complete entry, swinging his huge club, and in a general way clearing the stage for the actors proper, while he informed the company in smart verse that he was come, welcome or welcome not; concluding his speech with:

Make room, make room, my gallant boys,
    And give us space to rhyme;
We've come to show Saint George's play,
    Upon this Christmas time.'

The guests were now arranging themselves at one end of the room, the fiddler was mending a string, the serpent-player was emptying his mouthpiece, and the play began. First of those outside the Valiant Soldier entered, in the interest of St George–

Here come I, the Valiant Soldier;
    Slasher is my name;

and so on. This speech concluded with a challenge to the infidel, at the end of which it was Eustacia's duty to enter as the Turkish Knight. She, with the rest who were not yet on, had hitherto remained in the moonlight which streamed under the porch. With no apparent effort or backwardness she came in, beginning–

Here come I, a Turkish Knight,
Who learnt in Turkish land to fight;
I'll fight this man with courage bold:
If his blood's hot I'll make it cold!

During her declamation Eustacia held her head erect, and spoke as roughly as she could, feeling pretty secure from observation. But the concentration upon her part necessary to prevent discovery, the newness of the scene, the shine of the candles, and the confusing effect upon her vision of the ribboned visor which hid her features, left her absolutely unable to perceive who were present as spectators. On the further side of a table bearing candles she could faintly discern faces, and that was all.

Meanwhile Jim Starks as the Valiant Soldier had come forward, and, with a glare upon the Turk, replied –

If, then, thou art the Turkish Knight,
Draw out thy sword, and let us fight!

And fight they did; the issue of the combat being that the Valiant Soldier was slain by a preternaturally inadequate thrust from Eustacia, Jim in his ardour for genuine histrionic art, coming down like a log upon the stone floor with force enough to dislocate his shoulder. Then, after more words from the Turkish Knight, rather too faintly delivered, and statements that he'd fight St George and all his crew, St George himself magnificently entered with the well-known flourish–

Here come I, Saint George, the valiant man,
With naked sword and spear in hand,
Who fought the dragon and brought him to the slaughter
And by this won fair Sabra, the King of Egypt's daughter;
What mortal man would dare to stand
Before me with my sword in hand?

This was the lad who had first recognised Eustacia; and when she now, as the Turk replied with suitable defiance, and at once began the combat, the young fellow took especial care to use his sword as gently as possible. Being wounded, the Knight fell upon one knee, according to the direction. The Doctor now entered, restored the Knight by giving him a draught from the bottle which he carried, and the fight was again resumed, the Turk sinking by degrees until quite overcome – dying as hard in this venerable drama as he is said to do at the present day.

This gradual sinking to the earth was, in fact, one reason why Eustacia had thought that the part of the Turkish Knight, though not the shortest, would suit her best. A direct fall from upright to horizontal, which was the end of the other fighting characters, was not an elegant or decorous part for a girl. But it was easy to die like a Turk, by a dogged decline.

Eustacia was now among the number of the slain, though not on the floor, for she had managed to retire into a sitting position against the clock-case, so that her head was well elevated. The play proceeded between St George, the Saracen, the Doctor, and Father Christmas; and Eustacia, having no more to do, for the first time found leisure to observe the scene around, and to search for the form that had drawn her hither . . .

The remainder of the play ended: the Saracen's head was cut off, and St George stood as victor. Nobody commented, any more than they would have commented on the fact of mushrooms coming in autumn or snowdrops in spring. They took the piece as phlegmatically as did the actors themselves. It was a phase of cheerfulness which was, as a matter of course, to be passed through every Christmas; and there was no more to be said.

They sang the plaintive chant which follows the play, during which all the dead men rise to their feet in a silent and awful manner, like the ghosts of Napoleon's soldiers in the Midnight Review.[1]

So affected by the mumming plays of his youth, Hardy harked back to their formula in his last years for a wistfully autobiographical retelling of the Tristan legend, a difficult work which is little read nowadays, but which caused quite a stir when it was first published in 1923. The full title of this curious piece is The Famous Tragedy of the Queen of Cornwall at Tintagel in Lyonnesse: a new version of an old story arranged as a play for mummers in one act, requiring no theatre or scenery. *It was taken up with enthusiasm by the composer Rutland Boughton, whom we shall meet later on, and turned into a kind of Wagnerian opera, which he called a music-drama. Although regarded as Boughton's finest*

---

1   Hardy, T, *The return of the native* (1975 ed.), 142-57 (abridged).

work it languished unperformed for many decades and only in 2010 has it received a commercial recording.[1]

Hardy also prepared a version of the traditional play, 'Saint George', for a group of Dorchester amateur actors, the Hardy Players, to perform in their dramatization of The Return of the Native *in 1920. Christmas Day that year was a memorable occasion for everyone concerned. The local newspaper, the* Dorset County Chronicle, *takes up the story.*

A Most Exciting Christmas

HE HARDY PLAYERS visited the County Hospital on Christmas evening. The party first sang the old Mellstock carols at the foot of the main staircase. Then they gave in three of the wards the famous mummers play which was a prominent feature of the recent performance of *The Return of the Native,* and which was intensely enjoyed by the patients . . . After the delightful entertainment by the Mummers, the hearts of all the patients were cheered by the distribution of gifts by Father Christmas, realistically impersonated by Mr E J Stevens. He distributed his largesse with unstinted hand, and his geniality and merry quips were infectious. Further enjoyment was afforded by an excellent concert by the nurses . . .

Following their visit to the hospital the Players wended their way to Max Gate, and repeated the play as a tribute to Mr Hardy. Arriving at the house the Players first sang a carol, and when the last strains had died away the veteran author himself threw open the doors and with the utmost heartiness gave them the traditional welcome. The Players were invited to the drawing-room, and there before Mr and

1   Boughton, *The Queen of Cornwall.* Dutton Epoch 2CDLX 7256, released November 2010, New London Orchestra and London Chorus, conducted by Ronald Corp.

Mrs Hardy and a family party they gave the mumming scene, and, before such an audience, needless to say, played *con amore*, and Mr Hardy and his guests were delighted with the performance. The party were then invited by Mr and Mrs Hardy to 'a bite and a cup', and left amid an interchange of warmest appreciation and good wishes. The privilege of entertaining Mr Hardy under his own roof tree will be one of the Players' choicest memories.[1]

And so it was. No fewer than three of the company later recorded in print their recollections of the evening, including Father Christmas (E J Stevens) and his daughter in the 1960s, and the Turkish Knight (Gertrude Bugler) in 1982. Gertrude Bugler's stunning performances as Eustacia Vye, and later as Tess, captivated the octogenarian Hardy (and aroused his wife's jealousy). Here is her vivid account of that unforgettable evening (prompted in places by the words of the master), as she relived it over sixty years later.

It was a beautiful starry night when we met at the end of Prince of Wales Road opposite the junction of South Street and South Walk. The company comprised the singers of the 1918 revival of The Mellstock Quire and the mummers who had part in Mr Tilley's adaptation of *The Return of the Native*, which was performed in November 1920. The singers carried an old horn lantern slung on a pole, and a violin or violins; the mummers were resplendent in their uniforms, helmets, and swords, with gay-coloured ribbons everywhere. Our strangely visored helmets had been made by Mr Tilley from directions and sketches made by Thomas Hardy, who attended several rehearsals, as did Florence and her dog Wessex.

So we laughed and chatted as we moved up Prince of Wales Road to the Wareham Road, and before long we were at the white gate which opened to the short drive leading to the house. We crept

---

1   *Dorset County Chronicle* , 30 Dec. 1920.

up that drive in silence, and it seemed that all the lights of Max Gate welcomed us. The singers quietly grouped themselves round the lantern, and then, to use Hardy's own words, written so long before, there 'passed forth into the quiet night an ancient and time-worn hymn, embodying a quaint Christianity in words orally transmitted from father to son through several generations down to the present characters, who sang them out right earnestly'.

We were welcomed inside and shown where our stage was marked out by long strips of wood. Hardy at the rehearsal had suggested that we sang the words 'A-mumming we will go' as we entered, and again as we made our exit. He even hummed a tune for us, one we mostly knew as 'A-hunting we will go'; and of course we did just that. So we moved out to the porch in order to make what we hoped would be an impressive entrance. Father Christmas in his scarlet robe led the way with his huge club; then came the Valiant Soldier, the Turkish Knight, St George of England, and the Saracen. The Doctor in black, with his jar of 'alicampane' swinging from his waist, brought up the rear.

Father Christmas opened the play, saying:

Here come I, old Father Christmas;
Welcome or welcome not,
I hope old Father Christmas
Will never be forgot.
Make room, make room, my gallant boys,
And give us space to rhyme.
We've come to show St George's play
Upon this Christmas Time.

He swung his club, and stood with the Doctor at the back of the stage. The Valiant Soldier moved forward, saying 'Here come I, the Valiant Soldier, Slasher is my name', and so on. Eustacia (as the Turkish Knight) says:

Here come I, a Turkish Knight,
Who learnt in Turkish land to fight:
I'll fight this man with courage bold;
If his blood's hot, I'll make it cold.

Valiant Soldier replies, 'If then thou art the Turkish Knight, Draw out thy sword, and let us fight.' And fight they did, the issue of the combat being that the Valiant Soldier was slain by a preternaturally inadequate thrust from Eustacia, Jim coming down like a log.

The Turkish Knight then said he would fight St George and all his crew – 'Ay, country folk and warriors too'. St George entered magnificently with his well-known flourish,

Here come I, St George, the valiant man
With naked sword and spear in hand,
Who fought the dragon
And brought him to the slaughter,
And by this won fair Sabra,
The King of Egypt's daughter.
What mortal men would dare to stand
Before me with my sword in hand?

He and the Saracen fight. St George wins, but by now all the soldiers are on the ground, moaning and groaning. Father Christmas asks,'Is there a doctor to be found. To cure me of this grevious wound?' 'Yes', says the Doctor and, after some bargaining over the price he is to be paid, he administers a few drops of the 'alicampane' to each fallen hero. The groans cease.

Our audience laughed heartily as we came to life. To the slow chanting of the Doctor and Father Christmas, we rose slowly from the dead in the awful manner required. (The chant was suggested by Thomas Hardy at our rehearsal; it happened to be 'Langdon in

F', the favourite of Tess). With the points of their swords touching, the mummers then circled, singing right merrily, after their rapid recovery, 'And a-mumming we will go. 'Our audience was most appreciative. We then moved to the dining-room for refreshments. As our visors were just coloured ribbons attached to the large helmets, our faces were obscured, and eating and drinking, made difficult . . .

So now seats were found for us all, and hosts and hostess came to talk with us, and to tell us how much they were enjoying the evening, as we were. There were recollections of The Mellstock Quire, *The Trumpet-Major*, rustic scenes from *The Dynasts*, and the crisis in the proposal scene of *The Return of the Native*, when the electric lighting in the Corn Exchange at Dorchester failed, and poor Clym and Eustacie had to sit in darkness on the stage till candles were brought. That had happened only a few weeks before, but tonight we could laugh even at that. Hardy was interested in everything, and could remember as much as we did. I was sitting with some of the older players when he came our way, and he had a word for everyone. When he came to me he said, 'Won't you raise your visor for me, Eustacia, as you did for Clym Yeobright?' So I held the ribbons aside as I had done for Clym, and saw a smiling Thomas Hardy.[1]

On the following day, Boxing Day, Florence Hardy described the evening's events in a letter to a friend.

We, contrary to our usual custom, have spent a most exciting Christmas. Yesterday the Mummers (under our beloved Mr Tilley) came and performed in the drawing room here, to the intense joy of TH his brother and sister (whom I had here) and the rest of the household. And friends who accompanied them fiddled to us and sang carols outside – the real old Bockhampton carols. Then they

1 Bugler, Gertrude, 'Christmas night at Max Gate', *Thomas Hardy Society Review*, 1982, 235-7.

came in had refreshments in the dining room and we had a very delightful time with them – Miss Bugler looking prettier than ever in her mumming dress. TH has lost his heart to her entirely, but as she is soon getting married I don't let that cast me down too much . . . Will you be able to see it [in London] do you think or will you come down here to see it with TH at Weymouth? We shall be delighted to see you here whenever you are able to come. T is very well. At the party (of the Mummers etc) last night he was so gay – and one of them said to me that he had never seen him so young and happy and excited. He is now – this afternoon – writing a poem with great spirit: always a sign of well-being with him. Needless to say it is an intensely dismal poem.[1]

The collectors and revivers of mumming plays in the early twentieth century sensed that they were in the presence of something very ancient, a primordial ritual of death and rebirth and fertility. Parallels were drawn with the drama of ancient Greece and with tribal shamanism. Unfortunately for such theories, although mummers and mumming (and the similar activity, 'guising' – for 'disguising') are recorded in England as early as the thirteenth century, there is no evidence of a play until very much later. A fragment survives from 1738, but complete

1   Millgate, M (ed), *Letters of Emma and Florence Hardy* (1996), 170.

versions of the mumming play only begin to appear after 1750.[1] This makes the reminiscences in verse of a Dorset poet, William Holloway, of his childhood Christmases (he was born in 1761 near Blandford Forum) one of the earliest references to the play in Wessex.

Scenes of Youth
William Holloway

 OR YET FORGOTTEN be the festive eve,
To pageant mummeries dedicated still,
When Father Christmas to the neighbours round
His annual visit paid, in garb grotesque;
While, as he crack'd his merry jokes, and shook
His long white beard, the huddling children crept
Close to the mother's chair, and sought to hide
Beneath her apron blue each chubby face.
Prepar'd the way. . . behold a glitt'ring train;
In Sunday's best apparel, richly lac'd
Down ev'ry seam with paper, gold-emboss'd;
Of paper too aloft their ensign waves . . .
Their helmets shine with nodding plumes adorn'd,
Pluck'd from the barn-door cock, or turkey's tail;
With swords of wood, or lances, trembling white,
The peasant champions onward proudly stride,
With awkward gait, and mouth bombastic strains,
Expressive of defiance, daring loud
To single combat every bold compeer.
    Foremost, St George of England . . . he who slew
The venom'd dragon . . . shakes his dreaded lance:
Th' Egyptian Soldan, and the Norman Prince . . .

1   See discussion in Hutton, R, *The stations of the sun* (1996), ch.7, 70-80.

The Roman Soldier, and the Turkish Knight
Come next, exulting in their proud exploits;
With others, of inferior name and note,
But not less vaunting of heroic deeds.
Out fly their swords! the clatt'ring fight begins;
While many-a little bosom anxious heaves,
To mark the dire event. Fast drop around
The vanquish'd combatants, with quiv'ring limbs;
And soon the red-brick floor is all bestrew'd
With bloodless carcases, which mimic death,
Cautious, with-eyes shut up, and breath repress'd;
While o'er the fatal field of battle stalks
The doughty victor, insolently vain,
And, wrapt in self-importance, slow retires.
　　　Caught with the pomp and splendor of the scene,
Then would my kindled passions glow anew
With martial ardour, emulous of fame,
By judgment uncorrected . . . Such, too oft,
The Muse suspects, in nobler bosoms reign,
Prelusive to those sanguinary storms,
That waste mankind, and wrap the world in woe![1]

William Morris, who opened this exploration of mumming, was wrong in his assertion that 'mummer's books' did not exist. The words were sometimes printed in the form of broadsides or chapbooks, as this one, circulated by Nott, a Taunton printer, sometime after 1800. It mixes up with the traditional elements various subjects of national pride, such as contemporary battles (Trafalgar and Quebec), and guest appearances from real and imaginary heroes and villains. The result is an unusually high casualty rate, and a grand confusion of miscellaneous characters in search of a story line.

1　Holloway, W, *Scenes of youth*, 1803

Old Father Christmas
Or a New Play for the Christmas
Holidays

IRST: OPEN THE door of the room in which the company are, and begin with the following words:

Open the doors, and let us come in,
I hope your favours we shall win;
Whether we rise, or whether we fall,
We shall do our endeavours to please you all.
The merry time of Christmas is now drawing near;
I wish your pockets full of money, and your cellars full of beer,
And if you'll not believe what I do say,
Walk in, Old Father Christmas, and boldly clear the way.

Old Father Christmas
Here comes I, Old Father Christmas, welcome or welcome not,
I hope old Father Christmas will never be forgot;
Altho' I am come, I have but a short time to stay,
'Twas I, that led the King of Egypt away.
Room! Room! give a little room to sport;
For in this house I mean for to resort,
For to resort and merrily to play;
Walk in, the King of Egypt, and boldly clear the way.

King of Egypt
Here comes I, the King of Egypt, as plainly doth appear,
St George is my only son and heir.

Walk in, St George, and boldly act thy part,
That all this jovial company may see thy noble art.

St George
Here comes I, St George, that did from England spring,
Some of my mighty works for to begin.
First in a closet I was kept,
From thence into a cabinet,
From thence upon a rock of stone,
There did I make my sad and dismal moan,
Whilst many men did strive me to subdue,
I ran my firy dagger through and through;
I fought them all courageously,
And still came off with victory.
For England's right, for England's admiration,
Here I draw my bloody weapon with vexation.
Where is the man will me withstand?
Let him come in, and I will cut him down with my courageous hand.

Prince Valentine
Here comes I, Prince Valentine, so fair a man renown'd;
Soon shall thy haughty courage tumble down,
As for a fall thou shalt receive of me,
So let us fight it out most manfully.
Hold, hold, St George, let us shake hands before we fight;
Thou first challeng'd me, I next challenge thee,
So let us fight it out most manfully.

(St George and Prince Valentine now fight, and, after some struggling,
Prince Valentine is killed; but while he is lying on the floor, Prince
Amoric, his father, enters and says:)

Prince Amoric

As I was arising out of my bed,
I heard my only son was dead.
O cursed, cursed Christian! What hast thou done?
Thou hast ruin'd me, by killing my only son.

St George

He did me the challenge give. How could I him deny?
You know how high he was, but look how low he lies.

Prince Amoric

O help me, help me, Sambo! for never was there greater need.
Wilt thou stand idle, with thy sword in hand?
Come and fight, like a loyal subject, under my command.
I see him there dead, which makes my heart
To bleed. Distracted shall I run;
So I'll lie down, and die by my only son.

(Prince Amoric lies down by the side of Valentine, and dies.)

Sambo

Prince Amoric's law will I obey;
With my sword and spear I hope to win the day;
For yonder is he that spilt my master's blood,
And with his body will I make an ocean flood.

St George

O doctor! is there ne'er a doctor to be found,
Can cure these champions of their deep and deadly wounds?

Doctor

Yes, yes, St George, there is a doctor to be found,
Can cure these champions of their deadly wounds.

St George
What is thy fee?

Doctor
Ten pounds is my fee; five only will I take of thee.

St George
Where hast thou travelled?

Doctor
France, Italy, Germany, and Spain.

St George
What canst thou cure?

Doctor
The itch, palsy, and the gout,
All pains within, and pains without,
And if the devil is within, soon I'll fetch him out.
I have a little bottle in my pocket, call'd Virtue and Fame.
Here, Jack, take a little of my flip-flap, put it into thy tip-tap;
Rise, Jack Slash, and fight again.

(Prince Valentine and Prince Amoric now gets [sic] to life again, and rising, says:)

Prince Valentine
O terrible! terrible! Was like ever seen,
That men should be brought from their seven senses into seventeen?

Bloody Warrior
Here comes I, a Bloody Warrior, spent all my time in bloody wars,
And now I'm return'd, cover'd with wounds and scars.

I've serv'd King George both by land and by sea,
And now I'm content in Old England to stay;
But of all the battles that I have fought on my way,
Was the glorious battle in Trafalgar's Bay;
And as I'm return'd, in Old England to dwell,
I'll drink to the heroes who on that day fell.

Admiral Nelson
Drums, beat to arms!
Trumpets, sound to Fame!
I am a British hero,
And Nelson is my name.
Remember, on the 21st of October,
That being the very day,
Nineteen sail of the line,
Some we took, and some we sunk,
And some cowardly bore away.

Admiral Duncan
Drums, beat to arms!
Trumpets, sound to Fame!
I am a British hero,
Admiral Duncan is my name.

General Wolfe
Drums, beat to arms!
Trumpets, sound to Fame!
I am a British hero,
General Wolfe is my name.
I have scaled many rocks,
And climbed many walls;
Neither was I haunted nor daunted at all,
Till a bullet struck me on the gall.

As I lay bleeding on the wat'ry sands,
I heard a voice say 'Bear up, General Wolfe, and die in my hands'.

Little Man John
Here comes I, a little man, John Slasher is my name;
With sword and buckler by my side, I hope to win the game.

St George
I am St George, that man of courage bold,
And with my sword and spear have won three tons of gold.
I slew the Dragon, and brought him to the slaughter,
And by that means I won the King of Egypt's daughter.

Turkish Knight
Here comes I, the Turkish Knight,
Come from the Turkish land to fight,
To fight St George, that man of courage bold,
Altho' his blood be hot, I soon will make it cold.

St George
Hold, hold, proud Turk! pray don't you be so hot,
For in this room is one thou knowest not;
Here is one that will cut thee as small as the dust,
And send thee to the devil, to make apple-pie crust;
I'll cut thee and slash thee as small as the flies,
And send thee to the devil, to make mince-pies;
I'll cut thee and slash thee, and after I've done,
I'll fight the bravest champion under the sun.

Turkish Knight
You first the challenge gave, and I the challenge took,
And why should I of you refuse a stroke?
Draw out thy sword and fight, draw out thy purse and pay,

For satisfaction I will have before I go away.

St George
No satisfaction shalt thou from me have,
For in one moment I'll make thee an English slave.

(Here St George and the Turkish Knight fight.)

Turkish Knight (being wounded by St George, says:)
O! hold thy hand, St George; for one thing of thee I crave;
Spare but my life, and I will be thy slave.

St George
Get thee home unto thy Turkish land,
And tell what noble champions in England stand;
Ten thousand of such ones as thee I'll fight,
For to maintain the Crown of England's right.

Turkish Knight
Here I arise and go away;
God bless King George, and all his ships at sea.

Tom Bowling
Jolly sailor, jolly sailor, Tom Bowling is my name;
Here's me and men, and men like war,
Just come on shore, in hopes to beat eleven score.
We'll set our guns aboard of them,
We'll make a dreadful noise,
We'll make the King jump off his throne,
And all the people shout for joy.

Fire Poul
Here comes young Fire Poul, as you may understand;

Walk in, young Crumell, and take me by the hand.

Young Crumell
Here comes I, young Crumell, as you may plainly see;
I think, young Fire Poul, I'm man enough for thee.

St George
I am St George, and the battle soon will try;
He that is resolv'd to fight, come, fight with me and die.

Last: Gentlemen and Ladies,
You see the Turkish Knight is to be conveyed to the Castle;
Let your voices thro' this room ring,
And be so well pleased as to put something into our Christmas Caps, and say,
God save the King.[1]

So many mumming plays have been transcribed and preserved, from Wessex and elsewhere, that it is perfectly possible to summarise the action common to them all in a few words. This was done long ago, and is worth repeating:

The typical Mummers' Play opens with a naïve introduction in which one of the performers craves the spectators' indulgence, asks for room and promises a fine performance. When this is concluded the two protagonists appear, and after each has boasted of his valour they fall to fighting. In this duel one or the other is wounded or killed. A doctor is then summoned who vaunts his proficiency in medicine and proceeds to revive the fallen hero. Here the main business of the play ends. It is now the turn of minor characters to enter and provide

1   SRO DD/SAS C/2273 3/4.

irrelevant amusement of a simple sort. One of them collects money and the performance finishes with a song.[1]

So, mumming consists of a theme and variations. Here are a few of the latter from various Wessex locations, providing the 'irrelevant amusement of a simple sort'.

From Stourton, Wiltshire

Duchess
Here comes I, Miss Duchess, with my broom, broom, broom, To sweep the room clean for the Duke and the Captain to have room for to fight.

Duke
Here is the Duke, the Duke of Northumberland,
With my broad sword in hand.
Where is the man? I bid him stand.
I'll cut him in humerus, and as small as a fly;
I'll send him to the cook-shop for to make mince-pie.
So walk in, Captain.

Captain
Here comes the Captain, Captain Curly! Duke, I heard your voice from out the chimney.

Duke
Pray, what did you hear, Captain Curly?

---

1 Tiddy, R, *The mummers' play* (1923), 73, quoted by Hutton, R, *The stations of the sun* (1996), 70.

Captain
I heard the challenge of Captain Curly.
Here comes I, so light as a fly;
But I've no money, but what cares I!
Here comes I from the Isle of Wight,
Unto the Duke of Northumberland;
Here comes I to fight.
So mind yourself, and guard your blows;
Off comes your head, if not your nose!

After the Duke has been wounded Doctor Finley is summoned to dose him. Some of his treatments seems a little drastic:

Doctor Finley
I'll cure the hickly, pickly, palsy, or the gout.
I'll cure old Jack Daw with the toothache,
Or old Mag-Pie with the headache.

Captain
Pray, how do you that, Mr Finley?

Doctor
By twisting their heads off, and sending their bodies into ditch.

Next entered the most interesting character – the most interesting because the least obvious – Johnnie Jack. He carried a number of small dolls on his back:

Johnnie Jack
Here comes I, little Johnnie Jack,
With my wife and family at my back.
My wife's so big, my family's so small,
If I hadn't come when I had I'd have starved them all.

Out of five I saved but one;
All the rest is dead and gone.
So, ladies and gentlemen, have pity on me,
Poor Johnnie Jack, and his great wife and he.

Lastly comes Bighead:

Bighead
Here comes I, that's never been yet,
With my big head, and little wit.
My head's so big, my wit's so small,
I've brought my fiddle to please you all.[1]

From Lulworth, Dorset

In this version the Play of St George has become the Battle of Waterloo, and the characters changed accordingly. Here is a short extract.

Tom Fool
Here am I, Tom Fool. Haw, Haw, Haw. Is Mr Bull in?

John Bull
Yes, Tom, what may you want of him?

Tom Fool
I am come to tell you that Bonaparte has come
Over from France with two million of French.

John Bull
Never mind him Tom, nor all his army too,
Give me and my men the battle,

---

1 Adapted from Balch, E E, 'In a Wiltshire village', *Antiquary*, xliv (1908), 379-82.

We'll show them the British Rattle.

Tom Fool
Rattle, Rattle, that will not do,
When there is rattling, there must be fighting as well as rattling too.
Therefore I must see what I can do.
But hark! I think I hear them coming.

Bonaparte
Here am I, Bonaparte lately come from France,
To pay John Bull a visit, and learn him a new dance,
A dance that's never been danced before, my boys, by any man but me.
I'll strike stirs in all your hearts, and make you Britons flee.

Tom Fool
Ha, Ha, but when the French do come to England, they will come without a heart,
Therefore tonight Mr Bull and I will try to upset proud Bonaparte.
Although you call me Tom Fool, there's many a man been made fool by me,
And by my actions here tonight, that truth you'll plainly see.
As for that tyrant Bonaparte, I hope for to lay down,
And with my sword in hand this night, I'll lay thee on the ground.

John Bull
Be silent Tom, don't interrupt that noisy fellow's breath,
Be as it will, though, Tom Fool shall be that tyrant's death.

Bonaparte
Don't talk of fools, nor yet of death but learn this warlike dance,
For the time shall quickly come, when I am free in France.
Come on my bold hero.

Prince Bulow

Here am I, Prince Bulow from Flanders lately come,
Where the cannons they do rattle, and sound the warlike drum.
With my true courage, I follow Bony slow to your land to fight
For Bonaparte which is my whole delight.
Likewise you British dogs, I will defeat this night.

Duke of York

Here am I, the Duke of York, standing all on British land.
Proud Bonaparte I do defy, and all his daring band.
With British troops my boys, I went through Holland, France and Spain,
I will this night, with sword in hand, face Bonaparte again.[1]

From Symondsbury, Dorset

The Doctor, who is introduced as Mr Martin Dennis, is clearly a surgeon as well as a physician.

St George

Most noble doctor, if thou set those men on their pins again I'll give thee one hundred pounds: there is the money.

Doctor

So I will, my worthy champion. I am sure I won't want for whiskey for one twelve-month to come. For the first man I saw beheaded I put his head on again, and he is doing well and making his fortune and cream tarrity [?]

---

1   The full text is in Chandler, J, *Thomas Hardy's Christmas* (1997), 42-54, transcribed (with permission) from a typescript then in Dorchester Reference Library.

St George
Pray by what means is he doing well and making his fortune and
cream tarrity?

Doctor
As I must tell you, my worthy champion – in course of a hurry I put
his head on the wrong way – his mouth where his poll ought to be,
and he is now exhibited in a wondering nature.

St George
Very good answer, Mr Doctor. Tell me more of your miracles and rise
these warriors.

Doctor
I can cure love-sick maidens, jealous husbands, squalling wives,
brandy-drinking dames, with one touch of my ackmiseul [?] or one
sly dose of my Jerusalem balsam, that will make an old crippled dame
dance the hornpipe. So now to convince you of all my exertions, I will
arise Captain Bluster, Gracious King, General Valentine and Colonel
spring.

Next Father Christmas has a row with his wife, variously known as
Dame Dorothy or Old Bet. She refers to him as Jan.

Father Christmas
I have catched a fine dry jack hare,
And I intend to have him fried for supper,
And here's some wood to cook him with.
Look! See!

Old Bet
No, Jan, have him roasted nice.

Father Christmas
I tell thee I'll have him fried.

Old Bet
Was there ever such a foolish dish!

Father Christmas
I tell thee I'll have him fried; and if thee do'snt do as I do bid, Lord sown [?] thee, I'll hit thee in the head.

Old Bet
Do as you like, I do not care.
I never will fry a whole dry jack hare.

(Father Christmas knocks Old Bet down)

Father Christmas
Oh! What have I done! I have murdered my wife,
The joy of my heart and the pride of my life.
Now to the gaol I shall quickly be sent;
I did it in a passion, no malice I meant.
Is there a doctor can restore
My poor old wife to me again?
Fifty pounds would I give, and twice fifty more.

(enter Doctor – with a rather different bedside manner from that of his predecessor)

Oh! What, be you a doctor?

Doctor
Yes, I am a doctor of great fame, one who has travelled through Europe, Asia, Africa, and America, and by long practice have learnt

the best of cures most disorderly to the human body; been in the army some time, found nothing difficult in restoring a limb that suffered mortification, an arm cut off by a sword, or head been struck off by a cannon ball, if the application be not delayed until too late.[1]

From Lydiard, near Swindon

This play was collected by Alfred Williams, and included characters called Most High Proud (explained as the King of Spain), Beelzebub (reminiscent – in some respects – of the Cerne Abbas Giant),[2] and minor characters. Williams explained that these, the Tinker, Soldier, Doctor and Saucy Jack, were subservient to the principal action of the piece. Their activities were extended or curtailed according to circumstances and the degree of hospitality shown by the occupants of the house at which the play was presented.

Beelzebub
Here come I, Beelzebub,
On my left shoulder I carry a big nub,
And in my hand a dripping-pan,
Don't you think I'm a jolly old man?
My father's been and killed a fat hog,
And that you can plainly see;
My mother gave me the bladder
To make a hurly-ga-gee.
I saw a mouse by yonder wall,
He ran in, and that was all

---

1   Extracts from Udal, J S, 'Christmas mummers in West Dorset', *Somerset & Dorset Notes and Queries*, ix (1905), 9-19.
2   This theory, propounded by Stuart Piggott, is discussed by Hutton, R, *The stations of the sun* (1996), 78-9.

All
To my tol the rol, tol the rol the rido

(Enter Saucy Jack, with a bundle of dolls strapped on his back.)

Saucy Jack
Here come I, old Saucy Jack,
With all my family at my back.
Christmas comes but once a year,
And when it comes it brings good cheer –
Roast beef, plum pudding and mince-pie,
And who likes that any better than I?

(Here Saint George [a.k.a. Moll and regarded as female] and the Tinker quarrel and fight.)

Tinker sings
Good morning, Moll, and 'ow dost do?
And wher' bist thee agwine?
I got zummat to zay to thee
If thee canst spare the time.

All (chorus)
Fol the rol the rido, and that's the time of day O.

Saint George
What hast thou got to say to me,
Of any sort or kind?

Tinker
Why I should like to marry thee,
If thee oot but be mine.

St George
Dost thee think I'd wed with a clown,
That is not better bred?
For I must have a handsome man,
'Fore ever I will wed.

Tinker
What, byent I handsome enough for thee,
With my dandy leather breech?
The gold-laced band about my neck?
Look on the other twitch.

St George
Now I must have some butcher's meat,
And bread and butter fine,
And every morning a dish of tea,
To drink instead of wine.

Tinker
Won't good fat bacon sar thy turn,
Some delicate powdered beef,
Some bread and cheese, and milk, sweet Moll?
For that's a farmer's chief.

St George
If thou and I should ever wed,
As sure as thou art born,
A cuckold thou should'st surely be,
And thou should'st wear a horn.

Tinker
Then if a cuckold I should be,
Thou and I should never agree,

So let us kiss and part, sweet Moll,
And never wedded be.

All
For the rol the rido, and that's the time of day O.

(At this point Robin Hood and his merry men arrive).[1]

Oh No, it isn't!
Thomas Forder Plowman

By delving into the sub-plots and diversions of the mummers it becomes clear that, whatever affinity their play may ever have had with pagan fertility rituals, it had become much closer to another Christmas institution, the pantomime. Cross-dressing, knockabout humour, little songs and choruses – all these are pantomime trademarks. It is quite possible, in fact, that the two stem from a common theatrical tradition.

1   Williams, A, 'A Wiltshire mummers' play', *Wiltshire Gazette*, 30 Dec 1926, 3.

Pantomime developed in the eighteenth century out of harlequinade, a comic interlude between the acts of the main play staged in London theatres. Only later was it regarded as a play in its own right, and – because of its topsy-turvydom – it became associated with Christmas. At Bath the first pantomime seems to have taken place on Boxing Day 1850, and was advertised thus:

THEATRE ROYAL, BATH under the management of Mrs Macready.

The Nobility, Gentry, and Public are respectfully informed that the theatre will open on Thursday Dec 26 1850 with a new comic grand CHRISTMAS PANTOMIME, being a new version of the History of England – Romantically, though Historically, rendered – Local, yet Legendary – called HARLEQUIN TEMPLAR; or, Richard Couer de Lion taking in Bath on his way to Palestine; an Incident not to be found in either Hume, Smollett, Goldsmith, or Macaulay.

The Opening and Comic Scenes written and invented expressly for this Theatre; the Overture and Music composed, arranged, and selected by Mr. Salmon; the Scenery, entirely new, designed and executed by Mr. F. Thorne, Mr. Stanley, and Assistants. The Properties, Masks, and Paraphernalia, by Messrs Howey, Lodge, and Ashwell; the extensive Machinery, Tricks, and Transformations, by Messrs Norwell and Wiltshire; the Dresses, by Miss Quick and Assistants.

The HARLEQUINADE will be supplied by Metropolitan Performers of the First Celebrity. Clown: Mr. Grammani, Harlequin: Mr. Osmond. Pantaloon: Herr Karl. Columbine: Mlle. Rosins.

Thursday Dec 26, and following evenings. Previous to the Pantomime, the Comic Piece of 'THE INNKEEPER'S WIFE'. Characters by the Company. To conclude with the Farce of 'The Two Gregories'.

This was how it was noticed by the Bath Chronicle *the following week:*

The new Christmas pantomime was produced on the evening of Thursday last. 'Its title is 'Harlequin Templar; or Richard Couer de Lion taking in Bath on his way to the Holy Land'. The piece has been got up with great care and considerable cost; and its success has been complete. The introductory libretto is extremely comic, and it has been received with shouts of the heartiest laughter. As may be inferred from the title of the pantomime, there are numerous local allusions. These have been conceived in a spirit of capital humour, and are such as cannot give offence in any quarter. The scenery is very good – the dresses and disguises are capital – the fun never flags – and the tricks and transformations very cleverly executed. The music consists of adaptations of very pleasing popular airs; and this department of the entertainment is alone amply worth a visit to the Theatre. The various characters are supported with great vivacity. Each scene has its particular claim to approbation; but we may single out for especial notice the fight between the 'armies' of Richard and Saladin, than which we never witnessed anything more irresistibly ludicrous. It has nightly thrown the house into uncontrollable fits of laughter. We heartily recommend those of our playgoing readers who may not have seen the Pantomime not to lose the opportunity of doing so. They will have an abundant return of rich amusement for their money.[1]

The Bath pantomime became an institution, to such an extent that even someone who went on to be one of the city's mayors tried his hand at it in the 1890s. He was Thomas Forder Plowman, mayor in 1912, and in his autobiography he candidly mused on his shortcomings.

1   *Bath Chronicle*, 26 Dec 1850; 2 Jan 1851.

My theatrical experiences would hardly be complete if I did not confess that once upon a time I had the hardihood to attempt the regeneration of pantomime, and there were people good enough to think that I did accomplish something in that direction, but, if so, the effect was very transient. I must admit that, viewed from an author's standpoint, the result fell far short of my hopes and aspirations. In my simplicity I fancied that both the public and the profession might take kindly to a stage-version of a pretty fairy story, so presented that the main incidents, accepted and believed in from time immemorial, followed in proper sequence without incoherent interruptions, thus sustaining the interest in the plot to the finish. I thought, too, that the traditional old woman – a man in petticoats – with an acknowledged craving for alcoholic drinks, and a flightiness of disposition out of harmony with her years, might be made more sober and respectable. I likewise believed that the red-nosed 'knockabouts', who were wont to burst upon the scene clad in modern garments of a flamboyant type, might be dispensed with. I sought also to disestablish other freakish monstrosities, which I need not specify. Then it was part of my scheme that every rhyming couplet should have its proper number of feet, neither more nor less; that its scansion should pass muster; that the rules of rhyme should be strictly observed; and that the whole should go trippingly on the tongue. Of course, the popular songs of the day had to be utilised, but I adapted the words to the particular situation they were intended to illustrate.

Alas, I lost sight of the fact that the average pantomime company, wedded to ancient traditions, regarded what I looked upon as mere excrescences as absolute essentials, whilst the ordinary stage-manager cared for none of the things that I thought all-important! So my efforts to substitute something in the way of humour more subtle than horseplay and a mere kicking up behind and before, and to introduce a touch of sentiment here and there, often had to give way to interpellations [sic] that made me shudder and played havoc with my fairy-story. In a sylvan glade in Fairyland, a comedian, who had previously got into a brilliant check suit specially for the purpose, would suddenly burst upon the scene in order to impress upon the audience in song that 'At Trinity Church I met my doom', or to vocalise something akin to it, equally foreign to the situation. I would say to him, 'But, my dear sir, if you must sing that song, I will write words for it that shall be more in harmony with the spirit of the scene, and you can sing it in a garb appropriate to the piece.' This, he thought, would ruin everything. I could fight the matter ofttimes successfully at rehearsal, and then would behold the check suit and hear all about Trinity Church when it came to the public performance.[1]

To bring to an end this exploration of the theatrical side of Christmas here is a retelling of one of the favourite pantomime themes, Cinderella, set in Weymouth by Llewelyn Powys.

A Christmas Story
Llewelyn Powys

 ANET SPARKES WAS twelve years old, an odd little child with a pale face and the bright eyes of a bird. Her yellow hair was always tangled in elf knots and her hands were always grubby: for her mother, who took in other people's washing, did not have time to look after her properly. It was, in fact, Janet herself who had to be a dutiful mother to her younger sister Ivy. Every Saturday afternoon throughout the summer the two children might be seen walking past the Civil and Military Stores at Weymouth, on their way to the sea front. Here on the sands they would remain until late in the evening, when with reluctant steps they would go trailing back to their home next to a bootmaker's shop on the other side of the harbour.

---

1   Plowman, T F, *In the days of Victoria* (1918), 207-9.

Janet was an imaginative child and would often surprise her teacher by her intelligence. She possessed, for example, a really remarkable gift for learning poetry by heart. At the afternoon repetition lesson, when it was her turn to recite, her whole being would suddenly become illuminated so that the other children would stop coughing and stop shuffling their feet on the class room floor.

The two Sparkes children used to play always in the same place, a few yards from the donkey stands on the pier side. They were familiar figures to Joseph Hardcastle, the ice-cream man, to the Corporation deck-chair man who had eyes as far-sighted as a cock robin's, and to Mr Smallbones, the proprietor of the donkeys. Ivy was deeply attached to Daisy, the daughter of Mr Hardcastle, who was a few years older than herself; whereas Janet's whole attention was taken up with following the movements of the goat-carriage boy. She always knew when he was away with his carriage and when he was back at the stands, and was never tired of watching him sauntering carelessly by the side of his two lily-white goats.

The boy's name was Fay Merlinson, and he looked, with his sun-tanned skin and bare feet, as if he were an Arab lad who, after tightening the scarlet bellystrap of a desert camel, had been carried to Weymouth Esplanade on a magic carpet. It was perhaps his foreign appearance that so bewitched Janet. He certainly was very different from the boys she knew. He was as fond-of the donkeys as he was of his own goats. Without troubling to read the names on their forehead straps, he could recognize any one of them by merely glancing at its hairy, simple head. From his high position on the Esplanade he kept a sharp look out, and if he saw an ass being maltreated by its urchin postilion his voice would soon he heard oddly shrill in tone shouting at the boy. All the donkey boys feared and obeyed him. He seemed to be accepted by them as their natural leader. They called him Sea Crow. Janet longed to have him speak to her, but though he would often acknowledge her presence by a friendly nod, he never came down to her sand castles. As the summer advanced all Janet's romantic imaginings became centred about him and about his wooden goat carriage. This vehicle seemed to her as wonderful as the Godmother's carriage in the story of Cinderella. She could distinguish it from a great distance; its notched woodwork shining as if carved out of silver!

One evening in late August, when Janet was returning home alone, Ivy and Daisy having gone off together under the care of Mr Hardcastle, she saw the Sea Crow with his carriage approaching from the direction of the ferry. The mere sight of the boy made her shiver. She hardly dared to look up. They met at the entrance of the Alexandra Gardens, and she soon realized that he was stopping his goats. With the most courtly gesture possible he threw open one of the carriage doors and a moment later there she was in the upholstered miniature Lord Mayor's coach, her broken sandy shoes nervously resting on its handsome carriage mat. She had been transformed into a princess. She flushed with an unspeakable happiness.

The boy turned his animals at Devonshire Place and began following the Harbour in the direction of the Bridge. A crowd was collected near the Customs House, and when they came up they noticed that there were boys at the Quay's edge stoning a wounded sea-gull, which, unable to fly or swim, was being carried helplessly by the incoming tide towards the Backwater. A horror seized upon Janet. The Sea Crow gave repeated utterance to his shrillest calls and then began swearing at the boys ; while at the same time, giving the reins into Janet's hands, he leaped on to a coal barge and from there to a pleasure boat, where, with the dexterous twist of an oar, he lifted the unfortunate gull out of the water. Hardly three minutes could have elapsed before he was back at Janet's side laying the wounded bird in her lap. It was not a herring gull, indeed it was like no gull that she had ever seen. It might have been an albatross, it was so white, white as a Christmas goose!

They now went on their way, the white gull, the white carriage, and the white goats. He did not stop again until they had passed under Weymouth Bridge and had arrived at the deserted turning that overlooks the Backwater. The boy then took the bird up and said these words:

Yellow webs and yellow beak,
Mackerel eat for meat.
Wing and feather
Heal together.
Fly free
To the sea.

Immediately afterwards Janet saw the gull float away as if it had never been injured. It circled about a small tub-like fishing boat with sails white as its own wings, and then dived under an arch of the New Bridge to rise on the other side with the evening sunlight glancing bright upon the feathers of its head and back as it winged its way towards the Harbour mouth and the blue waves and the distant cliffs.

All through the melancholy autumn months that followed, Janet Sparkes would recall every moment of that happy twilight hour that the two had spent together. They had sat side by side in the unused doorway of the great seventeenth century warehouse and he had set about feeding the two goats with scraps of cow cake that he took from his ragged pocket. Janet had loved to examine the animals at such close quarters–their wrinkled horns curving backwards, their wide-open comprehending eyes! She even liked to watch the insistent way they nudged with their black noses for more! more! more!

The next day the Sea Crow was not on the donkey stands. She did not see him again after that evening. At last she persuaded Mr Hardcastle to make inquiries of him of Mr Smallbones. 'Oh, that lad never speaks out jonnick where he do come from. He always goes sudden-like and always returns sudden-like. But bless me, never let the maid fret; he'll be back next spring. I don't have to hear the cuckoo holla over Lodmoor many times before I see thik Sea Crow, as they call 'en, back again along be goat carriage.'

The autumn went by slowly and sadly for Janet, but at last December came. Mr Sparkes had for a long time planned to take his wife and two little girls to the Pavilion Theatre on Christmas Eve. Such a thing had never happened before. At tea-time on the evening of the long anticipated day Daisy arrived with an invitation from the Hardcastles for them all to come to supper after their entertainment. Janet realized how the appearance of Daisy had made Ivy yearn to have her friend with her at the play and with a great effort of will she explained to her mother that she was not feeling very well and would prefer to stay at home. It had been difficult to be so unselfish, and as soon as they had gone and she was alone in the empty house she lay on her bed in the dark and cried.

Suddenly she was aware of a sound of some movement outside her window. It was as if there was something on the flat roof of their neighbour the cobbler's shed. Then a mysterious light came flooding into her room and there, leaning against the broad sill where she kept shells and pebbles, was the Sea Crow! It seemed as natural as day. Just as on the former occasion, he flung open the small carriage door and in no time at all she was being borne up over the sloping roofs of the Weymouth houses. Often afterwards she tried to remember the manner of the goats' progress. They certainly did not fly. With their driver they seemed to glide through the cold atmosphere, their cleft hooves striking the crystal levels of the sky with a reiterated tapping. It was freezing hard but Janet was too excited to feel cold. She looked down at the lights of the town and at the great Bay spread out below her, with its beached shore curved like the bow of Apollo, merging into the white cliffs with their risings and fallings under the glittering stars of the winter night!

When they came to earth at last it was in the little spinney below Poxwell stone circle. Here by the small bridge that spanned the woodland stream was an open space. Janet Sparkes looked about her in amazement. On all sides were a gay little people mounted upon diminutive horses, animals exquisitely proportioned. It might have

been a Blackmore Vale meet in miniature if fairies could be believed
to take pleasure in hunting wild living creatures to death. The Sea
Crow stood at her side dressed now like a prince, and she herself was
wearing, she discovered, the most lovely clothes and a white fur cloak
that filled up the entire seat of her carriage. But what was even more
wonderful, the small moonshine wood was brightly lighted without
lights. All around her 'the bridles were ringing' and she could hear the
small palfreys champing and see them pawing at the mossy ground
with hooves round and polished. It was as though the fair unhallowed
flesh of these debonair riders possessed some mysterious luminosity
of its own, so that after the manner of glow worms their carnal
bodies had the power of giving out at will a charmed lustre. Janet was
spellbound; she looked from one to the other of the outlandish flower-
like profiles, admiring the gallantry, the courtesy of this company,
as, leaning lightly from their embossed and decorated saddles, they
indulged in their shrill banter. About her all the time was this natural
wood with patches of blackberry brambles showing dimly against
the trunks of tall trees, from the bare tops of which roosting wood
pigeons, disturbed by so unaccustomed a chittering below, would fly
off with the sound of their wings beating against the cold December
twigs denuded of leaves.

The cavalcade moved away at last and was soon advancing
along the downland ridge above the Ringstead Valley. The goat
carriage came last of all. Behind was a rout of wild animals that from
a traditional fealty to the Elfin Court always follow such processions.
Janet counted as many as twenty drowsy badgers, all of whom must
have passed out of long bristle-polished passages leading from their
vast sets under High Chaldon. There were a great many cliff foxes,
beagles of the god Dionysos, and hares from forms in neighbouring
flinty root fields, and rabbits from the warrens, and stoats and weasels
and rats, and even a house mouse, grown fat and adventurous from
larding her tiny curved ribs in Mrs Tom's generous pantry. The grass
eaters seemed to have lost all fear of the flesh eaters and gambolled by

their sides as if they knew on this night of all nights in the year their blood, by an express dispensation, could not be spilled.

How marvellous the sight was to the child! The royal trappings of the horses, the nodding feathers, the smooth frosty lawns of upland grass! How still it was too on those ancient hills! Not a sound came from the sea, and above her head shone the Christmas stars!

When the procession reached the corner where Queen Victoria's red pillar-box stands by the side of the track leading down to Holworth Dairy, a number of winter-coated heifers got up from where they were lying. One of them came close up to the goat carriage and then, snorting, frisked away over the jack-frost grass. The troop left the Merlin Thorn Tree on the right and turned down the valley leading to the green pond, and then in stately order went up the broad grassy track which, at an easy level, climbs to the down opposite the barn known as Shotts Barn. A bright light was pouring out through its wide open harvest doors.

What a scene it was when all was ready for the fairy theatre! At the north end was the stage, and at the other end was the eldritch audience. The old barn was illumined with candle stars of different colours held in the triple cups of innumerable carline thistles. Little Janet again glanced furtively around her, marvelling at the fuchsia-like forms of the dainty ladies whose physiognomies had never for a single hour been pinched or puckered with human woe. How they bent forward their pollen-powdered cheeks idling after their buskin gallants! A white screech owl had been disturbed in the rafters above, and Janet watched it, perched on its draughty stool under the slate roof, looking down on them with grave, perplexed eyes. Then the puppet players appeared and the company became silent.

When the play was over the fairies began to throng towards the door, gathering their petal-bright wraps of wool, fur, and feather about their sharp shoulders as the night air, coming in from the open downs, penetrated their bones light and hollow as quills of ivory. Janet was in dismay to think it was over so soon and begged her Prince to snatch for her one of the thistle sconces. With this trophy clasped in her hand she again seated herself in her carriage and followed the procession down to the green pond.

The Court did not return to Poxwell Wood. They broke up at the Roman Road, where it is the custom for the gipsies to have their camp.

The Sea Crow went over to take leave of his mother –that great fairy. Janet could see him bending over her hand with the grace of a drooping foxglove. She waited. The air blew cold against her forehead. She could hear a sheep coughing in its hurdled fold. So must they have coughed a few minutes before the shepherds heard the angels singing on the rocky downs above Bethlehem.

It was past midnight when Janet Sparkes was once more back in her bedroom. It was not till two o'clock that she went downstairs to open the front door to the others. They looked exactly the same as when they had left. Mr Sparkes's Sunday boots, thanks to the frost, were as bright-polished as ever. 'The theatre was lovely,' Ivy said, 'I do wish you had been there to see it.' It was on the tip of Janet's tongue to say 'I have been to a play too,' but an instinct warned her in time of the unwisdom of ever confiding to anybody this Christmas Eve's incredible adventure. Perhaps after all it had been nothing but a dream. Suppressing an inclination to burst into sobs, she ran upstairs to her room.

She was reassured utterly, for never did a Hebrew maiden, looking upon her seven candlesticks of Israel, the sacred Menorah, experience emotions more ecstatic than did little Janet Sparkes when she saw that there really and truly was, lying on her chest of drawers under her broken looking-glass, a common downland thistle, its prickles shining clear in the yellow light of her common bedroom candle.[1]

---

1   Powys, L, *Somerset essays* (1937), 199-209.

4
Winter Weather

HE SMALLEST BOUGHS and the tiniest twigs are coated on the upper part with a white rib of snow; for the flakes, scarcely slanting in their fall before the light air, rest on the first thing they touch; so that even the laurel leaves, which droop with the frost, are covered, and the crinkled holly-leaves hold the snow as if their spines grasped it like a claw. In the hedge the very peggles on the hawthorn bush are tipped – red fruit beneath, white snow above – and appear enlarged to twice their real size. The fields are levelled – the furrows filled and the clods hidden: a smooth white surface everywhere. Over the broad brook the branches of the trees hang low, heavily weighted, and dip their slender points in the water, black by contrast. Dark and silent, the stream flows without a ripple or a murmur against its frozen shores. But in the afternoon, when the sun shines in a cloudless sky, there floats above the current a golden vapour lit up by the rays. The sun sinks lower, and the disc becomes ruddy as it enters the mist above the horizon. Night falls, and the frost sharpens and the snow hardens on the boughs. Then in the morning as the sun rises the eastern side of the wood becomes glorified exceedingly. Each slender snow-laden branch – all the interlaced pattern of the trees – glows with an exquisite rosy light. Another day, a third, and still the beautiful snow lies everywhere. It shrinks a little, because now the tops of the larger clods in the ploughed fields are visible. There is a group of such dark clods in one place – eight or nine close together. Suddenly one moves: then another detaches itself and creeps a yard away: it is, in fact, a covey of partridges crouching hopelessly on the snow. These birds, like others that obtain their food on the ground, endure great privation when it is not only covered with snow but frozen hard beneath. It is indeed difficult to understand how they find sufficient to support life. They enter rickyards where the snow is partially cleared by the men; they venture, too, into gardens that are not immediately under the windows of a house. Their roosting-place – on the ground – is easily discovered during the snow, because it is partly scratched away and melted there and appears a darker patch in the white field. At other times the covey separates, and the various members spread about to feed, calling each other, and rejoining at dusk; but in bitter weather they remain together. To the hawthorn bush by the roadside, where the peggles are tipped with snow, a fieldfare comes as we go by, shaking down a shower of snow as he alights, but just beyond reach of the walking-stick. Though we pause and watch his motions he does not fly, but scrambles farther into the bush, bringing down fresh showers; so tame, or rather so bold, has hunger made him. The fieldfare is usually so wild that it is not possible to approach within gunshot, unless by a stratagem. Upon the lower branches of an elm – those that project from the trunk like brushwood – sits a redwing, his feathers puffed out, and betraying no trace of alarm. Though they come from the north, redwings seem among the first to suffer; a few days snow like this quite debilitates them, and they have not even the energy to escape. A stone, a stick, anything will bring them down; and they are killed in numbers by cats when they venture into gardens, as they constantly do. Another sits on the bank, partly hidden by the ground-ivy that there clothes a slight projection which, like a roof, has kept the snow from a tiny terrace. In the ditch, which is deep, the water is frozen, but the sides are a little moist near the bottom still, and to these places come the garden thrushes and blackbirds. At the gateway there is a short arched culvert for the water to pass through; it is dry now, and these birds enter the mouth, finding that in this cellar-like spot the frost is not so hard.

There is a place in the copse where, under the shelter of the trees and behind a thicket of briar and thorn, scarcely any snow has penetrated. It is overgrown with low brambles, and is several inches thick with dead leaves. These keep the frost away from the earth in the same manner as a mat, and here eight or ten blackbirds and thrushes are busily at work pulling up the leaves and searching beneath them. They quarrel constantly about the best localities, and drive each other away, fighting for existence. It is often remarked that the thrush dies quicker than any other bird in severe weather; and a comparison has been made between it and the tiny golden-crested wren, which scarcely heeds the frost or snow, as if the former was a delicate bird. The contrast is not just. The reason why the thrush dies so soon is because he is starved. Those who have watched the thrush at ordinary times must have observed the really immense quantity of worms, snails, and similar food he consumes. The moment the ground is frozen all this is shut off from him, and he languishes. If frost be accompanied by continued snow he perishes. But the elegant golden-crested wren is not starved: his food of insects is not buried by the snow or rendered inaccessible by frost. He may be seen entering every bramble bush, and peering under the leaves there which yet remain green. There are a thousand and one places where insects lie torpid – under leaves, in the crevices of bark, and so on – perfectly well known to this happy little creature. The birds that feed on the ground suffer most; next, those that put much reliance on seeds or grain; those that may be called tree birds do not endure so much. The blue tomtit literally looks everywhere: in the porch, under the rafters of cowsheds and outhouses, even inside the open box that protects the bell-wire at the outer gate, and may be seen clinging to the boards against which the bill-poster sticks his advertisements, and looks under the strips of torn paper.

Passing further up the road, the rooks have discovered an arable field, where, just before the snow fell, manure had been carted out and left in small heaps for spreading. These are now covered with snow, but near the bottom are perhaps not quite frozen. An oak-tree, white to the smallest twig, stands solitary in the midst. A whole flock of rooks are perched on it; every two or three minutes some descend to the immediate neighbourhood of the manure heaps, and after a short interval rise with a feeble caw and rest upon a branch. There is a perpetual stream of rooks like this passing up and down. The very bough the rook roosts on at night is coated with frozen snow, though his weight as he alights shakes it off in some degree under his claws. In the ash-trees by a farmhouse some hundreds of starlings are perched; the tree is black with them, and there is a long row on the railings round the rickyard beneath; but they are silent. At another time there would have been a continuous calling – a noise rising and sinking, a confusion of tongues: now they sit still and quiet. Then they would barely have remained in one place three minutes: now they do not seem to care to move at all. Their food, too, is cut off from them. Judging by the few flocks that are to be seen about, it would appear as if numbers must have left the district. So too, with the wood-pigeons. Just before the snow there were crowds of them in all the arable fields, to the annoyance of the farmers. Not a single flock is now visible. From out of a double mound one single wood-pigeon rises, so close that every marking of his feathers is apparent. He lifts himself heavily, as if wounded, but once in the air flies easily enough, though he goes but across a single field and alights in a tree: he is weakly for want of food.

Sheep-pens, where the snow has been removed by manual labour, or trodden down and melted by the sheep themselves, are favourite places with the birds in hard weather. The common wagtail is a frequenter of sheep-pens: half a dozen or more may be noticed at once on the ground there. Tat-tat – top-top-top! – a kind of quiet tapping sounds in the higher branches of a tall elm fifty yards away.

A bird is clinging to the side of a bough; his head is thrown back, and every few seconds he delivers a sharp blow with his beak, peers again, climbs further up, gives a series of quick raps, and then flies to the next tree. A slight shower of snow falls from the bough on which he alights; in a minute the tapping sounds again; and thus he visits every elm in the hedgerow. It is the nuthatch, and it is surprising how far the quiet tap-tap can be heard in the stillness. When the foliage is thick on the trees in summer, though the tap may be heard, it is not so easy to watch his motions; the fall of the leaf is like removing a screen. A rustling, scratching sound on the bank where it is overhung by a stole, and clear of snow, shows that the hedge-mice are about, despite the severe weather. Some one, perhaps a sportsman, has dropped an empty fuse-box, without a lid, in the hedge. The scratching proceeds from this box – there is a mouse in it. The tiny creature is so small that the box, which is merely supported by a few dead oak leaves, allows it to turn round easily. He scratches and sniffs at every corner – pauses, and scratches again, as if in desperate hope that there must be something eatable about it. At last he gives up the useless attempt, and disappears under the oak leaves. Some distance further there is another rustling: something here is darting to and afro with an eager motion under the ground-ivy. This time it's a weasel, whose hunting is greatly favoured by the snow. If it were deep it would not suit him; but two inches are just sufficient to weaken the prey, and yet cause him no inconvenience in chasing it. Rabbit-tracks are everywhere in the snow, and especially round and round a long narrow mound in the open field, where the farmer has stacked his roots and covered them with straw and earth as a protection against the frost.

By now the sun has reached the highest point of the low curve he describes on a December day, and the wind being still, there is a manifest rise in the temperature. The rays have a visible effect upon the thrushes and other birds that have hitherto moped on a bough. They are now searching for food with energy – the holly-tree in the garden, on which there are a few berries, attracts them. A blackbird, who has ventured almost to the house-door, flies up, goes no farther than the nearest bush, and, perching there, shows a tail one side of which is pure white. The left side of the tail has a white edging; all the other feathers are perfectly black. Till the snow and frost drove him to the close neighbourhood of the house this white-marked blackbird escaped notice.

There were no special signs of the approach of the hard winter till the northern winds began to blow, and continued so persistently. It was noticeable that while the frost lasted there was an utter calm, and the fields and hedges at night were almost spectral in their white robes and silence. The last swallow we noticed was on the 25th of October. A last stray blossom on the woodbine still showed on the 2nd of November. On the 12th of November the redwings were eating the red fruit of the briar for a day or two, it being cold; but they seemed to abandon the hedge berries (of which the crop is scant) directly afterwards, and did not touch them again until the frost began. On the 20th of November a flock of eight magpies appeared on a birch-tree in the midst of a furze common, and their evolutions were amusing to watch. Thrushes were singing freely on the 25th of November.

If a frost like that we have recently experienced in the south and the presence of snow for a few days cause so much distress among birds, it is easy to understand their sufferings and death in the north where the snow has lingered so long. Over two inches disappeared in a single day in the thaw of December 26th. In the afternoon the streams, suddenly swollen by the melted snow, overflowed their banks, and the ground thus irrigated was immediately resorted to by crowds of starlings and other birds.[1]

Few writers have had the ability to depict the countryside and its wildlife so vividly, and with such photographic observation, as the Victorian

---

1   Jefferies, R, 'Under the snow', *Chronicles of the Hedges* (ed. S J Looker, 1948), 125-30 [essay first published 1879].

novelist and essayist Richard Jefferies, who wrote that description, 'Under the Snow', for a magazine in 1879. It is something of a cliché for writers about Christmas to point out how rare it is in fact to witness a white Christmas – the odds are better if the whole twelve days of Christmas are included – but nevertheless snowfall, intense cold, and freak weather events are associated in everyone's minds with midwinter. And it is appropriate, therefore, to set the icy scene so that we can relish the warmth indoors. Here, then, is a selection of Wessex poetry, description and reportage appropriate to the season.

First a simple but moving poem by a complex man with a legal and civil service background, Maurice Hewlett, whose essays and novels are long forgotten, but who spent his later years at Broad Chalke in the Ebble valley of south Wiltshire. A keen gardener and countryman, he championed the Wiltshire labourer and served as a magistrate. This poem was published in 1920, three years before his death.

Soft Weather
Maurice Hewlett

HE WIND BLOWS mild
Out of the west,
Soft as the lips of a child
On a woman's breast;

And the gray earth
Stirs in her deeps,
In all her intimate valleys
Where the wind creeps,

Sighing in the bents,
Crying beyond,
Ruffling with soft laments

The still dew-pond.

The shepherds are telling
Of open weather
When the ewes and they in the shealing
Must labour together.

Come Christmas soon,
With an earth-sigh,
With a blurr'd ring to the moon,
And a mackerel sky;

And Christmas mirth
Stream over the hill,
And peace be yet upon earth
For men of good will![1]

Edward Slow was a contemporary of Hewlett's, and probably well known to him, since he had been mayor and alderman of Wilton, the nearest small town to Broad Chalke. He made up in enthusiasm for his lack of poetic talent, and he wrote in authentic Wiltshire dialect.

Tha Snow
Edward Slow

HA SNOW, THA snow, is vallen,
An my good deam, she be callen,
'Be quick, good man, hie out a tha starm,
An com to yer snug leetle cottage, za warm'.

---

1   Hewlett, M, *Flowers in the grass* (1920), 51-3.

Tha snow, tha snow, ael droo tha snow,
Away to his wirk tha poor man mist go;
Bit, ah, wen at nite a greets his snug cot,
An smills his hot zupper, his keers be vargot.

When tha snow lays deep and vrosts da bite,
An tha vields an downs be covered quite,
Tha leabourer sturdy, up in the vield barn,
Be-leabours ael day tha russet brown carn.

Tha vrost an tha snow tho cheerless they zeems,
Tha zweets that thay avs ther roughness redeems;
Var where will ee vine a cozier zite
Than a leabourer's cot on a cwould winter's nite.[1]

The best known of Wessex dialect poets was the scholar, schoolmaster and clergyman, William Barnes, rector of Winterbourne Came near Dorchester. He was a not only a master of dialect, but a fine poet, greatly admired by Hardy, who also wrote verse in standard English. This short meditation, looking from his study window, perhaps, across the frozen churchyard, foreshadows Hardy's famous new year poem, 'The darkling thrush'.[2]

1   Slow, E, *The Wiltshire Moonrakers edition of West Countrie Rhymes* (1903), 292.
2   See below, pp. 383-4.

A Winter Night
William Barnes

IT WAS A chilly winter's night;
    And frost was glitt'ring on the ground,
And evening stars were twinkling bright;
    And from the gloomy plain around
      Came no sound,
But where, within the wood-girt tow'r,
The churchbell slowly struck the hour;

As if that all of human birth
    Had risen to the final day,
And soaring from the wornout earth
    Were called in hurry and dismay,
      Far away;
And I alone of all mankind
Were left in loneliness behind.[1]

We move further west now, to Exmoor. Our reporter is the naturalist and countryman E W Hendy, who in 1930 brought together a number of his contributions to newspapers and magazines into a book, Wild Exmoor through the Year. *In it he depicted the activities of birds and animals month by month, with a gift for vivid description which transports the reader to his side to experience – in this instance – a December sunrise and snowfall.*

1   Barnes, W, *Poems* (1962 ed.), ii, 667.

Exmoor's Winter Pageant
E W Hendy

INTER, AMID THE moors and coombes of the West, is a time of happy surprises; for thanks to the mutabilities of our inconstant climate, it is the unexpected which always happens. In some years the mellowness of autumn lingers on till within a week or two of a green Christmas; you may find herb-robert, mallow, valerian, periwinkle, forget-me-not, campion and scabious – even a late foxglove – and a dozen other common flowers in bloom in the hedgerows. A sprig or two of bell-heather is always to be seen in some sheltered corner. Gorse is ever in flower, but it was a surprise to see a lady-bird amid its spikelets in November. I have found my first primrose on Christmas day.

To mankind, winter sunrises are more familiar than those of summer. We wake to find the room flooded with a subdued rosy radiance; above the rim of skyline streaks of tawny orange and glowering red sprawl like the glistening length of some gaudy dragon-salamander. Pines top the ridge in silhouette; below them the still darkened moorland shades from purple into velvety black; the arc above is packed with ruffled clouds, tinged with infinite delicacies of rose, from the faint blush of apple-blossom to the carmine of flamingo's wing; between them are rifts of metallic blue, unfathomably deep. And across this riotous pageant of colour rooks and jackdaws, tossed and buffeted by the wind, steer their clamorous journey to feeding grounds on emerald meadows by the sea's verge.

The country folk describe such a memorable dawn more succinctly; they say 'The reds are out,' and prophesy rain before evening. Often they are right, but it may portend only wind. In any event a change in the weather follows, soon or late. The next morning you may look out upon a dazzling wonderland of snow. The moor, all its rugged contours smoothed and softened, seems to have drawn nearer during the night, so clear and vivid are its outlines. With glasses, or even with the naked eye, you may see a line of black specks crawling downwards towards the woods which fringe the coombes; they are the red deer seeking the succulent ivy which clothes the stunted oaks; walk through any sheltered woodland and you will find the ivy leaves bitten off as high as a stag can reach, upright on its hind legs: if the snow lasts, deer become so tamed with hunger that they scarcely move at your approach.

On the meadows near the sea, where the snow lies but sparsely, and vanishes most quickly, birds, driven from more northern latitudes by stress of weather, congregate in multitudes – finches, waders, gulls, plover, and thrushes of all species. But the ravens and the rest of the crow tribe still haunt the moorland wastes: deep snow means dead sheep, and where these are the carrion eaters are gathered together.

Walking one morning after a blizzard, I took a pathway which led me down into the Horner Woods, and in a moment I was in a fairy land. Each crinkled branch of stunted oak was limned in snow, and where a cluster of dead leaves had given the flakes a resting place the laden branches were bent and curved; from the ancient oaks and alders which clothe the lower slopes the unwonted burden had ruthlessly torn great limbs. Halting some thirty yards down the path I looked back along an alley completely arched over with crystalline tracery, and at the end of the vista was a glimpse of a glistening waste of moor, rising gently to a sky of a very pale and filmy blue.

Tales of cars and lorries embedded in snowdrifts on the moorland roads led me the next day to climb Porlock Hill and see for myself. As I trudged upwards I began to think that perhaps the stories were exaggerated; the half-thawed surface was slippery, but until I reached the one thousand feet line the snow was only an inch or two deep. A two-seater car, containing two cheerful optimists, passed me about half-way up. But, once on Porlock Common, there was a change. Soon I heard the two-seater grunting and groaning; as I came round a corner I saw it endeavouring to back out of a drift. Eventually its efforts were successful, and it retreated whence it came, with the occupants perhaps a trifle dashed in spirit. Drifts began to cross the road, first one, then two, and at length three feet deep. Soon it became impassable. I had hoped I might penetrate as far as Oare Post and enjoy that wonderful prospect over the heart of Exmoor. I persevered for another half-mile, and then had to give it up, for now the snow was over my knees.

Retracing my steps, I met another fellow-creature whose intrepidity put the two motorists to shame. He had pushed a bicycle, to whose handlebars was attached a bass bag which contained a turkey, up the thousand odd feet from Porlock. And he proposed to traverse some ten more snowy miles to Lynton. I did my best to dissuade him with dismal tales of cars buried in unfathomable depths at Lillycombe and Culbone Stables, and pointed to a darkening sky which looked ominous. But, unpersuaded and indomitable, he decided to continue his trek. Whether he spent the night in a snowdrift, his head pillowed upon the turkey and stags nibbling at his frozen whiskers, I cannot say. If my sanguine traveller ever reached Lynton he deserved to enjoy his Christmas dinner; it was well-earned.[1]

1   Hendy, E W, *Wild Exmoor through the year* (1930), 290-3

Somehow, one feels that becoming snowbound on Exmoor in the 1920s was regarded as a harmless adventure. At an earlier period severe weather could be a matter of life and death. In the 17th century, before newspapers as we know them existed, people learned about heroic or amazing events, and were fed propaganda, by chapbooks – cheap crudely-printed pamphlets hawked around the countryside by pedlars and chapmen. Very popular were those containing tragic stories, sometimes known as 'penny dreadfuls'. Here is one, from 1685, which not only tells us a good deal about human suffering when winter weather set in, but also describes the regular pattern of long-distance travel, here interrupted, between Wessex and the capital.

A True Relation

 TRUE RELATION OF a great number of people frozen to death near Salisbury, and in several other parts of the West of England, on Tuesday, the twenty-third of December, 1684, besides horses and much other cattle.

The dismal truths contained in this paper will need no preamble to induce a belief thereof in the reader; they are no stories of what happened in former kings' reigns, or an account of things done in Prester John's dominions, easier to be believed than disproved. But a dreadful relation fit to be recorded in the chronicle for after ages, and a present astonishing dispensation of God Almighty, which calls for the serious consideration of all Englishmen.

On Tuesday, the 23rd of December, 1684, the weather being cold and freezing, there likewise happened a terrible, and certainly the most dreadful storm hath in these nations been heard of in the memory of man. To give the particulars from every part of the kingdom, would take up many sheets; and what I yet have exactly, is from the western parts thereof.

The carriers from London, to Exeter, Taunton, Shaftesbury, Bath, and Wells, etc., going as usually out from London on Saturday, and particularly the 20th of December, 1684, and in pursuance of their respective journeys, being on Tuesday the 23rd with their horses and passengers, to pass the Downs on this side Salisbury: such of them as escaped, and returned to London, do relate the manner of the storm in those parts to be as followeth, viz. That the wind being all day north-east, and violently cold, about two in the afternoon it began to snow very fast, and held on till two or three a clock next morning, the wind continuing fierce, and blowing it in such heaps, that in some places the snow lay as high as a house top, in others the ground scarcely covered, which so altered the roads, especially upon the Downs and Plains, that (although some of them had weekly used the same roads for thirty or forty years together) none of the said carriers could that night either find the way to their inns, or any towns they might get shelter, but themselves, their passengers, and horses forced to wander about till many of them were frozen to death, who before the storm began, were hearty and healthful. Each of the said carriers labouring, and being lost several miles distant from the other.

Mr Mathews the carrier of Shaftesbury had his unfortunate lot within fifty-six miles of London, two miles on this side Stockbridge, who albeit he escaped with life, yet his hands are frozen up, that he hath lost the use of them, and two of his horses dyed with extremity of cold upon the Downs that very night.

Mr Morris the younger carrier to Exeter; also Mr Clark the elder, who carries to Shaftesbury, Evil [Yeovil], and other parts, with their horses and passengers were lost upon the Downs, six miles beyond Stockbridge; there in like manner wandring all night to an again, by continual action and labour were preserved alive.

Mr Collins the Taunton carrier, and Mr *** the carrier to Bath and Wells, with their gangs of horses and passengers travelled that day, about two miles distant from each other; were passing between

Andover and Amesbury, and when first lost, judged they might want five or six miles of Amesbury.

The Wells carrier being foremost, had two of his company frozen to death, viz. his own son, a youth about thirteen or fourteen years of age, and a young man, a passenger aged about twenty years; which persons were not parted from the rest, or smoothered in the snow, but absolutely frozen to death, as they rode or walked along in company. This distressed carrier's bowels yearning as he saw his son grow stiff and faint, got him up, and carried him rill he dyed in his arms, and after he was dead, carried him on horseback; until extremity of cold forced him to let him drop upon the Down and leave him.

Neither had Mr Collins who carries to Taunton and Tiverton less misfortune; a man and his wife, two hearty antient people, being of his passengers, and riding on single horses, altho' very healthful and well in the morning, and chearful in the afternoon, yet by the continued cold and stragling of the poor horses, or by their own growing feeble to manage them, lost sight of the gang, and wandred by themselves, till at length they lay down and dyed one at the feet of the other.

Mr Collins himself and servants, when within three miles of Amesbury, hapned upon a parish where they hired a guide for ten shillings, who undertook to lead their bell horse, and conducted them a mile and a half of the three; when going faster than they could follow, Mr Collins beg'd of him for Gods sake to go no faster than they were able to come with the other horses.

But the guide, alledging his own life was in danger, kept on his pace, and got safe to the Bear Inn at Amesbury by nine o'clock at night; Mr Collins, his servants and horses wandering till six in the morning, and then discovering an old barn, broke into it for shelter till day light, one of his said servants is like to loose the use of his limbs, and Mr Collins with the rest, meetly (under God) by violent labour and busling saved their lives.

The servant of the Lady Fines of New-Tony, in the county of Wilts, having been that day at Salisbury market, in his return with a cart and two horses, lost himself upon the same Down, and having tyed his fore-horse-head to the cart, was found dead near them, by eight of the clock that evening, and being within half-a-mile of Amesbury: the servants of the Bear Inn, coming out to look for the carriers, found him in manner as aforesaid.

A shop-keeper living near Chauke [Broad Chalke], a place in those parts, also perished in coming from Salisbury market.

Six or seven country-people, in passing from Chard to Ilmester, though but three or four miles distance, were by the way frozen to death.

One Mr Knight of Evil [Yeovil], a market-town of Somerset, in a letter to a friend in this city, affirms, about thirty people from that town and parts adjacent, that went the same day to markets, or after other concerns, were not heard of, except some few found dead.

About Tiverton many in like manner perished as they went from markets. Between Plymouth and Exeter many smoothered in the snow. From almost every part of the western road, we have the like dreadful news, which all happened upon the very same day, and the truth thereof ready to be testified by hundreds that are since returned to this city, besides the carriers herein mentioned, who are themselves men of great credit.

London: printed by George Larkin, at the Lower-End of Broad Street, next to London-Wall. 1685.[1]

However vague, misinformed and sensational such reports may be, their message – that life on the road could be perilous – was forcefully made. Compare that with this treatment of a similar misfortune, commemorated in cider-fuelled song and then filtered (and perhaps cleaned up) through a Somerset folklorist's notes.

1   Anonymous broadside (Wing T2281) printed by George Larkin, 1685; reprinted in *The late flood . . . an account of the disastrous inundation* (1841).

The Snow Dumpling
Richard Walter

Y THE ROADSIDE between Stoke [sub Hamdon] and Cartgate,[1] adjoining the lane leading to Rixon, there formerly (1830) stood a thatched cottage, in which lived Jack Hayne, a pensioner [i.e. a former serviceman], commonly known as 'Captain' Hayne, and his wife Betty, who lived a cat-and-dog life. Betty used occasionally to go to Yeovil shopping, and on one occasion during a snowstorm was benighted on her way home over Ham Hill and was lost until morning. This inspired the following verses:

> I'll sing ye a song, 'tis a rather rum joke,
> About an old 'ooman that lived up to Stoke,
> Who went into Yeovil for 'baccy to smoke,
> And some snuff and some tea which she put in her poke.
> (Refrain):   Ri-too-ral-loo-ral-loo-ral-lay,
>   Ri-too-ral-loo-ral-lay.

---

1 Now on, or very close to the A303 dual carriageway, north-east of Stoke sub Hamdon.

The wind did blow and the snow came down,
'Twas as dark as pitch afore she left town;
She took but a drop o' good gin at the Crown,
And away she toddled o'er Odcombe Down.
   Ri-too-ral, etc.

It was such a night as one seldom sees,
The snow was deep, and hard it did freeze;
So she lighted her pipe to keep out the breeze,
But at every step she was up to her knees.
   Ri-too-ral, etc.

She lost her way, but she struggled on till
She got to the top of Hamdon Hill,
When she made a slip, and against her will
Down she rolled like a rat in a mill.
   Ri-too-ral, etc.

The snow gathered round her and formed a ball,
As round as a dumpling but not so small.
It rolled and rolled until the wall
At the bottom received it and stopped its fall.
   Ri-too-ral, etc.

When Betty had finished her comical roll,
She thought that her quarters were rather droll;
So she up wi' her stick and she poked a hole
To let out the 'baccy smoke – cunning wold soul!
   Ri-too-ral, etc.

She thought it a long and a terrible night,
For her nose and her knees were doubled up tight;

But still she kept puffing wi' all her might,
And wondered how long afore 'twould be light.
    Ri-too-ral, etc.

Next morning Jack Hayne came whistling wi' glee;
He was 'mazed such a smoke from a snowball to see;
He gave it a kick – Lor' how stared he!
When out bundled Betty as brisk as a bee.
    Ri-too-ral, etc.[1]

Folklore collecting was very much in vogue in Somerset in the 1920s, when that song was recorded.[2] Its devotees uncritically collected superstitions and ghost stories, the retelling of which they embroidered into a cosy fireside setting. Tales of the supernatural have long been associated with the Christmas season, deriving in part, no doubt, from the dark and cold nights at this time of year; but also subconsciously because they seem to chime in with the recurring themes of death and rebirth, and of normality turned on its head. Here are two Somerset examples, the first involving a nocturnal trek through prodigious snow from Chard to Crewkerne, only a few miles south-west of Betty, the human snowball.

The Old Man's Christmas Story
G F Munford

 YE! DRAW AROUND the fire, and I will tell the tale once more. I always think of it at Christmas time, and at the very sight of a snowflake that night's adventure rushes into my memory and makes me shudder.

1   Cary, D M, *Some ballad-legends of Somerset*, (Somerset Folk Series 14, 1924), 118-19.

2   See Raymond, W, 'Somerset and her folk movement'; in Clark, E V, *Walter Raymond: the man , his work and letters . . .* (1933 ed.), 187-98.

I forget the year now, but it was during that memorable winter when there were twenty feet of snow upon the ground – when the tops of the trees were the only traces of vegetation – when the hedges were totally covered with the purest of white mantles, and no guide was left for the traveller but his own untutored instinct.

There never could be a brighter moonlight night, and when I set out on my journey from Chard to Crewkerne – about ten o'clock – the moon, which was nearly full, shone with such lustre upon the snow that the pure soft silvery light flung a kind of enchanted halo over the earth. If only for the scenery, my memory of that night will never fade.

Fear! I knew not what it meant, and cared but little for the ghosts and hobgoblins which are known to haunt that road – for, to tell the truth, I did not then believe in them. I was well wrapped up, and, with a stout stick as my only companion, I started with a light heart across the unbeaten desert of snow which lay before me – walking as straight as I could in the direction in which I knew Crewkerne lay.

For the first three or four miles I was confident of my own sagacity, but, after walking about an hour and a half – having seen no trace of a house, not even Windwhistle Inn, which I fully expected to pass – I began to fancy that I had taken the wrong course. I was getting terribly tired – for it was hard work to wade through the snow – and my heart began to beat fast as I thought of the probability of being lost and of the horror of death from cold and hunger. All the courage I had at starting evaporated – I was fairly unmanned – and I stood still in that bleak snowy desert, not knowing which way to steer, and almost cried. I thought of my home and of the comforts which I knew awaited me there, and cursed my foolhardiness for venturing across the pathless waste. The owls, who could find no resting-place except on the tops of the tallest trees, were loud in their midnight revels, and kept up a continual 'Ch'wit! ch'woo!' as if in mockery of my perplexity.

Whilst my thoughts were racked with the dilemma, and I was considering whether I should turn to the right or left, or whether I should keep in the way I was going, or re-trace my steps, I saw, far off in the pale moonlight, what appeared to be the chimney of a cottage, and hastily made my way thither, with the view of ascertaining the direction I ought to take for Crewkerne. It was a cottage, and what was more, it was inhabited. But it was literally snowed in, and the only means of going in or coming out of the house was through the bedroom window, and at that I rattled violently to arouse the occupants of the room.

It was some time before I received my answer, although I plainly heard the rough voice of a man, the tremulous notes of a woman, and the plaintive whispers of several children – all of whom were evidently in a state of great alarm. Thinking that my intrusion had been the cause thereof, I shouted, asking for two or three hours shelter, and telling them that I had lost my way.

The rough voice was in favour of admitting me, but I heard the woman say, in an earnest tone: 'For God's sake, Robert, don't think of such a thing! It's that dreadful smuggler's ghost again! Oh, we will leave this terrible place!' And then she burst out crying.

'Nonsense!' replied her stern companion. 'Ghosts can't talk! 'Tis a poor traveller who has lost his way. Let's pull up the curtain and open the window. If it's anybody who means any harm he shall soon feel the contents of this pistol!'

He was, I suppose, about to open the window, but the entreaties of his wife, and the screams of his children – all of whom declared that it was the 'smuggler's ghost' – prevented him from doing so.

'If you won't give me shelter,' I said, 'will you do me the favour to tell me the direction I must take for Crewkerne.'

'Keep a little to your left, and follow straight on,' replied Robert. 'You will then come to Coombe Farm, when you'll know where you are.'

'Yes, if ever I get there. But where am I now?'

'At Purtington. Keep to your left and you'll make no mistake. Good-night.'

'Good-night,' I growled, surlily enough, you may depend upon it – for I thought them unnaturally inhospitable.

I followed in the direction I was told without the slightest hope of ever finding my way, and wondering deeply what on earth the people could have meant by their strange behaviour and by their allusion to the 'Smuggler's Ghost'. 'Ch'wit! Ch'woo!' rejoiced the owls, as I again plodded mechanically on. My limbs were stiff with cold, and I felt dreadfully afraid that I should fall across the ghost to which those nervous people had alluded. Snow, snow, everywhere – except up there, where the moon and stars looked down upon me in silent majesty! So overwhelming was the scene that I believe I should have swooned and dreamed of being in fairy-land but for the hideous screaming of the owls.

In the midst of the dismal chorus, a fearful heart-rending scream burst upon my ears – a long agonizing shriek – too wild for human utterance. It began in the distance, travelled with the chilly night-air across my path, hung among the far-off hills, came back again and again, and ultimately died into a groaning wail!

Whilst I stood paralysed with fear, a riderless horse, saddled and bridled, plunged out from among the tops of the trees of Blackmoor Copse, on my right, and dashed at full speed towards the spot on which I was rivetted. Another horse, but with a rider on its back urging it at full speed, came close behind. And yet a third, also with a rider, plunging recklessly after the second! I was not alone then, but I prayed for my solitariness to return.

Oh, 'tis too, too horrible to tell! The first horse – as if mad with fright – ran close to me, snorted a deathly dampness, and dashed on, and on, and on! I saw it no more.

The second horse was ridden by a grim surly-looking fellow, with a pistol in his belt and a dagger by his side. He had on a slouched hat, and pulled it over his eyes as if to hide his face. But the diabolical leer in his countenance could not be hidden with a thousand coverings! Oh, how he urged his horse and kept looking behind him as if fearful that his pursuer would overtake him! And what a sense of strangling suffocation was flung over me as the fiendish form glided close to my side! I could not move – try how I would.

The third whirled past me with the same haste, and he, I saw, was dressed in the uniform of a coastguard. His hand eagerly grasped a pistol, and his face bore a wild and excited look I shall never forget, but not half so fiendish as the other.

The first horse took a circular direction, as if uncertain which way to go. On and on they plunged. The pace increased. And they were both coming towards me again! I fell upon my knees – I could not help it – and the owls laughed with joy. A strange thing was that the horses made no noise. The trampling of the animals could not be expected to sound amongst the soft snow, but there was no jingling of rein or stirrup, and neither rider uttered a word. Yet their looks betrayed a fearful meaning.

On and on! The pursued horseman urged his steed at the rate of an express train, and was bearing towards me at a frightful pace. But his pursuer gradually gained, and just as the grim-looking rider came close to me – crouched trembling amongst the snow – the pistol of the coastguard flashed its fatal messenger and put for ever a stop to the speed of the horse he was pursuing.

In an instant – in the twinkling of an eye – the rider leaped upon his feet, drew his pistol, and shot the horse of the coastguardsman dead! Another mysterious thing was that the pistols made no reports. But the long forked tongues of fire were plain enough, God knows!

I thought it must be a horrible dream, and mechanically moved my arms as if to wrap myself in the bedclothes. There was another moment's lull, in which both riders confronted each other with savage looks, each holding a dagger in his hand in readiness to strike a blow. Oh! What a deathly atmosphere surrounded me! All my imaginary bedclothes failed to keep it off. And the moon shone on those lifeless horses, and on those diabolical human forms – but no shadow was cast, no noise was heard – except the dismal chanting of the owls.

'Am I going mad?' I thought, 'or is it a frightful nightmare?' For I could not rise from my crouching position, although I saw those two men within a few yards of me engaged in a deadly struggle!

They closed. The one with the slouched hat then got the better of his antagonist, and, with a horrible leer of fiendish triumph, struck the dagger violently into his bosom!

There was another wild agonizing cry, which echoed and re-echoed along the snowy expanse, and which must have startled every living thing for miles – the owls again laughing their unearthly laugh of exultation!

The murderer wiped his dagger upon the ground – leaving a long red track – and hurriedly glided away, taking no notice of me, the unwilling witness of the foul deed.

All was done in much less time than I can tell it. But it seemed an age to me, and I was so petrified with fear that I thought I should have turned into a stone. After the murderer had departed, I felt much relieved, and the power of which I seemed deprived returned.

So I rose to my feet and went to the murdered man, thinking that I should perhaps be of some service to him. But, from what I have since heard, I was nearly fifty years too late!

I stopped and endeavoured to take hold of the arm that was stretched out upon the snow. But, good God! I found that I grasped at nothing! There was the form – stark and motionless – the rigid features in the horrible contortion, as if writhing in agony! – there was that blood oozing out of the wound and making a dark trail along the pure white snow! – and there were the two horses lying lifeless at his feet! I then became aware that what I had seen was only a phantom tragedy!

'Ch'wit! Ch'woo!' laughed the owls again. And the keen frosty air became full of such fiendish yells as pierced my very soul. All around me, and in the distance, there were such loud and discordant noises as if the orchestra of Hell had been let loose! I could endure the scene no longer – my nerves were completely unstrung – and I swooned by the side of those livid phantom corpses! – on a desert of snow, and with an uninterrupted chorus of owl-music as a dismal lullaby.

It must have been some time before I rallied, for when I awoke the day was beginning to break, and I was so benumbed and stupefied with cold that I hardly had the power to move. My brain was in a whirl. I looked around, but could see no evidence of a struggle. No corpses were there then, and no tracks upon the snow were discernible except those I had made myself. I then found that I was in Coombe Farm Valley, and I made my way home as fast as the weakened state I was in would allow me.

The story is not quite finished. I naturally fell ill and was seized with a fever brought on by the exposure and fright, and was ill for many weeks. When I first told my adventure, it was thought to be the invention of a disordered brain. But as soon as I was well enough – by which time the snow had disappeared – I found out the people who lived at the cottage to which I had applied for shelter.

Robert remembered my calling perfectly well, and told me that not long afterwards, on that very night, three horsemen passed his cottage in full chase.

'They were the ghosts of three men who often ride by this way in the middle of wintry nights,' said he. 'The first always stops opposite my house and hastily motions as if to ask for shelter. Immediately afterwards, the two others come on at full gallop, and all three bound off across the country. They do say that they are the ghosts of two coastguardsman and a smuggler who murdered them about fifty or sixty years ago. But about that I know nothing. All I know is that they often chase each other across the valley. And the reason I did not let you in was because my wife and children were afraid that you were the ghost of the smuggler seeking for shelter.'

I told him what I had seen, and he assured me that the tragedy had often been witnessed exactly as I have described it.[1]

---

[1] Munford, G F, *Ghosts and legends of south Somerset*, 1922, 21-30 (Somerset Folk

Just to make the story sound more authentic, and virtually impenetrable to anyone not acquainted with the way the locals spoke, some folklorists coated their accounts with a thick layer of dialect. This ghost story, from Pensford in north Somerset, is best read out loud after a few drinks – and even then it can be a struggle.

The Week before Christmas
H Hay Wilson

ERE BE DORIS feared to go whoam alone. Boys have been a tellin' her pack o' lies about the ghost to Parsonage Lane.' Doris's rosy face was tearstained and pale when Mary Andrews looked at her, rather awe-stricken.

'My dear lamb,' she said, 'thou shouldst mind Them as do guard thee, and not fear what thou canst not understand.'

'Now, Mary, you be foolish,' said John impatiently. 'Why don't 'ee tell the maid right out as there bent no such things as ghosteses, and they gurt loobies should hev' a swap behind the ear for trying to frighten little maids. Run along, my dear, and goos wi' uncle Jem,

Series 3)

he'm gwain home-along just now.' And Doris trotted away after her uncle.

'Policeman do say he do know thiccy ghost,' John went on angrily, ' – 'tis naught but a gurt ivy-bush do stand high up pitching forward in hedge above Weaver's trap where the road do fall by the water-gout. He do stand up there above the rexen so dark, and pleeceman say he do often vancy 'tis Varmer a standing there by gate, and do look up to speak to'n, and 'tis but the ivy-bush. And there bent no other ghost there, not as he do know by.'

Granfer Dyer was of another opinion. 'There'm more sights abroad than what us do always know,' said he, taking his pipe out and looking at John. 'And Weaver's Fatherlaw could have told 'ee better, for he did know my Veyther. Hevn't I a' told 'ee o' the zight my Feyther did see over to Park at Christmas time?'

John snorted, but said no more, because Granfer Dyer's story was an institution in the village.

'It were the week before Christmas,' said the old man, 'and my Veyther he were a terr'ble one for the Methodies, and he'd a-druv over to a meetin' to Bristol, and were coming back late, past Rectory and down by Five Gates, where 'ee know there'm a old road do come out that did used to be the old ancient way for all travellers before roadses were made proper. An' there'm an bit of him do come out all alone by himself in middle o' Park field, where they fir-trees do make a lew place for cattle, and do look still as if had been a bit o' old road as somebody had forgotten about. It were a regular mirky night wi' clouds heavy above, an' Veyther said 'a could see the lights of Bristol a'glowen in sky low down as it med be a furnace, gurt ways off, an' a big smeech o' cloud hangen over 'en, as do when rain be gathering, an' the sight o' thiccy glow did make Veyther think on the gurt vire as Parson do talk on, where the wicked go. It mid a been thic Methody chap he just a-heard did zet Veyther's thoughts like that, but he were a wonderful religious man, were Veyther, tho' 'piniated, an' did fetch all o' we hard over the head with gurt Book when us didn't versy right, Zundays. An' he were so sober a man as walked, and never a bit market-fresh.

'Well, there were Veyther wi' Hell-fire in's head which weren't a convanient thing to zet 'en home by of a dark night, but he would hev' knowed the way blind-mobbed, and so did old mare. Well, he were come so far's Five Gates, where old road do come out 'way past they Knaps like gurt emmetbuts where bones do lie buried, and 'ee do know 'tis tur'ble lonesome. Veyther he did zwer' around for to go down Hen Lane, an' 'tis so narrow's a want-wriggle, an' dark, one do seem buried like a carvy-zeed in a cake down there o' nights. So Veyther did cast a look over's shoulder to see there weren't nothin' behind 'en as shouldn't be there, for they lights in sky did zim to run in's head, and after he did turn away from they did seem like the darkness held 'en round so tight's a cheese – 'Tes mirky there when do fall night. Sure enough he did see summat, an' that were a two-double pair o' lighteses behind 'en, as it mid be of a gentleman's carriage, tho' Veyther did know gentry don't often go by there unless they'm miswent. An' 'tweren't old Squire neither for Veyther did know as he he'd took sick an' wer' bad a-bed, and volk dedn' look to see 'en last the year out. An' it were the week before Christmas. Well, Veyther were frightened to see quality that way, but it dedn scare 'en nowise, an' the lights were martal bright. But he did vind a quare thing, and that was, tho' night were so still 'ee could hev' heard a berry dapping in the hedge, yet a' couden' hear a pat o' the harses' hoofs, nor yet a sound o' wheels, and road be riddly down to they knaps.

'Well, a diden' think so much o' that, and old mare were getting on at a tidy pace, when something did make Veyther twirdle hisself round on seat to look behind, and there, if they lighteses hadn't turned into Hen Lane too an' were coming along fast behind 'en, an' now he did hear the harses' hoofs a'trampling fast and nigh to 'en. 'My dear life,' thinks Veyther, 'however shall we get 'n passed.' For the lane be that strait two carts can't pass, nor yet hardly a rave-waggon get along. Now, Veyther haden' the bad manners to be keepin' back quality behind 'en, so he did fetch the old mare a whack, as weren't used to that from he, and her did fling up her heels and set off at a pace. An' Veyther look round again, and see they lighteses gettin' nearer and hear harses a tramplin' and gallopin' like the wind, so he did whoop to they to keep back till could pass, but they didn' heed 'en and came on gallopin' like the wind. They did get so near, Veyther could see four harses an' a big coach, real magnifical, behind 'en, an' that scared 'en a bit for there weren't such in they parts. An' 'a could see mimmickin' yellows in tight breeches an' high boots a' sittin' on harses' backs, an' the tails o' the leaders did swish across 'en an' 'pear to dout the flame for a two-three seconds, and then did glimmer out again a-swinging to the gallopin' of the harses. But the back-lamps of the carriage did shine steady like the flame of a gurt cat's eye in the dark. Veyther he dedn' like the 'pearance of 'n, an', thinks he, they'll surely run we down, though the mare did vlee as if she had Old Vengeance at her tail. So Veyther did see they were nigh upon Summerlease by Wapsill's gate, where there'm a passing place and road be wide for maybe two acres and a ben. Now, they'll can pass, thinks Veyther, an' good riddance. So he did zwer' aside to let 'en pass. An' old mare wooden' stop, yet the pace they harses were a'gwain were nigh twice so fast as her. So Veyther couden' believe's eyes when did look back an' see coach weren't the leastest bit nigher, an' they harses a' gallopin' like the wind. So did try to pull up old mare, but she were ugly after the blow, an' wooden' bide still.

'Well, thinks Veyther, at Forty Acre they'm bound to pass we, an' when they got past Bloody Paddock, where Forty Acre do lie after the garden spot, Veyther did put all his heft on reins and pulled old mare on to grass wi' her nose over gate, so's her couden' get no farther, bein' too witty a beast to try an' climb. An' there her stood a' sweatin' and a' heustering while Veyther were glad to think they'm bound to pass now. He did look around, and they so close, could see the steam rise on harses' flanks and dim the light behind, and there were they unchristian lanterns o' the riding-boys a'dancing wi' the harses stride, an' the tails o' the leader a' douting them every minute, an' harses all the while a' gallopin' like the wind. They wer' so close as I be to you, or most near, an' 'ee do know, there'm a road do turn out by Bloody Paddock an' run along towards Tip. And 'tis hill-land there by, and all moory where water be ponded, and the road so rough wi' all the ravvle o' the guar'. An' top of 'en, the tip o' redding stuff do stand nigh to little wood that Parson do say be part of old road of ancient days.

'Now just when Veyther did think they would be past 'en, come the moon a'ridin' out from behind a cloud, and did shine sudden so bright as had been high-by-day, and he did look round for the coach, and would you believe 'en, thic coach dedn' niver pass Veyther, for while he did look around the four harses did zwer' an' dash down by thic little narrow old way like a rabbit down a wriggle an' – 'Massy a' me,' think Veyther, 'sure they'm zogged an' stooded,' for he couldn' hear the tramplin' nor the wheeels a' rolling no more. He stood there up in cart, did say, as he med lieu' been a pillar o' salt, wi's head twirdled round over's shoulder, an' mouth open so wide's a bat could lieu' flown in at 'en. At last he did think to pull mare's head round an' set her home again, and her by now so quiet's a christened babby.

'So he turned about, and when did look up towards top (the moon were gone in by then) there were lights a' flashing far off to other end of the lane nigh to Manor House, and they were going slow and stiff towards Tip, and there'm a gate by there, thou knows, do lead up to Tip, but 'tis always barred when miners be gone home. But Veyther could see from below, coach did dash through gate place just so fast as had galloped down road, an' they queer lanterns a' jumping and swinging, and the leader's tails a' swishing across them. They did head straight for the wood, a' gallopin' like the wind, and when they reached the lew place, that were the last Veyther saw o' the lights, for they went out, 'a said, in the night like a candle flame a' blown out, an' the dark did shut down over 'en like a sack over a live coal.

'Veyther, he did stand in a maze, an' the old mare too, when sudden he did hear steps, and there was a man coming in front of 'en, after the hedge an' going fast, tho' as if he were a bit catching. When did get near, Veyther see it were P'liceman Pascoe, an' him a' pankin' like a ewe in a thunderstorm – he were a stout man – an' his face so white's milk, as Veyther could see by's one lamp. 'Where be gwain, Pleeceman?' Veyther axed of 'en, but Pleeceman didn' answer, and Veyther were scared to see 'en, knowing 'en to be so valiant a man as walked, though not too well liked on account of his never drinkin' wi' nobody. But he'd fear no man's face nor yet not a company. Well Pleeceman Pascoe did grip old mare's bit as if he were glad of the feel of her, and pank – he were a stout man – so Veyther did ax of 'en after a bit would he get up an' hev' a lift. Pleeceman did get up beside Veyther and sit there an hickey as if he were cold. And when they did get whoam to house, Pleeceman purled on's feet as did get down, and Veyther axed of 'en to come in an' sit down, 'for I'm feared,' says he, 'you've had a turn.' Wi' that Pleeceman turn to Veyther, and 'a says, – 'Mr Dyer,' he says, 'you know I be a sober man.' 'Why, for sure,' says Veyther, 'an' some don't like 'ee the better for it,' he says, meanin' to comfort 'en like. 'Well,' says Pleeceman, looking a bit pearter, 'I'll tell 'ee what come to I this night, an' the first night ever I didn' knawe if the world were real about me.'

"It were up to Manor House,' he said, 'to end of Long Walk, where wall be almost ruinous, and there'm a little thatchers summer-house like a hay-pook in the moor of a gurt beech. Well, Squire's gardiner did 'quaint I last night as some shark had been round to poultry yard and had boned seven pullets, and 'tweren't a fox for was footmarks. So I think – here'm a rare place to climb in by – for 'ee know, old Squire be such a hunks he woulden' niver mend's fences.' Well, end o' it were Policeman Pascoe did clamber through fence, careful like – he were a stout man – and did peek wi's lantern inside summer-house to see if were anyone there. An' just then what do 'a hear but steps a' coming along Long Walk, gurt ways off, near to house. So Pleeceman, he thinks, 'I'll catch the villain,' a says, an' did step inside summer-house so slick's a weasel an' did quat down amid scruff and twigs within.

There were a gurt brack where haps were off door, and 'a could look drough, and all were so still, 'a could hear a bird peat in the rexen. The steps did keep a' cumin' nigher so slow he could tell 'en one by one, and, thinks he, 'a'll soon be nigh.' Then moon did come out sudden and so bright as 'twere high-by-day, and Pleeceman could count every mop o' grass on path, and, thinks he, 'Als lucky I did get inside while 'twere dark, an' the villain cann't hike off nowise.' An' still the steps kept coming nigher. An' just when they did turn corner there were Pleeceman feeling so sprack's a cat over a mouse, biding still wi's eye at the brack. An' steps come louder, and slower, an' yet slower, an' did go, slow, right a' past the door of the summer-house all in the moonlight, an' there were Pascoe a' lookin' right upon 'en as did pass by an' – eh, my dear life, there were nothing there and nobody at all in sight, and yet they footsteps did stop, and pass on, an' go away in the moonlight, though there weren't nobody there, says Pleeceman, his voice going up in a sob like a sick child's.

'Veyther said 'a did feel the flesh fair creep upon 'is bones when did look to Pascoe's face an' see it all wet wi' the terror of what he hadn' seen, an' just then they did hear harses' feet come clatterin' up to the house in the night. An' 'twer' the gardener from the Manor to say how old Squire had died in a fit sitting in's great chair an' looking so grim as he did when did turn his son out o' doors, and would Veyther ride wi' 'en for doctor, for he were feared to go alone in the dark. So they all dree did go, for none o' 'en woulden' be left alone wi' the terror o' what he'd seen in's head. An' it were the week before Christmas, an' there were still thiccy glow in the sky did make Veyther think all the while o' the gurt flame where the wicked do go.'

Granfer stooped to relight his pipe and looked across at John on his couch rolling sightless eyes at him in the darkness. 'Tis a wholesome thought for the most of us,' said John.[1]

1   Wilson, H Hay, *A Somerset sketch book* (1912), 128-37.

'Wholesome thoughts' – of the afterlife, perdition and the supernatural – will recur from time to time through this exploration of Christmas and New Year. But for the time being let us celebrate the winter weather and, in particular, the opportunity it presents for vigorous, if hazardous, exercise. Two of north Wiltshire's most celebrated writers and contemporaries of the younger Hardy were Richard Jefferies (who opened this sequence) and Francis Kilvert. Both described the exhilaration of winter skating on frozen lakes. Jefferies, born in 1848 at Coate, which used to be a great deal further away from Swindon than it is now, was the son of a small farmer. He worked first as a journalist, and then made a precarious living writing essays, novels and books about natural history and the countryside. His description of the 'elastic air' filling the skater's lungs as he builds up to full speed carries with it a sad pathos ('Oh that such a sense of vigour could but last'), because his best work was written under the death sentence of tuberculosis, and this essay was not published until 1909, over twenty years after he died.

Skating
Richard Jefferies

HE RIME OF the early morning on the rail nearest the bank is easily brushed off by sliding the walking-stick along it, and then forms a convenient seat while the skates are fastened. An old hand selects his gimlet with the greatest care, for if too large the screw speedily works loose, if too small the thread, as it is frantically forced in or out by main strength, cuts and tears the leather. A bad gimlet has spoilt many a day's skating. Nor should the straps be drawn too tight at first, for if hauled up to the last hole at starting the blood cannot circulate, and the muscles of the foot become cramped. What miseries have not ladies heroically endured in this way at the hands of incompetent assistants! In half an hour's time the straps will have worked to the boot, and will bear pulling another hole or even more without pain. On skates thus fastened anything may be accomplished.

Always put your own skates on, and put them on deliberately; for if you really mean skating in earnest, limbs, and even life, may depend on their running true, and not failing at a critical moment. The slope of the bank must be descended sideways – avoid the stones concealed by snow, for they will destroy the edge of the skate. When within a foot or so, leap on, and the impetus will carry you some yards out upon the lake, clear of the shadow of the bank and the willows above, out to where the ice gleams under the sunshine. A glance round shows that it is a solitude; the marks of skates that went past yesterday are visible, but no one has yet arrived; it is the time for an exploring expedition. Following the shore, note how every stone or stick that has been thrown on by thoughtless persons has sunk into and become firmly fixed in the ice. The slight heat of midday has radiated from the surface of the stone, causing the ice to melt around it, when it has sunk a little, and at night been frozen hard in that position, forming an immovable obstacle, extremely awkward to come into contact with. A few minutes and the marks of skates become less frequent, and in a short time almost cease, for the gregarious nature of man exhibits itself even on ice. One spot is crowded with people, and beyond that extends a broad expanse scarcely visited. Here a sand-bank rises almost to the surface, and the yellow sand beneath causes the ice to assume a lighter tint; beyond it, over the deep water, it is dark.

Then a fir-copse bordering the shore shuts out the faintest breath of the north wind, and the surface in the bay thus sheltered is sleek to a degree. This is the place for figure-skating; the ice is perfect, and the wind cannot interfere with the balance. Here you may turn and revolve and twist and go through those endless evolutions and endless repetitions of curves which exercise so singular a fascination. Look at a common figure of 8 that a man has cut out! How many hundreds of times has he gone round and round those two narrow crossing loops or circles! No variation, no change; the art of it is to keep almost to the same groove, and not to make the figure broad and splay. Yet by the wearing away of the ice it is evident that a length of time has been spent thus for ever wheeling round. And when the skater visits the ice again, back he will come and resume the wheeling at intervals. On past a low waterfall where a brook runs in – the water has frozen right up to the cascade. A long stretch of marshy shore succeeds – now frozen hard enough, at other times not to be passed without sinking over the ankles in mud. The ice is rough with the aquatic weeds frozen in it, so that it is necessary to leave the shore some thirty yards. The lake widens, and yonder in the centre – scarcely within range of a deer-rifle – stand four or five disconsolate wild-duck watching every motion. They are quite unapproachable, but sometimes an unfortunate dabchick that has been discovered in a tuft of grass is hunted and struck down by sticks. A rabbit on ice can also be easily overtaken by a skater. If one should venture out from the furze there, and make for the copse opposite, put on the pace, and you will be speedily alongside. As he doubles quickly, however, it is not so easy to catch him when overtaken: still, it can be done. Rabbits previously netted are occasionally turned out on purpose for a course, and afford considerable sport, with a very fair chance – if dogs be eschewed – of gaining their liberty. But they must have 'law', and the presence of a crowd spoils all; the poor animal is simply surrounded, and knows not where to run. Tracks of wild rabbits crossing the ice are frequent. Now, having gained the farthest extremity of the lake, pause a minute and take breath for a burst down the centre. The regular sound of the axe comes from the wood hard by, and every now and then the crash as some tall ash-pole falls to the ground, no more to bear the wood-pigeon's nest in spring, no more to impede the startled pheasant in autumn as he rises like a rocket till clear of the boughs.

Now for it: the wind, hardly felt before under shelter of the banks and trees, strikes the chest like the blow of a strong man as you rush against it. The chest responds with a long-drawn heave, the pliable ribs bend outwards, and the cavity within enlarges, filled with the elastic air. The stride grows longer and longer – the momentum increases – the shadow slips over the surface; the fierce joy of reckless speed seizes on the mind. In the glow, and the speed, and the savage north wind, the old Norse spirit rises, and one feels a giant. Oh! that such a sense of vigour – of the fulness of life – could but last!

By now others have found their way to the shore; a crowd has already assembled at that spot which a gregarious instinct has marked out for the ice-fair, and approaching it speed must be slackened. Sounds of merry-laughter, and the 'knock, knock' of the hockey-sticks arise. Ladies are gracefully gliding hither and thither. Dancing-parties are formed, and thus among friends the short winter's day passes too soon, and sunset is at hand. But how beautiful that sunset! Under the level beams of the sun the ice assumes a delicate rosy hue; yonder the white snow-covered hills to the eastward are rosy too. Above them the misty vapour thickening in the sky turns to the dull red the shepherd knows to mean another frost and another fine day. Westwards where the disc has just gone down, the white ridges of the hills stand out for the moment sharp against the sky, as if cut by the graver's tool. Then the vapours thicken; then, too, behind them, and slowly, the night falls.

Come back again in a few hours' time. The laugh is still, the noise has fled, and the first sound of the skate on the black ice seems almost a desecration. Shadows stretch out and cover the once gleaming surface. But through the bare boughs of the great oak yonder the moon – almost full – looks athwart the lake, and will soon be high in the sky.[1]

Whereas Jefferies went skating for the excitement and exercise, Francis Kilvert, curate at Langley Burrell near Chippenham, saw it as more of a social occasion (the difference between skiing and après-skiing springs to mind). In these diary entry from December 1870, set in Lord Cowley's park at Draycot Cerne, the recurring Christmas theme of things turned upside down (in this case almost literally) is to the fore.

An Attenuated Tom Cat
Francis Kilvert

UESDAY: AFTER DINNER drove into Chippenham with Perch and bought a pair of skates at Benk's for 17s. 6d. Across the fields to the Draycot water and the young Awdry ladies chaffed me about my new skates. I had not been on skates since I was here last, five years ago, and was very awkward for the first ten minutes, but the knack soon came again. There was a distinguished company on the ice. Lady Dangan, Lord and Lady Royston and Lord George Paget all skating. Also Lord and Lady Sydney and Mr Calcroft, whom they all of course called the Hangman.[2] I had the honour of being knocked down by Lord Royston, who was coming round suddenly on the outside edge. A large fire of logs burning within an enclosure of wattled hurdles. Harriet Awdry skated beautifully and jumped over half-sunken punt. Arthur Law skating jumped over a chair on its legs.

1 Jefferies, R, *The hills and the vale* (1909), 22-7.
2 William Calcroft (1800-79) was a famous hangman, who carried out some 450 executions between 1829 and 1874.

Wednesday: An inch of snow fell last night and, as we walked to Draycot to skate, the snow storm began again. As we passed Langley Burrell Church we heard the strains of the quadrille band on the ice at Draycot. The afternoon grew murky and when we began to skate the air was thick with falling snow. But it soon stopped and gangs of labourers were at work immediately sweeping away the new fallen snow and skate cuttings of ice. The Lancers was beautifully skated. When it grew dark the ice was lighted with Chinese lanterns, and the instense glare of blue, green, and crimson lights and magnesium riband made the whole place a light as day. Then people skated with torches.

Sunday: When Perch came back from skating at Draycot last night, he amused us with an account of Friday's and Saturday's doings on the ice. On Friday they had a quadrille band from Malmesbury, skated quadrilles, Lancers, and Sir Roger de Coverley. Then they skated up and down with torches, ladies and gentlemen pairing off and skating arm in arm, each with a torch. There were numbers of Chinese lanterns all round the water, blue, crimson and green lights, magnesium riband, and a fire balloon was sent up. Maria Awdry, forgetting herself and the passage of time, inadvertently spoke to Perch calling him 'Teddy' instead of 'Mr Kilvert'. Having done which she perceived her mistake, turned 'away and smote herself on the mouth', while Perch 'looked at her with a face like a stone'. While people were standing about in groups or skating up and down gently young Spencer skated up suddenly with outstretched arm to shake hands with Teddy. At the critical moment his skate hitched and he lost his balance and made a deep but involuntary obeisance before Perch, describing 'an attenuated arch', with his fingers and toes resting on the ice. People hid their faces, turned and skated away with a sour smile or grinning with repressed laughter. Perch stood still waiting for the 'attenuated arch' to unbind itself and retrieve its erect posture, 'looking on with a face like a stone'. Gradually the 'arch' rose from its deep obeisance. The arch was the arch described by an attenuated tom cat. During the torch skating Harriet Awdry hurled her half-burnt torch ashore. Lord Cowley was walking up and down the path on the bank watching with great impatience the skaters whom he detests. The fiery torch came whirling and flaming through the dark and hit the noble diplomatist sharply across the shins, rebounding from which it lay blazing at the foot of a tree. Lord Cowley was very angry. 'I wish these people wouldn't throw their torches about here at me,' grumbled his lordship. 'Come away and hide behind the island or he'll see you,' said Perch to Harriet. So they glided away and from the cover of the island they watched Lord Cowley angrily beating the blazing torch against the ground to try to put it out. But the more he beat it, the more the torch flamed and showered sparks into his face. Harriet described the incident thus, 'I hit old Cowley such a crack over the shins'.[1]

Kilvert was a fervent admirer of William Barnes, and went to visit his fellow-clergyman, almost forty years his senior, at his rectory near Dorchester in 1874. He described him in his diary. 'His face was handsome and striking, keen yet benevolent . . . a very remarkable

1   Plomer, W (ed.), *Kilvert's diary* (1960 ed.), i, 287-91.

and a very remarkable-looking man, half-hermit, half-enchanter.[1] To bring this sequence of wintry incidents to a close, and to draw us into Christmas day itself, here is Barnes in sentimental mood.

The Holly Tree
William Barnes

 REEN HOLLY, GLITT'RING in the gleams
Of gloomy winter, when the beams
Of western suns break wan between
The wat'ry clouds, and winds blow keen
Through leafless hawthorns, growing high
In hedge below thy chilly sky;
Thy life betokens, as we tread
The trackless beds of leaves all dead,
That though, in wint'ry winds, they now
Have wither'd on their shaken bough,
The shrouds that shed them at our feet
Will share again the quick'ning heat
Of lofty suns, and groves shall grow
All green again in summer's glow.
O holly green, unheeded child
Of heathy slope, and woodland wild,
Of evergreens with limbs bent low
By loads of lightly-sinking snow,
But few are left, O lonely tree,
With less of heed or help than thee.
The clinging ivy-stem, that cleaves
To cloud-high trees, with glist'ning leaves,
Or with its crooked limbs o'ercrawls

---

1 Ibid. ii, 439.

The crevices of lofty walls,
Holds steady by its trusty stay
When storms begloom the winter's day.
The mistletoe, disowning earth,
The air-fed child of lofty birth,
Keeps on her sunny tree her seat
Unsoil'd by touch of earth-borne feet;
While o'er the grey old headstone grows
The green-bark'd yew, wall'd in from foes
In hallow'd ground, to hang its head
Unharm'd, o'ershadowing the dead.
The forest fir that seems to mock
Its foes upon the ragged rock,
With twisting roots holds firmly fast
By faithful cliffs, and bears the blast;
And weatherbeaten walls inclose
The winter laurel from its foes,
Where, near the house, its scanty screen
Beskirts the walk upon the green;
And some fair girl, who first has felt
Her fulfraught heart with true love melt,
When fields are wearing, wide below
Her window, glitt'ring coats of snow,
Steals meekly from her mother's eyes,
To meditate by twilight skies;
And walks, unoccupied by aught
But one dear name, in blissful thought
Of bridal days still breaking blest
To bring her joy and leave her rest.
But no strong fence nor faithful tree
Affords a saving strength to thee,
Green holly, standing on thy hill
Unheeded, but preserv'd from ill

By thorn-sharp prickles thrilling keen
A threat'ning foe, fair evergreen;
Thus showing, holy shrub, the low
Unshielded souls o'erwhelm'd with woe,
That God in love will never leave
O'erlook'd his children when they grieve.
When winter brings the welcome morn
That warns us of a Saviour born,
And meeting kindred bring to mind
The mercy God has shown our kind,
Thy ruddy berries, set around
The room, are shaken by the sound
Of festive laugh, and freaky joke,
Of frolic-loving younger folk,
While mothers, smiling side by side,
All see their daughters' mirth with pride,
Enjoying o'er, in melting mood,
Their mirthful games of maidenhood,
Forgetful of the time to go
Through gath'ring sheets of glitt'ring snow;
Till low Orion faintly lights
Their lonely road, from western heights.
So live undying to adorn
Our day of joy thou tree forlorn;
Still meeting mirth and hearty cheer,
And music welcoming the year,
In happy homes where love may glow
In hearts but little tried with woe.[1]

1   Barnes, W, *Poems* (1962 ed.), ii, 667-9.

5
Christmas Shopping

LEGANT AND USEFUL HOLIDAY GIFTS: The gift a person makes is in keeping with the taste and thought of the individual who makes it. Expense has nothing to do with it. In this age many pretty and useful things are not expensive. A common person may make a common present, but one with a refined mind will always exercise good taste and good sense in what he gives. It is a mistake to throw away money on gifts which are useless, for while they may give pleasure to the recipient, the only gifts which afford anything more than a passing pleasure are those which are useful. Among the latter class are good instructive books, or better still, some useful toilet requisite, like a box of Toilet 'Vinolia' Soap, which cannot fail to please, and is strongly recommended for winter use by medical men to keep the skin smooth and free from roughness. The Vestal Vinolia Soap is also a charming article.[1]

With its moralizing and scorn of poor taste, its scientific approval and assumption of purity (Vestals were virgins), this Christmas advertisement published in a Salisbury newspaper in 1892 reflects the values of the late-Victorian society at which it is aimed. Every year magazine editors call for 'folksy' articles to fill their Christmas issues, and it is very easy for local historians to trawl old newspapers and get

---

1 *Salisbury & Winchester Journal,* 24 Dec. 1892.

up a piece poking fun at previous generations. The humour, I suggest, lies partly in the seemingly unsophisticated advertisements, but also in the then-and-now comparisons, sometimes worlds apart, sometimes remarkably similar. Here is such a piece, which I wrote for Wiltshire Life *in 2004.*

Another catalogue comes in the post. I glance through it, mutter gloomily about Christmas shopping, and toss it in the bin. Was it always this commercial? Let me take you back one hundred years, to see how the festive season was advertised in the Wiltshire newspapers of 1904.

Although the shopkeepers 'have been on the look out for several months collecting the latest novelties' (according to Jenkins and Pinder of Salisbury), Christmas shopping did not get under way until December. True, the *Wiltshire Chronicle* in Trowbridge had taken delivery a week earlier of its stock of Raphael Tuck and Sons Christmas cards – no less than 1,700 distinct sets – including humorous cards, 'a commendable feature being that there is nothing approaching vulgarity in any of the designs'. But only on 3rd December did it begin its columns of 'Christmas Notices'. The new fashion of 1904 was to send as cards pictures of yourself, and the *North Wilts Herald* in Swindon offered to make 48 cards for five shillings within seven days from 'a good portrait of yourself or someone dear to you'. The Fisherton Photo Studio in Salisbury would take the picture for you, but intending sitters were advised to be taken early in December to prevent disappointment.

The tone of Christmas advertising was frightfully polite. A W Godfrey, purveyor, of Devizes, 'has much pleasure in again thanking his numerous customers for their increased and hearty support during the past year, and respectfully begs to inform them that the quality of his purchases for the Xmas season is of the BEST and CHOICEST, as heretofore'. Charles Sloper, his neighbour in the Brittox, offered 'something useful and in good taste for a little money', and predicted,

"'THANKS AWFULLY, just what I wanted." This is the kind of thanks YOU will receive if you purchase your gift from our unique assortment.' Good taste was vital, as Stevens of Chippenham knew. 'For Gentlemen only – The handiest and neatest tie for the double collar is undoubtedly the little gem which we are selling under the name of the "Tricky Bow". We have them in exclusive patterns, each one smart and in good taste.' Class-consciousness lurked too. Holland (County Cigar Stores, Chippenham and Devizes) proclaimed that, 'Our No. 1 Mixture is now patronised by most of the gentlemen in the neighbourhood', but hastened to add, 'We can suit every class of customer'.

Food was foremost in many Christmas thoughts. Occasionally the advertisers seem to score an own goal. 'Rowntrees elect Cocoa, makers to the King. For the people *the best is not too good.*' Or, as Bowyer, Philpott and Payne of Trowbridge put it: 'Inspect our stock, and compare our quality and price before buying elsewhere'. Rose & Son of Devizes made much of their new technology: 'The premises are lit by electricity generated by our own plant', and their cold store, 'fitted on the most modern lines', could chill 10,000 pounds of meat daily. And why not telegram your order for sausages, which would receive prompt attention? The meat was precisely sourced. You could choose a cut of beef from, 'a very fine cross-bred shorthorn and polled Angus maiden heifer; champion, Norwich Show; 2nd prize, Birmingham Show', etc, exhibited by Mr Alexander of Holt. In Trowbridge you could actually get to know your victim: 'Garlick & Sons beg to inform their kind supporters that they have already secured a grand herd of the choicest Aberdeen, Angus, Devon, Shorthorn and Heavy Steers and Heifers: N. B. A few of the cattle will be exhibited alive in front of the shop on Saturday next.' Or, as Charles Hamlin of Salisbury explained, with 'Gip', the quickest fattener, you could do the job yourself 'By giving their pigs "Gip" the cottager can now fatten two pigs instead of one, and thus make money. Xmas pigs – are you getting yours ready?'

Yes, Christmas catering is a serious business. 'What would Christmas be without plum puddings?' asked Jenkins and Pinder, corner of Endless Street and Winchester Street, Salisbury. 'There will be thousands of them disposed of on Xmas day which stands for tens of thousands of hours in preparing, unless the ingredients have been prepared by A RELIABLE FOOD CHOPPER. The old method of chopping suet, powdering bread, chopping candy peel, raisins and currants takes up many hours, but if done with one of our famous CHOPPERS the work of hours are reduced to minutes. If you live in this age of speed buy a CHOPPER, which is not only useful in making Xmas puddings, Mince pies, sausages, pork pies etc, but is useful all the year round. What a gift it would be for mother! The price is 3s 4s 5 s 6s. Every size useful.'

Well, I am sure that mother will be delighted – or at least she would have been if you had given it to her before she made the plum pudding! And anyway, doesn't she have servants to do that sort of thing?

On the matter of presents here are some 1904 suggestions which you may not have thought of: a silver muffineer (to keep your muffins hot, of course); a bath chair in good order; a wringing and mangling machine; a Tortoise stove no. 4 (second-hand); a toque or a fascinator (both women's headgear); an inkstand; a special 'Britannia' phonograph; a model Swindon electric tram (with rails complete); a sable muff, gaiters for boys and girls ('appropriate for this bleak season'); or a lamp for the dog-cart. Or maybe, 'a special lot of Stiltons (Rich, Ripe and Blue) from ninepence to one shilling, from Singers' Stores, Chippenham (frequent deliveries). Or perhaps hamper no. 4 ('a very suitable present'), consisting of three bottles each of port, sherry and claret, one each of whisky, brandy and gin, all for a guinea.

That will take care of the grown-ups. Now for the children: 'Xmas Stockings. As every year we have the largest and very best money can buy. "Mother, remember you buy MY stockings at

Tomkins & Barrett's [Regent Street, Swindon]." "Oh, drat you, go to sleep, do." "Well, mother, they are just beautiful, and fancy ½d to 2/6 each."

Keep trying, dear, what you need is a frosty letter from Santa: *'Santa Claus' letter to the young folks of Salisbury*. Christmas is nearly here and I should like you to know that I will call with my sack at Fowler and Bailey's bazaar, Catherine Street before visiting your homes on Christmas Eve. So if you'll get your father and mother to hint to Messrs Fowler and Bailey the toys and other pretty things you would like best, no doubt they and I can arrange that your stockings shall be well filled by Christmas morning. *Yours frostily, Santa Claus.'*

And so, after the tree, the novelties, the present-opening and the food, romance is in the Christmas air. Fortified no doubt with a pull of P P Pratt's 'Wee Drappie' (a special blend of four whiskies, three and sixpence a bottle from the Wiltshire sole agent, Dowding & Son of Chippenham), our hero contrives to find himself alone in the drawing room with his sweetheart. He is attired in his new gentleman's hosiery (heavily spliced in the most wearable parts, suitable for any season, from the Scotch Wool and Hosiery Stores, Salisbury), and she cuts a fine figure in her Y & N Diagonal Seam corsets (will not split in the seams, nor tear in the fabric, four and elevenpence upwards).

'Oh! Gertie,' he begins, 'do marry me, and I will buy the furniture at Case & Sons (Contractors to HM War Office), West End Furnishing Stores, Salisbury, whose advice is, "Don't hesitate, Come along, talk the matter over with us. We are ready to furnish your home from top to bottom, cheaper than you would get it elsewhere."' How can she resist?

And with that he reaches into his pocket for the 'New Ivy' engagement ring (hall-marked, 18-carat, twenty-one shillings, real stones, from Hilser, of Church Walk, Trowbridge). And a happy new year to you both. Jolly & Son's sale starts next week, and everything must be cleared by stocktaking.[1]

Much of the modern Christmas, whether we delight in it or detest it, is already there in 1904. The cards and the food and the alcohol are there in abundance, the latest gadgets and technical innovations, the pointless gifts (who really needs a muffineer?), the stockings and Santa Claus, the nagging children, the apparent bargains, the 'buy early for Christmas' imperative. But it is all tinged with a class consciousness which today is hidden – or at least sublimated. The shopkeepers are obsequious to a fault, there are gentlemen, hard-pressed mothers, other classes, and cottagers. Christmas is a mirror of the society that creates and continually re-creates it. But for some of these invented traditions it is possible to trace their origins – the Christmas card, for instance.

The First Christmas Card

LAME FOR THE pandemonium of Christmas shopping can be laid squarely, and on the highest authority, at the door of the three wise men (but not, with hindsight, perhaps so wise after all) who came from the east bearing gifts. But who is responsible for the scramble to meet the deadline of the latest posting date for Christmas? Who invented the Christmas

1   *Wiltshire Life*, Dec. 2004.

card? There is nothing in the Biblical story about sending cards –
indeed without postage stamps and letter boxes, to say nothing of
printing, cardboard and envelopes, the commercial Christmas card
is a difficult theological concept. But Somerset historians have always
maintained that it was a wise man from the west, a native of Bath,
who first had the idea.

Sir Henry Cole was an affable, bewhiskered Victorian gentleman
who died in 1882 with a splendid string of achievements attached
to his name. He had helped to set up the Public Record Office, to
introduce postage stamps, and to organize the Great Exhibition of
1851; he founded the South Kensington museums, raised the money
to build the Royal Albert Hall, and initiated what became the Royal
College of Music. In his spare time he learnt etching, published
illustrated books for children, won a prize for designing a tea service,
and fathered three sons and five daughters. And in retirement he
organized a cookery school, and was a director of a company which
reprocessed sewage. Bath, where he was born in 1808 (the son of
a dragoon guards captain and his wife), should feel proud to have
produced such a man.

Oh yes, and he invented the Christmas card. His autobiography,
which was issued soon after his death, devotes only one line to the
fact, with an illustration, and a footnote explaining that by the 1880s
more than twelve million extra items of post were being sent each
Christmas week, with a stamp value of £58,000. The first of Cole's
cards, issued in 1846 (according to the caption in his memoirs), has
three illustrations. Its centrepiece depicts a benign wine-drinking
paterfamilias amid a tableful of children and other relatives, and he
is flanked by smaller pictures of the hungry being fed and the naked
being clothed. The design was drawn for him by an artist, John Calcott
Horsley, and a thousand copies were issued for sale as part of his
children's magazine venture, under his pseudonym Felix Summerly.

Modest though they are, Somerset people have from time to
time ventured into print to claim this 'First' for their county. For

example, in the *Somerset County Herald* in January 1904 Sir Henry Cole's first card, of 1846, was described, along with the observation that it was not until 1862, sixteen years later, that commercially produced cards came into general circulation, with designs of holly, mistletoe and robins.

Twenty-one years after this newspaper entry, in 1925, the matter was re-opened. A correspondent who styled himself 'SANTA CLAUS' (so he does exist, after all!) wrote in to ask:

> I have heard it said that the custom of sending Christmas cards originated in Somerset, and that the first cards of the kind ever known were made by a Somerset man less than 100 years ago! I find it difficult to believe this, and should be glad if you or any of your readers could tell me if there is any truth in this story. SANTA CLAUS.

Santa, via the *Somerset County Herald*, received four letters in reply – others may have been stuffed up the chimney, of course. Two reiterated Sir Henry's claim, and a third noted that the early Christmas cards had been disliked by his extremely evangelical family as being a high-church product of the Oxford Movement. But the most interesting reply came from the redoubtable Willis Watson of Crewkerne.

> I have always been under the impression that the Christmas card originated at Bath, and that the names of J C Horsley, RA, and Sir Henry Cole were associated with it. And I had written a reply to Santa Claus to this effect. Within a few minutes of completing my task the post brought me the *Newcastle Weekly Chronicle* for Saturday December 19th. A notes and queries column is a feature of this paper, and, naturally, I always turn to this. Judge my surprise when I noticed the heading of the first note was 'The First Christmas Card'. What a strange coincidence

– the very words I had myself written but a few minutes before! [Perhaps Santa had dropped a line to the Newcastle paper as well.] I read the note in the *Chronicle*, and I destroyed the one I had intended for the *Herald*. If the *Chronicle* correspondent is correct, Somerset can no longer claim to be the birthplace of the Christmas card. I am wondering whether Newcastle can either, because, after all, with the art of printing invented in the fifteenth century, it would be risky to assert that no member of the craft during the period 1471 to 1845 printed a message of goodwill to his nearest friends at Yuletide, and even included an illustration by way of a wood-cut. Here is what E. Wells says in the *Newcastle Chronicle*.

'Christmas cards, which have regained much of their old popularity, were first printed in Newcastle. In 1845, the Rev Edward Bradley, known as a writer as 'Cuthbert Bede', sent designs for Christmas cards to Mr Lambert, the well-known publisher and stationer at Newcastle, and they were printed for private circulation. This was repeated in 1846, and in the following year the printers conceived the idea of putting designs on the market. In 1847-8 they offered the cards for sale, and these were the first cards offered to the public. This origin of Christmas cards was vouched for by Mr Thomas Smith, who in 1845 was Messrs Lambert's foreman printer, and who, soon afterwards, started in business on his own account.'

It will be noticed that the Newcastle cards were not publicly sold until 1847-8 [Willis Watson continues], so Somerset beats Newcastle by a year on this point. The Newcastle cards could not have been the first cards offered to the public, because it is not quite reasonable to think that Sir Henry Cole would have had 1,000 cards printed in 1846 for private circulation. But at present, it seems as if the honour of designing the first card belongs to Edward Bradley, as his is dated 1845, three years before he took his BA degree in

University College, Durham, and when he was at the age of eighteen years.

So Somerset honour was satisfied, but only by a whisker. And there the matter seemed to rest until January 1935, when 'H.C.' (perhaps one of Santa's mischievous relatives?) wrote to the *Somerset County Herald* with exactly the same inquiry. This time a new threat emerged. The then current issue of *The Stamp Lover*, as 'READER' pointed out, included a reproduction of the earliest known Christmas card. It was by a sixteen-year-old boy, W.M. Egley, and it was dated – horror! – 1842. Worse still, as 'F.F.' elaborated in his reply to the newspaper, Egley was born in Doncaster; and there was another hat in the ring, too. In 1844 W.A. Dobson, Queen Victoria's favourite painter, and a native of Germany although of English parentage, painted a card and sent it to friends instead of his usual Christmas letter. But all these contenders – Egley's and Dobson's, and Bradley's too – 'F.F.' dismissed as 'a purely private affair'. Cole's, however, was the real thing, and 'it may therefore be said that as a commercial proposition Christmas cards owe their inception to a Somerset man'.

Yes, that was Willis Watson's patriotic verdict, too. He had not been idle in the cause of Somerset's vindication since the previous threat. He had apparently found a letter published in *The Times* in January 1882 (in fact it was 2nd January 1884). It was from a Joseph Cundall of Surbiton Hill:

> The first Christmas card ever published was issued by me in the usual way in the year 1846 at the office of Felix Summerley's Home Treasury, at 12 Old Bond Street. Mr Henry Cole (afterwards Sir Henry) originated the idea. The drawing was made by J.C. Horsley, RA; it was printed in lithography by Mr Jobbins, of Warwick Court, Holborn, and coloured by hand. Many copies were sold, but possibly not more than 1,000. It was the usual size of a lady's card.

So perhaps Willis Watson had trumped his opponents and won the trick for Somerset. But he still had misgivings. After rehearsing the contents of his 1925 reply he ended with a question: 'If anyone has access to Sir Henry Cole's autobiography, perhaps some reference to Christmas cards could be found and decisive evidence forthcoming that the Christmas card really had its birth in Somerset.' And indeed it does – in a way. The card was issued, its caption maintains, in 1846, but the footnote mentioned earlier concludes by claiming that it was designed in 1845. A misprint, perhaps? The plot thickens.

What none of our heroic Somerset correspondents knew was that the battle they were fighting had already been won, many years earlier. First the artist Horsley, as an old man in 1883, had written to *The Times* explaining that, although he had designed and drawn the first Christmas card, it was entirely Sir Henry Cole's idea. And then it had been left to Sir Henry's daughter, Henrietta Cole, to strike the opposition a fatal blow. In November 1903 she wrote to *Notes and Queries*:

> I may say that I have in my possession one of these cards, coloured, and sent by Mr Horsley to my father, with the inscription 'Xmasse 1843', three years earlier than the first issue of the cards; and, wishing to verify the date, I consulted my father's diaries, and found the following entry: '17th November, 1843, Mr Horsley came and brought design for Christmas card'.

She was quite right. By the time that a definitive history of the Christmas card came to be written, in 1954, several examples of the card bearing the date 1843 had come to light. So that had put paid to Dobson's claim (1844), and to Bradley's (1845). Only the boy-artist W.M. Egley (1842) was still in the running. And even his supporters had to admit that the 2 in 1842 was cramped – it could be an 8, or even a 9. That matter had been settled in 1935, when a Mr H.J. Deane wrote to the *Sunday Times*. He possessed one of Egley's cards, and Egley himself had written on the back, 'Christmas Card – the Second ever published. Designed and etched by W. Maw Egley, 1848, India proof'. So Egley himself, perhaps anticipating this barrage from scribbling antiquarians, had already conceded defeat. And now it is Sir Henry Cole, the native of Bath, who appears proudly each year in the *Guinness Book of Records* as the man responsible for the first Christmas card – which, as we now know, was sent out in 1843. And don't let anyone try to persuade you otherwise![1]

Notice, however, that wise old Willis Watson, the avid devourer of 'Notes and Queries' had his misgivings about asserting a negative – had no-one printed a message of goodwill before Cole's idea. Just possibly he had in the back of his mind a note published by its Dorset editor in Somerset & Dorset Notes & Queries *in 1898.*

The Christmas Piece
C H Mayo

 HE PRESENT SEASON reminds me of what was a familiar object in my boyhood [Mayo was born in Salisbury in 1845][2] at this time of year – The 'Christmas Piece'.

The 'Christmas Piece', as it was called, was a Broadsheet, measuring about 20½ inches by 16¾ inches (I take the dimensions from some specimens now before me) with a blank space in the midst round which was a border of rude engravings, still more rudely painted by hand in gaudy colours, representing a set of subjects from

---

1 Compiled from various sources, including Buday, G, *The history of the Christmas card* (1954); *Fifty years of public work of Sir Henry Cole*, 2 vols. (1884); *Notes & Queries*, 9th ser., xii, 14.11.1903; news cuttings in Somerset Studies Library; *Oxford Dictionary of National Biography*.

2 *Somerset & Dorset Notes & Queries*, xix (1929), 193 (obituary).

the Bible or a series of historical scenes derived from other sources. The story of Daniel was a favourite. The boys, who were the purchasers of these artistic productions, wrote upon the blank space within the illustrated border, a specimen of their calligraphic skill, which might take the form of the Lord's Prayer, the Apostles' Creed, or some other short composition. The signature of the writer was also added. The 'Christmas Piece' was then complete, and was carried about shortly before Christmas, from house to house, in the form of a roll, with a view to extract a pecuniary reward from the admiring householder to whom it was exhibited at that open-hearted season. I remember this happening in the forties and fifties at Salisbury. Others may remember the same elsewhere. The same 'Piece' often did duty in several seasons.

I have before me some (unused) specimens, which were given me a few years ago by the son of the late Mr. Penny, bookseller, Sherborne. They represent: Christ the Good Shepherd; Balaam Blessing; the life of Joseph; the besieging of Jerusalem by Nebuchadnezzar; the Ten Commandments; the Crusaders and the life of Richard the First; the life of King Henry the Eighth; Queen Elizabeth.

The arrangement is similar in all these broadsheets, viz., a long hand-coloured woodcut stretches across the top of the sheet, and forms the most striking object in the 'Piece'. Six smaller engravings, also coloured, three on each side, form a right hand and left hand border; and the foot of the sheet is occupied with a long, more or less emblematic illustration, but on a much smaller scale than the head-piece.

The engravings are rude enough, and the colouring has only its brilliancy to recommend it. The head-piece representing the siege of Jerusalem by Nebuchadnezzar, is violently anachronistic, as several banners of the besiegers bear the S.P.Q.R. [abbreviation used by the Roman army].[1]

---

1 *Somerset & Dorset Notes & Queries*, vi (1899), 174-5.

Such printed sheets have been noted elsewhere. According to a standard history of Christmas, over 100 designs were issued by an engraver, James Cole, during the early 19th century, to be written on by children and given to their parents for Christmas.[1] Was Mayo's recollection of their true purpose, to extract money from grown-ups, a peculiarity of Salisbury's mercenary boys?

But to return to Sir Henry and his invention. A great man, no doubt, but not perhaps the most popular customer when he nipped into the post office to send his cards. In fact the vogue for sending Christmas cards seems not to have taken off until the 1870s, a few years before his death, but then his invention led to frantic scenes, and every Christmas local newspapers carried reports of the heroic exploits of postal staff. It has even been suggested that the Robin Redbreast, so often found on cards, was a reference to the postman who delivered them.[2] Let's join the queue in Weston super Mare post office in 1894 (courtesy of a somewhat verbose Weston Mercury *reporter).*

Christmas at the Post Office

 HADES OF GIBBONS! Shades of Matthews! Less than forty years ago the whole of the business at the Weston super Mare Post Office was not only conducted but carried out by the late Miss Gibbons, she being the only recognized Government Post Office clerk for this district in those days, whilst the duty of delivering such missives as persons residing at a distance from time to time forwarded to their limited acquaintance at Weston super Mare was undertaken by Her Majesty's solitary representative in that department, who was better known as 'Jemmy', as a prefix to the surname of Matthews, than by any other designation.

1   Pimlott, J A R, *The Englishman's Christmas: a social history* (1978), 75.
2   Ibid. 104-5.

Less than forty years have passed away since those worthy officials were in sole charge of Her Majesty's mail in our midst, and what do we find at the present day? Why, a staff of over sixty men and boys engaged in connection with the Weston super Mare Post Office, including a postmaster, a sub-master, fifteen clerks, thirty postmen, nine telegraph messengers, and a whole host of supernumeraries for exceptional work.

The season of Christmas is one when the services of these latter are especially called into requisition, and the calling up of these 'reserves' no doubt materially strengthened the standing army in their attack on, and subsequent defeat of, the foe, in the form of an overwhelming mass of correspondence. The seven days prior to the week immediately preceding Christmas Day chanced to be the 'out season count-out', the information obtained by such counting being forwarded to St Martin's-le-Grand, so that headquarters may ascertain the amount of work despatched by our local postal force: to ascertain that there are not included on the staff other than real working-bees with plenty of work to do, and so decide that none are too liberally paid by the so-called 'Working Men's Government' of the present day. The 'count' referred to showed that during the week over 63,000 letters and newspapers – to say nothing of parcels – were received and delivered in Weston super Mare, and that within the same interval over 58,000 documents of a similar character were despatched. These figures will give some slight idea of the work carried on at our Post Office 'out of the season'; to the extent to which such work is increased when Weston is 'in season' we will leave our readers to imagine.

But it is more with regard to the Christmas season that we have now to speak, and we are reliably informed that during the week preceding Christmas Day, the work at the Post Office – both in the receiving and despatching departments – was fully five times the ordinary average; or, in other words, 315,000 letters received and delivered, and 290,000 despatched. In the *Pirates of Penzance* we are reminded in song and verse that, 'a Policeman's life [*sic*] is not a happy one': what shall be said of the Post Office officials, at a season of the year when the greater number of the community are on pleasure bent? It is at this festive season that the officials in our great state-managed business are hard at work sorting and preparing for delivery the thousands and millions of missives which on Christmas morn are to bear the message of 'Peace on earth, goodwill toward men'. Let us hope that, as a slight acknowledgement of the valuable services rendered by the civil, obliging, and by no means overpaid servants of Her Majesty, that the 'postman's knock' will remind householders that they have a social duty to perform.

The laborious duties of the clerks may be imagined when we state that on Christmas Eve at the General Post Office no less than £76 worth of stamps were retailed. On Christmas morning the delivery at Weston super Mare commenced at 10.30, when each regular employee was allowed a 'super' to carry the heavy baggage – in fact, a biped luggage van – and with his assistance the whole of the heterogeneous mass which had arrived by the night mails was successfully distributed to those entitled to receive them shortly before two o'clock in the afternoon – the mass in question comprising about 80,000 letters and parcels. The work of the department in Weston super Mare was greatly facilitated by the prevalence of mild weather, which enabled the mail carts to arrive and depart with punctuality, whilst with regard to the train service there was little to complain of as compared with some previous years – the greatest delay being under one-and-a-half hours.

The actual posting of letters for the merry season was late, which was attributed to Sunday coming before the Eve of Christmas, and during the whole of the 24th letters were poured in in shoals so long as the office remained open. With the assistance of four supplementary stampers the whole of the 'receipts and disbursements' were successfully dealt with, and the damaged consignments are next to nothing. Letters and Christmas cards bearing such a vague address as 'From Frank to Percy' failed to find the persons for whom they were intended, but these instances were few and far between, whilst some singular addresses were readily deciphered by those accustomed to the work, or several would have been minus a practical remembrancer of the season.

The new Post Office – the site for which in the centre of High Street has been acquired for nearly two years – not being in a sufficiently advanced state to be designated 'the receipt of custom' for the parcel post department, a large room opposite the present contracted premises was again utilized, and so relieved the congestion which would otherwise have occurred at the Post Office proper. The average business in this department is about 1,900 parcels per day received, and 1,400 transmitted. During the five days preceding Christmas 5,600 parcels were received, containing, for the most part, game, geese, turkeys and plum puddings. The whole of these practical reminders of the season were delivered in good time, and in each instance, we venture to imagine that to the recipients, the 'postman's knock' was the most musical tone that had previously been heard this year.[1]

The ever-growing popularity of the Christmas card from the late 1870s coincided with the arrival of Santa Claus, complete with stocking, reindeer and chimneys, from the United States. Unknown in Britain before about 1878 he rapidly assimilated 'Old Father Christmas', the figure of Christmas personified in the mumming plays, so that by 1900

1   *Weston Mercury & Somersetshire Herald*, 29.12.1894.

they were indistinguishably the same.[1] We have encountered him in 1904 writing frostily to children on behalf of a Salisbury department store, and even pretending to visit the shop with his sack on Christmas Eve. Soon he was to be found in person at every store and important Christmas event, a larger-than-life, benign giant of jollity, whose mask only occasionally slipped.

Alarming Incident at Bazaar
'Father Christmas' lit a cigarette

N ALARMING INCIDENT occurred at the bazaar in the Burnham-on-Sea Town Hall on Saturday [8 December 1945]. When 'Father Christmas' impersonated by Mr Percy Sealey, of 29 Abingdon Street, was lighting a cigarette, his whiskers caught fire. The hall was crowded and grown-up people nearby with great promptitude threw clothing over him, and the flames were quickly extinguished.

'Father Christmas' was rushed to the Burnham-on-Sea Hospital, but happily not detained and he was able to return home comparatively little the worse for his experience. He received slight burns about the back of the neck and left hand, and shock. He attended at the hospital on subsequent days of the week to have the injuries dressed.[2]

During the 1870s and 1880s, too, the 'traditional' gifts of food and drink for feasting at Christmas and New Year were being supplemented by the giving of Christmas presents. Shopkeepers naturally encouraged this development as a boost to their business, and have done ever since (as have compilers of books like this!). In the larger, fashionable towns, such

---

1   Pimlott, J A R, *The Englishman's Christmas: a social history* (1978), 111-19.
2   *Burnham-on-Sea Gazette*, 15 Dec 1945 (thanks to David Bromwich for this reference).

as Weston super Mare in 1894, rival shopkeepers paid for extravagant newspaper advertisements, even resorting to verse.

Muscatels in Clusters

CHRISTMAS NOVELTIES. Cosaques! Cosaques! Cosaques! An immense and choice selection, from 5d to 5s per box. Fancy boxes of Chocolates and Metz Fruits, from 3d to 21s. A large stock of Fancy Tins of Biscuits, and Iced Cakes, including Banquet, Chatsworth, Almond Iced, Richmond, Festival, etc. etc. Muscatels in clusters, or layers, from 10d per lb. Carlsbad, Elva, and French Plums. Finest Stilton, Gorgonzola, Camembert, and Cheddar Cheese. An early inspection is respectfully invited. Price list on application. CLARKE & NORMAN, 18 REGENT STREET, WESTON SUPER MARE

Christmas 1894. CHARLES WIGMORE, Fruiterer and Potato Salesman, 23 Meadow Street, Weston super Mare. In returning Thanks to his numerous Customers for their past Patronage and Support, begs to say that he has a good supply of English and Foreign Fruit, and all kinds of New Nuts, reliable for Christmas use; also a large assortment of First Class Potatoes, namely Schoolmasters, Beauty of Hebron, Magnum Bonum, Bruce, etc., and of the finest quality, which cannot fail to give entire satisfaction. English-fed Turkeys, Geese, Chicken and Ducks at lowest possible prices. An inspection respectfully solicited. Note the address: 23 MEADOW STREET, WESTON SUPER MARE

Xmas 1894. Useful presents. Ladies in search of useful articles for presents should call and see WM. C. THOMAS'S Stock, which is now replete with an immense variety of articles suitable to the occasion, at Popular Prices. Ladies' Fancy Aprons, Servants' Aprons,

Pinafores, Servants' Caps, Silk Squares and Mufflers, Lace Fronts and Collarettes, Purses, Fans, Handkerchiefs, Handkerchiefs in Fancy Boxes, Wool Wraps, Gloves of every description, Hosiery, Umbrellas, Jackets, Capes, Mantles, Silk Blouses, Skirts, Fur Boas, Collars and Muffs, Millinery, Mob Caps, Dress Lengths, Cosies, Cushions, Antimacassars, Curtains, Table Covers, Down Quilts, etc. etc. 4 HIGH STREET, WESTON SUPER MARE

Buy your Christmas Presents at SYDENHAM & SONS, Furnishing and General Ironmongers, Brass Pole Makers, Plumbers, Gasfitters, etc. Special discount of 3s in the £ off all Lamps during this month only. See our Special Carpet Sweeper, manufactured expressly for Christmas Presents. No advance in price. 5 MAGDALA BUILDINGS (Three doors from Shaftesbury Hotel), WESTON SUPER MARE.

Christmas 1894, at the WESTON BAZAAR.
Who has not heard of the Weston Bazaar?
Or seen the delightfully dazzling display?
The choicest collections that come from afar
Of home manufactures a gorgeous array!
Of many ingenious and novel inventions
To charm young and old at the time of 'Good Cheer'.
Our choice is so large that the closest attention
To what we may briefly enumerate here,
Is not half so good as a casual inspection,
A gentle walk round to behold our display;
There's no entrance fee and we make no collection,
In fact our friends tell us we give things away;
All the most popular games of the day,
All that's alluring, instructive, or pleasant.
Charming the serious, amusing the gay;
Suited alike to the peer or the peasant,
Spoof Anno Mundi, Go Bang Cannonade,

Flitterkins, Ludo, Reverie, Glissade,
Chess for the serious, Snap for the jolly,
Pliffkins for Harry, Patcheel for Polly.
If undecided just send for a list,
A chance like the present should never be missed.
Boxes of puzzles for those who desire
To seek entertainment at home by the fire.
Boxes of cubes, Architectural bricks,
All that is novel in Conjuring Tricks;
Dolly's own Mail Cart and Dolly's delight,
Dolls with three faces, with two and with one,
Dolly's that cry in their terrible plight,
After they're purchased they soon may have none.
As for our varied assortment of Cards
Christmas and New Year, they tell us our show
Is quite unapproached in the town, as regards
Their beauty, and that's saying much as you know.
MORAL: If you would please, you had better by far
Take all the dear children to Coulsting's Bazaar.
Rocking Horses, Mail Carts, Bicycle Horses, Doll's Houses, and all the
large and useful Toys in immense variety at the WESTON BAZAAR,
24 HIGH STREET. Look at our show in the windows opposite, No.73,
and then come and walk round the Bazaar.[1]

1   *Weston super Mare Gazette,* and *Weston Mercury & Somersetshire Herald,* issues
    of 15.12.1894 and 22.12.1894.

The range of seasonal foodstuffs available from a small-town grocer can be gauged from this Warminster catalogue of 1900. Note that Christmas shopping (here and generally) did not really begin in earnest until the second or third week of December.

Evaporated Apricots and Plain Grosvenor

ILSON & MAYO beg to intimate that they have just completed their purchase of FANCY and other GOODS, suitable for Christmas Trade, the quality of each article being the very best obtainable. The Goods will be Displayed on a Stand, inside the Shop, from December 14th, and the favour of your kind inspection is requested at an early date.

Bonbons: a large and varied stock from 6d to 2s 6d per box.

Dessert Fruits: French Plums in 2lb and 4lb boxes (loose 6d per lb); Elvas Plums, 2lb boxes; Tunis Dates, 1lb and 2lb fancy carton; Taffilat Dates, very choice (cheaper qualities at 3d per lb); finest pulled Figs, 2lb boxes; finest layer Figs, 1lb and 2lb boxes; cooking Figs, 3d and 1d per lb; Muscatells, choicest quality 1s 3d per lb, special value 1s per lb, good quality 10d per lb; Metz Fruits, in ¼lb, ½lb, 1lb and 2lb fancy boxes; also Crystallized Angelica, Apricots, Cherries, Chinois, Ginger, and Glacee Cherries.

Huntley and Palmer's Specialities: Cakes: Iced Almond, Chatsworth, Fruit, Marlborough, Mairfair [*sic*], Balmoral, Novelty, Rutland; Plain Grosvenor, Royal, Fruit, Genoa, Madeira, Bristol, Sandringham, Lisbon, Eton, Palace; Biscuits: a very handsome selection of fancy tins in all shapes and sizes.

Nuts: Black Spanish, Barcelona, Brazils, Shell Almonds, Chesnuts [*sic*], Wallnuts [*sic*].

Oranges, Lemons, Apples, Grapes, Normandy Pippins, Evaporated Apricots, etc, etc.

Wine, Spirit, & Beer Department: Spirits: all are well matured and the age is from five to eight years, no new qualities kept in stock. Wines: a large stock of very choice qualities, including a few special lines as under: Tarragona (our importation), 1/6 quart bottle; Pale Sherry, 15/-, 18/-, 20/- per dozen; Choice Port, 24/-, 30/-, 36/- per dozen; Claret (1893 vintage), 18/-, 20/- per dozen; Bass's Best Pale Ale, imperial half pint and pint bottles; Bass's Light Table Ale, imperial pint bottles; Imperial Ale (speciality 2/- dozen) pint bottles; Guinness's Stout, imperial half pint and pint bottles.

Provisions: Choice Blue Stiltons direct from Dairies in Leicestershire; Choicest Gorgonzolas; Choicest Cheddars; Choice Somersets; Very Fine Truckles.

Bacon: Prime Wiltshire, smoked or plain; Choicest Irish Smoked Hams; Own-Cured Plain Hams and Bacons.

Pork Pies: our own make, already noted throughout the town and neighbourhood.

Please order requirement for Christmas a week beforehand.[1]

Towns throughout Wessex, such as Warminster, catered not only for their own townspeople, but also for the surrounding villages, to which many tradesmen took regular deliveries. Village shops, too, responded to the increasing demand at Christmas. 'Kington Borel is not to be found on the map', wrote Heather Tanner in the foreword to Wiltshire Village, *which was first published in 1939, '. . . for it is not any one village, but rather an epitome of some of the villages of north-west Wiltshire. The book is to be regarded as fiction rather than as local history; but, like all fiction, it is based on fact.' Here is her description of the run-up to Christmas at 'Kington Borel' between the wars, which was served from the local town, 'Bramelham' – her name for Chippenham.*

---

1   Catalogue in Waminster Dewey Museum, by permission of Warminster History Society.

Christmas comes to a Wiltshire Village
Heather Tanner

HE SCARCITY OF berried holly in the hedges is one of the many signs of the near approach of Christmas. There are more fat geese and turkeys going to Bramelham market; the bus is fuller on Fridays, and the spicy smell of boiling puddings is wafted from the housewives' coppers. There are larger crowds than usual round the butcher's van that calls at Kington Borel on Saturday afternoon. Mrs Coates wants her middle cut of brisket of beef, to be rubbed with black treacle, spices and saltpetre every day till Christmas Eve, when she will boil it with the hock in readiness for the visit of her son and his family. Mrs Dingell has ordered pig's cheek to make into brawn, and there is a general demand for suet. Dusk has fallen before the van has finished its round, and it is illuminated cosily from within. The light falls on the upturned faces of some dozen children and dogs clustered expectantly at the open double doors: they are waiting for the women to finish haggling over the price of backbone, cuttings or shin. At last it is their turn. The butcher doles them out – children and dogs alike – a large lump of suet apiece. 'Does 'em good,' he says. 'Keeps 'em warm.' Too pleased for thanks, the children run off, sucking their suet as they would a cornet ice, and the van moves on to Stanley Fitzurse.

Christmas is a busy time for Annie Comely, and the shop is more crowded than ever. Pink Christmas stockings dangle from a coloured paper-chain stretched across the already low ceiling; the inkpot gets mislaid behind the raisins, and there is only just room among the brown paper parcels and the home-made plum cakes on the counter for the tray of Christmas cards, gay with unseasonable roses and pansies and shiny with embossed celluloid. Sometimes the post office till runs out of small silver, and some must be borrowed from the caramel tin containing the shop takings – a procedure frequently entailing much mental arithmetic, in which the co-operation of all the waiting customers is sought. But nothing seems to disturb Mrs Comely's equanimity. She has been postmistress ever since the death of her mother eighteen years ago, and even when Mrs Archard was alive Annie helped whenever she was home; it was she, in fact, who had bought the letter-box for her mother with her first savings in service: she had paid two pounds to have it set in the wall beside the shop window. There were fewer letters to cope with in those days, but the work was harder, for there was no red mail van and the Archard household had to be sorters and postmen combined. Today the van takes letters along the chief roads and Mrs Comely delivers those for the centre of the village while her husband minds the shop; but at Christmas, when the head office at Bramelham needs all the extra help it can get, the village returns to the old way, and the younger Comely children go the long round that used to be their aunt's daily walk.[1]

In 1939, when that account was published, things were about to change. No more abundance of food, no more carefree jollity. Ena Berrett was

1 Tanner, H and R, *Wiltshire Village* (1939), 138-40, by permission of University for the Creative Arts, Farnham.

a young schoolteacher at Hilperton near Trowbridge, and her wartime diary records the daily privations and dangers leading up to Christmas 1940.

Two Oranges
Ena Berrett

HURSDAY 19 DECEMBER Mr Pearson has been trying to get some sweets and oranges for the children but the shops had none. However he managed to get 10 lbs from Rose and Pavey's who make sweets in the town [Trowbridge]. We counted them out and put an equal number in each bag.

Friday 20 December Today we broke up for a fortnight. The children went home very pleased with their sweets and calendars they had made. It is a cold cloudy night. The siren sounded at 5.45 p.m. and the all clear did not go until 10.35 p.m. There were no search lights and we did not hear many planes, but we heard two bombs fall – one was rather loud.

Saturday 21 December The bomb we heard last night fell on Mr Harding's farm at Beanacre. They say the windows in the farm house are broken. I went to Trowbridge on the bus to help my friend in her shop [Brown's in Roundstone Street]. Fruit is very scarce. Customers could only have two oranges and two onions each. It was a fine evening so I walked home – the sky was full of search lights – they searched the sky for the planes I could hear throbbing overhead.

Sunday 22 December A bitterly cold day – very few in church. The wireless went off the air after the 9 p.m. news.

Monday 23 December This morning Mr Evans the L.C.C. [London County Council] teacher came to see me about a party for the evacuee children. The director of education for the L.C.C. is in Devizes during the holidays to see that the evacuee children in the area are being well entertained. I went to Trowbridge again to help my friend. Chicken are 2/3d per lb this year. There was an alert from 6.30 p.m. until 1 a.m.

Tuesday 24 December Spent another busy day in the shop – each customer was allowed two oranges.[1]

Finally in this section, and to prepare us for the themes of Christmas day, here is Llewelyn Powys recalling in 1925 a trip with his brother Theodore on Christmas Eve from his home at Chaldon Herring near Lulworth to Dorchester. Shopping is involved, but in a minor capacity, as a sledge-hammer is not a typical Christmas purchase. This piece, from the autobiography of a philosopher weakened by tuberculosis and confronting his own mortality, is far more about religion, self-analysis, reflection and humanity. It is a strange and skilful essay in contradictions. The atheist reads the Bible on Christmas Eve to praying virgins who will not give birth, and chooses a passage which condemns the feasting and drinking and music-making which is about to take place in the name of Christianity. And there are other strange juxtapositions, which by re-reading it you will discover for yourself.

1   Wiltshire & Swindon Archives 1442/1.

A Christmas Eve
Llewelyn Powys

T LOOKED AS if we were going to have a green Christmas. For days on end it continued to rain, so that presently we could hardly conceive the smoke from the chimneys blowing from any other direction than the southwest. Theodore and I planned to do our shopping on Christmas Eve. On December twenty-fourth, therefore, we had an early breakfast and set off over the moor to catch the train into Dorchester. It was not raining when we started, though the sky was heavy with clouds. As we were shutting the white gate out of the garden, the postman arrived and handed me a letter from Switzerland. I opened it, to find that Wilbraham, who in desperation had fled back to Davos Platz, was dead.

As we passed the Vicarage gate, I noticed how out at the elbow, out at the knee, out at the heel, Theodore was. In those days I had not yet learnt how little it matters whether a man has a good cloak over him or not. From my childhood I had always entertained certain middle-class prejudices, and I was still too close to Sherborne and Cambridge not to set considerable store by a new pair of breeches. He took my protest in good part; but even as I was speaking, I felt ashamed; aware as I was, that however ragged his jacket might be, he himself remained inflexibly loyal to a certain poetic conception of the world which in its intolerance of the vulgar and commonplace set him once and for all outside ordinary standards.

When the train drew up at Moreton, we got into a carriage with some country people, who were also going into the town to do their shopping. Theodore remarked how one of the children, a little girl of fourteen years, was still wearing her summer hat, a shady straw hat, which looked pathetic enough when we got out at the South Western Station, to find that it had again begun to rain. Presently we were walking along one of those stately avenues, the trees of which were planted by French prisoners at the time of the Napoleonic wars. Over the high wall which surrounds its garden I saw the solidly built Victorian chimneys of the house in which I was born. How often have I not tried to reconstruct for myself that occasion when opportunity was given for me to be created. By what auspicious hazard was a way prepared, during the autumn of the year of our Lord 1883, for me to appear on this round world, the eighth child of Charles Francis and Mary Cowper, a unique composite of the dust of a million progenitors, allowed, in its turn, an ephemeral existence, in which to see, to smell, to hear, to taste, and to touch? Surely the brave nature of the reversion granted to me on that far-off night cannot be gainsaid. Let these devilish, badger-headed scientists reduce all matter to a series of revolving electrons, it still remains a sublime miracle of miracles that man, with brittle egg-shell skull, should have been raised, should have raised himself out of the dust! To open delicately contrived eyelids on this earth, on this fifth-smallest of the planets, which like a flock of frightened birds keep sailing about the sun, is surely a chance beyond all chances. It would be better to be a midget than a dead stone, it would be better to be a mud-eating lobworm under the ground than a dead stone, better to be a white-bellied beetle in Pit Pond than a dead stone, and better, how much better, to be a cogitating mammal, firmly set upon his heels, capable of prevision, capable of retrospection, capable of wittolry.

And the fact that I was eventually born in the month of August, 'born in a corn-field,' as John declares, has always been a satisfaction to me. Down in the West of England those four weeks have a character of their own. They know nothing of the mystical intimations which belong to the spring, and yet, at the same time, they are void of the sombre hints of cold annihilation that one comes to associate with the fall of the year. This month of Caesar Augustus is a hot, good-natured, casual month. During its thirty-one days the foison of many a broad acre grows ready for the harvest; indeed, the countryside, far and near, lies basking under its hedges, like some swart, amorous dairy-wench, in sultry contentment, her vagrant longings at last completely satisfied. In the month of August the power of the Priest is at its nadir. Let him raise pale, vestmented hands before never so many ornate altars, let him thunder in the garb of an evil crow from never so many Puritan Pulpits, it will profit him little. Behold! the grain grows golden in its husk, the green apples swell on their whorled twigs, and the shell of each hazelnut is neatly fitted with its ivory kernel. What have we to fear?

It was growing dark before we were ready to leave the gay, lighted streets, which, in spite of the heavy downpour, were so filled with festive faces. Theodore had bought a sledge-hammer for breaking up his coal, and with this primitive implement over his shoulder we began our walk, the rain blowing in gusts against our muffled figures, the naked hedgerows on each side of the old Wareham highway only dimly visible. A glimmer of light shone through the trees surrounding Max Gate. We thought of the old man [Thomas Hardy], in there, sitting by his apple-wood fire, brooding on God knows how many past Christmas nights; the old man whom we so loved and honoured, wise as the oldest owl in Yellham Woods. On we went, the sentinel elms by the field-gates appearing and disappearing. Now and then, a tranter's van would overtake us, its dim, swaying lantern throwing upon our drenched forms a momentary illumination. As we came up over Broadmayne hill we remembered that we knew the clergyman of the place, an eccentric, bigoted, old-fashioned Calvinist, who lived with his two daughters, whose wits, together with those of their father, had been well-nigh turned by so much reading of the Bible. We determined to call at his house. It stood a little way back from the village street, a dark, gloomy vicarage, with the plaster falling from its walls. We turned towards it. On that Christmas Eve it presented to us a perfectly negative front. No light shone from any of its windows, from any of those tall, black, upstair windows, whose heavy sashes were surely never opened to let fresh air into the bare, loveless bedchambers they sheltered! We pulled at the bell. A hollow clack-clack-clack sounded, like the falling of a tin plate on a scullery floor. We waited. We could hear singing in the village; but except for this, and the sound made by a broken gutter emptying its water into the blackness of some shrubs to our left, there was nothing to disturb the forlorn quietude of the place.

We turned to go, and then, from somewhere, from some room far removed from the lidless windows at which we gazed, we heard the unmistakable sound of a door opening. A moment later and one of the girls was at the threshold, holding in her hand a guttering candle, the light of which made visible each raindrop falling at that particular moment between our eyes and her small, soberly dressed figure. We were conducted into the kitchen at the back of the house. The old man was out, they told us. He had gone to the bedside of a dying woman. The two girls made us welcome. They put a heavy iron kettle on to a fire, made in a grate which still held the grey ashes of many previous fires. I don't think I ever enjoyed a supper more than this one with these two extraordinary girls, whose minds had been given so odd a twist by the theological whimsies of their father, and whose demure bodies were so obviously never destined to be held in the free, unscrupulous arms of a lover. Our sudden appearance, out of the dark night, evidently excited them, and they set before us a fine feast, with toast, and bread-and-butter, and goose-eggs, and 'braun of tusked swyne.' With shining eyes, and quaint mouths awry with merriment, they listened to the stories of our day's adventures, their work-boxes and the garments they were making for the poor of the parish put away for once, on the side of the dresser. With a look of infinite deference on his astounding pigwiggen features, Theodore listened to everything either of them said; indeed, with his sledge-hammer leaning against his chair, he addressed them as if they had been princesses in disguise.

Before we left, the elder of the two put a large black-covered Bible before him, requesting that a chapter should be read. And so it came to pass that I found myself on this anniversary of Our Lord's birth listening to my brother's well-modulated voice intoning the sacred Scriptures. He selected to read from the sixth chapter of the Book of the Prophet Amos; and it seems to me that I can still hear the voice of this atheist, who is by his nature so profoundly religious, 'reading a chapter' over that kitchen table. We all four of us knelt on the uncarpeted floor. I watched a small mouse that kept running out from behind a basket of sticks. Once my eye rested on the figure of Joan, who knelt before me in rudely cobbled boots, with clasped hands raised above her head. And I suppose, until I am dead, the august, admonitory words that came to my ears will be associated with a little, frolicsome Christmas-mouse, with a bespattered window as seen under a coarse calico blind, with the ecstatic look on a praying woman's face. 'Woe to them that are at ease in Zion . . . that lie upon beds of ivory, and stretch themselves upon their couches, and eat the lambs out of the flock and the calves out of the midst of the stall; that chant to the sound of the viol, and invent to themselves instruments of music, like David, that drink wine in bowls, and anoint themselves with the chief ointments . . . which rejoice in a thing of nought, which say, Have we not taken to ourselves horns by our own strength?'[1]

1   Powys, L, *Skin for skin*, 1925, 115-24

6
Birthnight

HE FEW REMAINING days before Christmas passed by quickly. For a week the children had gone round to the farms every night, singing and begging. They carried lanterns made of swedes hollowed out, with a piece of candle fitted inside, and held them by the stump, warding off the draught with their hands. Then came 'Gooding Day' or 'Begging Day' – which is always eagerly looked forward to by the village children – and finally, the day before Christmas itself and the date of the proposed meeting at old Elijah's house.

A little before four o'clock the sun set, dropping down behind Lushill, and soon afterwards the station lamps at Highworth were lit, showing afar off like the lights of a ship at sea. The interior of Gramp's cottage was warm and bright. A fire of logs blazed up the chimney-back and a large lamp stood in the centre of the table beneath a rather low ceiling. Numerous pictures and photographs hung on the walls around. Above them were set sprigs of holly and mistletoe, or little boughs of ivy. On each side of the chimney was a recess fitted with cupboards and shelves containing dishes and chinaware, mugs and tumblers, gleaming in the merry firelight. The small clock on the mantlepiece was twenty minutes ahead of time. This is not an uncommon thing to find in the cottages, for the villagers love to be deceived in the matter of moments, and to feel that the hour is not really as far advanced as is indicated by the hands of the instrument.

Inside the door was a thin partition to protect the fireplace from draught. Behind this old Elijah always sat, and never thought of shifting his position out of consideration for any.

Each of the visitors to the cottage had brought Gramp a small present. Clothes he needed not, nor yet a new pair of boots, for he seldom wore anything but slippers, either indoors or out. Books and newspapers were useless to him, for he could not see to read, and he had a sufficient stock of knowledge crammed into his old head to last him for the rest of his days. This his children and grandchildren knew, and so did not trouble to buy him anything that would be of no use. Instead they brought him a few good things to eat – cakes and oranges, a piece of beef for Christmas dinner, several ounces of tobacco, and a little flask of whisky. With all these Gramp was greatly pleased, though it was easy to see that he most preferred the tobacco and the small flask of barley juice, which, after all, was quite natural for one of his years. His delight in the tobacco was unbounded. 'Ho! ho! ho! H'm! h'm! h'm!' chuckled he, taking up the packages and holding them in his mouth one after another, and tossing his head the while, before he stowed them away on the shelf beside his pipe and spills, and sat down in the arm-chair with a triumphant expression upon his countenance.

Gramp was the hero of the hour. This he knew, though he tried to be natural and to conceal his joy at having the company present. His daughter called him 'a regular owl' toff and teased him about wanting a 'hair-cut'. The children laughed and chattered like magpies, but old Elijah smiled the smile of one who is master of the situation and sat quietly and comfortably in his chair, smoking, and awaiting a convenient time for beginning the entertainment. He was dressed in corduroy trousers, with woollen waistcoat and cardigan jacket, and he had on a new felt hat such as is worn in the fields at haymaking. His wooden pipe was laid aside for a new clay with a long stem. His long snow-white hair fell gracefully over his shoulders and gave dignity to his form; he was really a grand old man, whose worth could not be over-estimated.

When the table had been cleared of the tea-things there came a lull in the conversation. Then Mrs Lawrence, Gramp's daughter, gave the fire a vigorous rout, brought more coals and set on the kettle again. Suddenly, without warning, Gramp burst into song with a clear, ringing voice, and we knew the time for festivity had arrived. He only sang one verse of the ditty. This was concerning two farmers who took refuge in the church porch during a heavy thunder-shower.

Several suggestions were made as to songs. One asked to hear 'The Jolly Tinker', or 'Preaching for Bacon,' others preferred 'Lord Bateman,' 'On the Banks of Sweet Dundee,' 'Butter and Cheese and All,' 'The Carrion Crow and the Tailor,' or 'The Oyster Girl,' all of which Gramp knew. Finally the matter was left for himself to decide.

Then Gramp said: 'Zeein' as we got a goodish company I thenks we ought to hae healths fust an' drenk to one another.'

A jug of ale was accordingly brought and the tumblers were reached down from the shelf. A little weak whisky and water, with sugar, was made for old Elijah. Then the glasses were clinked, and the young people stood up to drink.

'Now, then! What is it to be?' inquired Gramp of the first. Then the granddaughter replied:

> Here's a health to the world, as round as a wheel,
> Death is a thing we all shall feel;
> If life were a thing that money could buy
> The rich would live, and tile poor would die.

'Aa! Tha's a very good un. Go on wi' t'other,' said Elijah. Here the grandson spoke:

> Here's success to the plough, the fleece, and the flail,
> May the landlord ever flourish and the tenant never fail.

'Aa! Tha's a owld un, that is. I've yerd my grandfather saay 'e many a time when I was a bwoy. Wha's the next un?'

Elijah's son spoke next:

'Here's a health to that as'll do that good when the body and soul is taken from it!'

'H'm, h'm, h'm. Tha's a teert un. Don' know the meanie' o' 'e – No.'

'Yes you do know, too. What is it as does a ooman good when 'er baby's born? You knows as my mother allus used to gie a cup o' hot beer to the ooman as soon as the child was born when 'er went a nursin.'

'Ah! ah! ah! To be sure. I forgot that. Tha's as much as to say: "Yer's a health to the cup o' beer as dons the ooman good when 'er baby's barn." Go on wi't.'

> Here's to the man with a ragged coat,
> And with no means to mend it,
> And here's to the man with plenty of cash,
> And who doesn't know how to spend it.

'H'm! h'm! 'E dwun' live at our 'ouse, nat the last un, awhever. 'Ev 'e all done? Spose 'tis my time now then?' said grandfather, rising from the chair and taking up his glass from the table, while all eyed him eagerly. Holding the glass on high and inclining his head a little to one side, old Elijah delivered his toast:

> Here's to the inside of a loaf and the outside of a gaol,
> A good beefsteak and a quart of good ale,

cried he, and drank off the contents of the glass amid much laughter.

'But you got neether beefsteak nor yet ale, for you drunk whisky an' water,' cried Mrs Lawrence.

There was no holding Gramp after that. His old face wore an ineffable expression, and he shook with frequent laughter. First he sang 'Paddle your own Canoe, my Boys,' then ran into 'The Four and Nine,' and ended with 'Blow the Candle out.' Afterwards followed a short bit of patter, then came 'Parson Jingle Jaw's Adventure' and the song of 'Sweet Peggy o,' newly remembered after sixty years.

Just then a galloping of horses, accompanied by a loud rumbling sound, was heard outside.

'There goes the mailman from Lechlade! 'E's late to-night,' cried the hostess, looking up at the clock on the mantelpiece.

'Aa, 'e got a smartish load. 'E'll 'ev a job to get up Hywuth 'ill to-night. But dur-saay a got double 'osses. What! be 'e off a'ready, then? Thought 'e was gwain to stop a bit,' continued Elijah, as one of the company prepared to leave.

'Another half an hour and it will be Christmas morning,' replied he.

'Well! good-bye to 'e, if 'e must go. Look out for the owl' black dog o' Engleshum,' said Gramp, and the visitor, after wishing every one 'Goodnight,' and 'A Merry Christmas,' opened the door and left the cottage.

The night was calm and clear. Above Coleshill Wood the yellow half-moon was rising, topsy-turvy; the stars glittered brightly overhead in the frosty sky. Down below the sound of the Cole leaping through the hatches could faintly be heard, otherwise there was perfect silence. The street lights were out in the town on the hill, but the old church tower stood black against the sky and was visible several miles off. As I passed beneath the dark trees a black dog came running by, and I thought of Gramp's parting words at the cottage, in which he referred to the Inglesham Ghost, though that was probably one let loose from the neighbouring farmyard.

Old Elijah became so merry after my departure that he stayed up till after two o' clock, and it was feared that he would not go to bed at all. Even after he was put there he kept singing, and only fell asleep an hour before daybreak, to wake again with a song when the postman's rat-tat came at the door signifying the arrival of the Christmas letters and parcels.[1]

Elijah Iles, known as Gramp, died in 1917 at Inglesham in the Thames valley, north Wiltshire, aged 95. The poet, country-writer and folksong collector Alfred Williams had discovered this indomitable folk-singer and rustic raconteur a few years earlier and held him in very high regard. He wrote in an obituary: 'When all the Elijah Iles's have gone from our midst valuable links with the past will have been severed, and we shall be the poorer for it. It is by those who have travelled the road of life that we may best be made acquainted with its pleasures and hardships.'[2] The Christmas Eve party here described probably took place in 1914.[3]

Since the fourth century the Christian church has regarded 25 December as the birthday of Jesus. Because the gospel narratives describe a night-time birth, the early hours of Christmas morning or, more particularly, the midnight hour when Christmas Eve becomes Christmas Day, have come to be seen as the anniversary of that moment of birth – the cosmic moment, for Christians, when the world changed. The birthnight is then a time of mystery, of remembrance, of celebration. Hardly surprising, therefore, that writers have woven their stories and thoughts around this night. Two of the most attractive and beloved of birthnight narratives, the oxen kneeling in their stalls and the carollers going their rounds, will always be linked in popular imagination with Wessex, and with Thomas Hardy. But there are others, and in this and the next section, 'The Oxen' and 'Going the Rounds' are set in a broader context.

1 Williams, A, *Round about the upper Thames* (1922), 295-313 (abridged).

2 http://www.wiltshire.gov.uk/community/getfolkbio.php?id=109, accessed 4 Sept 2010.

3 Williams, having finished employment at Swindon railway works, was actively collecting folksongs in the Lechlade area during December 1914: http://www.alfredwilliams.org.uk/life.html, accessed 4 Sept. 2010; see also Clark, L, *Alfred Williams: his life and work* (1945), 78-80, 100-1.

Hardy set more than twenty poems against the background of Christmas and the New Year. This was partly because, as a working writer, he responded to magazine editors' calls for seasonal contributions; but a far more potent stimulus for an artist of his temperament was the cauldron of conflicting emotions which Christmas brought (and still brings) with it. William Barnes, whose Dorset dialect poetry Hardy greatly admired, felt this emotional charge too, but there was more honey, and less vinegar, in his nostalgic Christmas reflections. Here Barnes recalls one who, like Old Elijah, had 'travelled the road of life'.

Grammer's Shoes
William Barnes

DO SEEM TO zee Grammer as she did use
Vor to show us, at Chris'mas, her wedden shoes,
An' her flat spreaden bonnet so big an' roun'
As a girt pewter dish a-turn'd upside down;
 When we all did draw near
 In a cluster to hear
O' the merry wold soul how she did use
To walk an' to dance wi' her high-heel shoes.

She'd a gown wi' girt flowers lik' hollyhocks,
An' zome stockens o' gramfer's a-knit wi' clocks,
An' a token she kept under lock an' key, –
A small lock ov his heair off avore 't wer grey.
 An' her eyes wer red,
 An' she shook her head,
When we'd all a-look'd at it, an' she did use
To lock it away wi' her wedden shoes.

She could tell us such teales about heavy snows,
An' o' rains an' o' floods when the waters rose
All up into the housen, an' carr'd awoy
All the bridge wi' a man an' his little bwoy;
> An' o' vog an' vrost,
> An' o' vo'k a-lost,
An' o' pearties at Chris'mas, when she did use
Vor to walk hwome wi' gramfer in high-heel shoes.

Ev'ry Chris'mas she lik'd vor the bells to ring,
An' to have in the zingers to hear em zing
The wold carols she heard many years a-gone,
While she warm'd em zome cider avore the bron';
> An' she'd look an' smile
> At our dancen, while
She did tell how her friends now a-gone did use
To reely wi' her in their high-heel shoes.

Ah! an' how she did like vor to deck wi' red
Holly-berries the window an' wold clock's head,
An' the clavy wi' boughs o' some bright green leaves,
An' to meake twoast an' eale upon Chris'mas eves;
> But she's now, drough greace,
> In a better pleace,
Though we'll never vorget her, poor soul, nor lose
Gramfer's token ov heair, nor her wedden shoes.[1]

Now for two short stories set on this mystical night. The first, by the master, was presumably a commission, since it was published in 1877 in the first issue of a children's annual, entitled Father Christmas: Our

1   Barnes, W, *Poems* (1962 ed.), i, 167-8.

Little One's Budget.[1] *At the time Hardy was completing another and better known Christmas-inspired work,* The Return of the Native. *It was never included in his collected works, and it seems to have been completely forgotten (possibly even by Hardy himself) during his lifetime. Only two copies are known to survive, and it was not reprinted until 1942.*

The Thieves Who Couldn't Stop Sneezing
Thomas Hardy

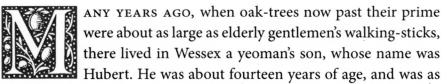

ANY YEARS AGO, when oak-trees now past their prime were about as large as elderly gentlemen's walking-sticks, there lived in Wessex a yeoman's son, whose name was Hubert. He was about fourteen years of age, and was as remarkable for his candour and lightness of heart as for his physical courage, of which, indeed, he was a little vain.

---

1   This title seems to be a very early example of the trend which was beginning to link Father Christmas, via Santa Claus, with children's presents.

One cold Christmas Eve his father, having no other help at hand, sent him on an important errand to a small town several miles from home. He travelled on horseback, and was detained by the business till a late hour of the evening. At last, however, it was completed; he returned to the inn, the horse was saddled, and he started on his way. His journey homeward lay through the Vale of Blackmore, a fertile but somewhat lonely district, with heavy clay roads and crooked lanes. In those days, too, a great part of it was thickly wooded.

It must have been about nine o'clock when, riding along amid the overhanging trees upon his stout-legged cob Jerry, and singing a Christmas carol, to be in harmony with the season, Hubert fancied that he heard a noise among the boughs. This recalled to his mind that the spot he was traversing bore an evil name. Men had been waylaid there. He looked at Jerry, and wished he had been of any other colour than light grey; for on this account the docile animal's form was visible even here in the dense shade. 'What do I care?' he said aloud, after a few minutes of reflection. 'Jerry's legs are too nimble to allow any highwayman to come near me.'

'Ha! ha! indeed,' was said in a deep voice; and the next moment a man darted from the thicket on his right hand, another man from the thicket on his left hand, and another from a tree-trunk a few yards ahead. Hubert's bridle was seized, he was pulled from his horse, and although he struck out with all his might, as a brave boy would naturally do, he was overpowered. His arms were tied behind him, his legs bound tightly together, and he was thrown into the ditch. The robbers, whose faces he could now dimly perceive to be artificially blackened, at once departed, leading off the horse.

As soon as Hubert had a little recovered himself, he found that by great exertion he was able to extricate his legs from the cord; but, in spite of every endeavour, his arms remained bound as fast as before. All, therefore, that he could do was rise to his feet and proceed on his way with his arms behind him, and trust to chance for getting them unfastened. He knew that it would be impossible to reach home on foot that night, and in such a condition; but he walked on. Owing to the confusion which this attack caused in his brain, he lost his way, and would have been inclined to lie down and rest till morning among the dead leaves had he not known the danger of sleeping without wrappers in a frost so severe. So he wandered further onwards, his arms wrung and numbed by the cord which pinioned him, and his heart aching for the loss of poor Jerry, who never had been known to kick, or bite, or show a single vicious habit. He was not a little glad when he discerned through the trees a distant light. Towards this he made his way, and presently found himself in front of a large mansion with flanking wings, gables, and towers, the battlements and chimneys showing their shapes against the stars.

All was silent; but the door stood wide open, it being from this door that the light shone which had attracted him. On entering he found himself in a vast apartment arranged as a dining-hall, and brilliantly illuminated. The walls were covered with a great deal of dark wainscoting, formed into moulded panels, carvings, closet-doors, and the usual fittings of a house of that kind. But what drew his attention most was the large table in the midst of the hall, upon which was spread a sumptuous supper, as yet untouched. Chairs were placed around, and it appeared as if something had occurred to interrupt the meal just at the time when all were ready to begin.

Even had Hubert been so inclined, he could not have eaten in his helpless state, unless by dipping his mouth into the dishes, like a pig or cow. He wished first to obtain assistance; and was about to penetrate further into the house for that purpose when he heard hasty footsteps in the porch and the words, 'Be quick!' uttered in the deep voice which had reached him when he was dragged from the horse. There was only just time for him to dart under the table before three men entered the dining-hall. Peeping from beneath the hanging edges of the tablecloth, he perceived that their faces, too, were blackened, which at once removed any remaining doubts he may have felt that these were the same thieves

'Now, then,' said the first – the man with the deep voice – 'let us hide ourselves. They will all be back again in a minute. That was a good trick to get them out of the house – eh?'

'Yes. You well imitated the cries of a man in distress,' said the second.

'Excellently,' said the third.

'But they will soon find out that it was a false alarm. Come, where shall we hide? It must be some place we can stay in for two or three hours, till all are in bed and asleep. Ah! I have it. Come this way! I have learnt that the further closet is not opened once in a twelvemonth; it will serve our purpose exactly.'

The speaker advanced into a corridor which led from the hall. Creeping a little farther forward, Hubert could discern that the closet stood at the end, facing the dining-hall. The thieves entered it, and closed the door. Hardly breathing, Hubert glided forward, to learn a little more of their intention, if possible; and, coming close, he could hear the robbers whispering about the different rooms where the jewels, plate, and other valuables of the house were kept, which they plainly meant to steal.

They had not been long in hiding when a gay chattering of ladies and gentlemen was audible on the terrace without. Hubert felt that it would not do to be caught prowling about the house, unless he wished to be taken for a robber himself; and he slipped softly back to the hall, out at the door, and stood in a dark corner of the porch, where he could see everything without being himself seen. In a moment or two a whole troop of personages came gliding past him into the house. There were an elderly gentleman and lady, eight or nine young ladies, as many young men, besides half-a-dozen men-servants and maids. The mansion had apparently been quite emptied of its occupants.

'Now, children and young people, we will resume our meal,' said the old gentleman. 'What the noise could have been I cannot understand. I never felt so certain in my life that there was a person being murdered outside my door.'

Then the ladies began saying how frightened they had been, and how they had expected an adventure, and how it had ended in nothing after all.

'Wait a while,' said Hubert to himself. 'You'll have adventure enough by-and-by, ladies.'

It appeared that the young men and women were married sons and daughters of the old couple, who had come that day to spend Christmas with their parents.

The door was then closed, Hubert being left outside in the porch. He thought this a proper moment for asking their assistance; and, since he was unable to knock with his hands, began boldly to kick the door.

'Hullo! What disturbance are you making here?' said a footman who opened it; and, seizing Hubert by the shoulder, he pulled him into the dining-hall. 'Here's a strange boy I have found making a noise in the porch, Sir Simon.'

Everybody turned.

'Bring him forward,' said Sir Simon, the old gentleman before mentioned. 'What were you doing there, my boy?'

'Why, his arms are tied!' said one of the ladies.

'Poor fellow!' said another.

Hubert at once began to explain that he had been waylaid on his journey home, robbed of his horse, and mercilessly left in this condition by the thieves.

'Only to think of it!' exclaimed Sir Simon.

'That's a likely story,' said one of the gentleman-guests, incredulously.

'Doubtful, hey?' asked Sir Simon.

'Perhaps he's a robber himself,' suggested a lady.

'There is a curiously wild wicked look about him, certainly, now that I examine him closely,' said the old mother.

Hubert blushed with shame; and, instead of continuing his story, and relating that robbers were concealed in the house, he doggedly held his tongue, and half resolved to let them find out their danger for themselves.

'Well, untie him,' said Sir Simon. 'Come, since it is Christmas Eve, we'll treat him well. Here, my lad; sit down in that empty seat at the bottom of the table, and make as good a meal as you can. When you have had your fill we will listen to more particulars of your story.'

The feast then proceeded; and Hubert, now at liberty, was not at all sorry to join in. The more they ate and drank the merrier did the company become; the wine flowed freely, the logs flared up the chimney, the ladies laughed at the gentlemen's stories; in short, all went as noisily and as happily as a Christmas gathering in old times possibly could do.

Hubert, in spite of his hurt feelings at their doubts of his honesty, could not help being warmed both in mind and in body by the good cheer, the scene, and the example of hilarity set by his neighbours. At last he laughed as heartily at their stories and repartees as the old Baronet, Sir Simon, himself. When the meal was almost over one of the sons, who had drunk a little too much wine, after the manner of men in that century, said to Hubert, 'Well, my boy, how are you? Can you take a pinch of snuff?' He held out one of the snuff-boxes which were then becoming common among young and old throughout the country.

'Thank you,' said Hubert, accepting a pinch.

'Tell the ladies who you are, what you are made of, and what you can do,' the young man continued, slapping Hubert upon the shoulder.

'Certainly,' said our hero, drawing himself up, and thinking it best to put a bold face on the matter. 'I am a travelling magician.'

'Indeed!'

'What shall we hear next?'

'Can you call up spirits from the vasty deep, young wizard?'

'I can conjure up a tempest in a cupboard,' Hubert replied.

'Ha-ha!' said the old Baronet, pleasantly rubbing his hands. 'We must see this performance. Girls, don't go away: here's something to be seen.'

'Not dangerous, I hope?' said the old lady.

Hubert rose from the table. 'Hand me your snuff-box, please,' he said to the young man who had made free with him. 'And now,' he continued, 'without the least noise, follow me. If any of you speak it will break the spell.'

They promised obedience. He entered the corridor, and, taking off his shoes, went on tiptoe to the closet door, the guests advancing in a silent group at a little distance behind him. Hubert next placed a stool in front of the door, and, by standing upon it, was tall enough to reach to the top. He then, just as noiselessly, poured all the snuff from the box along the upper edge of the door, and, with a few short puffs of breath, blew the snuff through the chink into the interior of the closet. He held up his finger to the assembly, that they might be silent.

'Dear me, what's that?' said the old lady, after a minute or two had elapsed.

A suppressed sneeze had come from inside the closet.

Hubert held up his finger again.

'How very singular,' whispered Sir Simon. 'This is most interesting.'

Hubert took advantage of the moment to gently slide the bolt of the closet door into its place. 'More snuff,' he said, calmly.

'More snuff,' said Sir Simon. Two or three gentlemen passed their boxes, and the contents were blown in at the top of the closet. Another sneeze, not quite so well suppressed as the first, was heard: then another, which seemed to say that it would not be suppressed under any circumstances whatever. At length there arose a perfect storm of sneezes.

'Excellent, excellent for one so young!' said Sir Simon. 'I am much interested in this trick of throwing the voice – called, I believe, ventriloquism.'

'More snuff,' said Hubert.

'More snuff,' said Sir Simon. Sir Simon's man brought a large jar of the best scented Scotch.

Hubert once more charged the upper chink of the closet, and blew the snuff into the interior, as before. Again he charged, and again, emptying the whole contents of the jar. The tumult of sneezes became really extraordinary to listen to – there was no cessation. It was like wind, rain, and sea battling in a hurricane.

'I believe there are men inside, and that it is no trick at all!' exclaimed Sir Simon, the truth flashing on him.

'There are,' said Hubert. 'They are come to rob the house; and they are the same who stole my horse.'

The sneezes changed to spasmodic groans. One of the thieves, hearing Hubert's voice, cried, 'Oh! mercy! mercy! let us out of this!'

'Where's my horse?' said Hubert.

'Tied to the tree in the hollow behind Short's Gibbet. Mercy! mercy! let us out, or we shall die of suffocation!'

All the Christmas guests now perceived that this was no longer sport, but serious earnest. Guns and cudgels were procured; all the men-servants were called in, and arranged in position outside the closet. At a signal Hubert withdrew the bolt, and stood on the defensive. But the three robbers, far from attacking them, were found crouching in the corner, gasping for breath. They made no resistance; and, being pinioned, were placed in an out-house till the morning.

Hubert now gave the remainder of his story to the assembled company, and was profusely thanked for the services he had rendered. Sir Simon pressed him to stay over the night, and accept the use of the best bed-room the house afforded, which had been occupied by Queen Elizabeth and King Charles successively when on their visits to this part of the country. But Hubert declined, being anxious to find his horse Jerry, and to test the truth of the robbers' statements concerning him.

Several of the guests accompanied Hubert to the spot behind the gibbet, alluded to by the thieves as where Jerry was hidden. When they reached the knoll and looked over, behold! there the horse stood, uninjured, and quite unconcerned. At sight of Hubert he neighed joyfully; and nothing could exceed Hubert's gladness at finding him. He mounted, wished his friends 'Good-night!' and cantered off in the direction they pointed out as his nearest way, reaching home safely about four o'clock in the morning.[1]

Anyone writing stories of Dorset life invites damning comparison with Hardy, but this did not deter several others, famously John Cowper Powys and John Meade Falkner. Further down the literary scale came spinners of melodramas and sentimental tales, such as Mary Blundell, who adopted the pen-name M.E. Francis. Here is part of one of her short stories, or 'idylls of country life', from a collection, Dorset Dear, *published in 1905. As a study of feminine guile employed to good effect at Christmas it is gently, but skilfully, written, and has a certain charm.*

The heroine, Mrs Sibley, is employed by the widowed sexton, John Foyle, to be his housekeeper and to look after his children. She, too, is widowed, her husband having recently died after some years in an asylum. Her matrimonial designs on her employer are discussed with a confidante, Martha Fry.

---

1   Reprinted in Dalziel, P (ed.), *Thomas Hardy: the excluded and collaborative stories* (1992), 52-65.

Mrs Sibley and the Sexton
M.E. Francis

ASN'T HE SAID nothin' – nothin' at all?' inquired Mrs Fry, resting a plump hand on either knee and leaning forward.

'Not a single word,' replied her friend; 'that's to say, not a word wi' any sense in it. An' Sibley have been gone six months now, mind ye.'

'So he have!' replied Mrs Fry. 'An' ye mid say as you've been so good as a widder for nigh upon six year – ye mid indeed. A husband what's in the 'sylum is worse nor no husband at all. An' ye've a-been keepin' house for Foyle these four year, haven't ye?'

'Four year an' two month,' responded Mrs Sibley. 'There, the very day after Mrs Foyle were buried he did come to me an' he says so plain-spoke as anything, "Mrs Sibley," he says, "here be you a lone woman wi'out no family, an' here be I wi' all they little childern. Will 'ee come an' keep house for I an' look after 'em all? Ye'll not be the loser by it," says he. So I looks him straight in the face: "I bain't so sure o' that, Mr Foyle," I says. "I do look at it in this way, d'ye see. A woman has her chances," I says. "I don't think Sibley 'ull last so very long – they seldom does at the 'sylum – an' then here be I, a lone woman, as you do say. I mid very well like to settle myself again; an' if I go an' bury myself so far away from town in a place where there's sich a few neighbours, I don't see what prospects I'll have."'

'Well, that was straightforward enough,' commented Mrs Fry. 'He couldn't make no mistakes about your meanin'.'

'He could not,' agreed Mrs Sibley triumphantly; 'an' what's more, he didn't. He up an' spoke as plain as a man could speak. "Well, Mrs Sibley," he says, "there's a Fate what rules us all.' He be always a-sayin' off bits o' po'try an' sichlike as he gets from the gravestones, ye know.'

'Ah,' remarked Mrs Fry nodding, 'being the sexton, of course, it do come nat'ral to 'en, don't it?'

'"There's a Fate what rules us all," he says,' resumed Mrs Sibley, '"an' we didn't ought to m'urn as if we had no hope. If you was a free 'ooman, Mrs Sibley – well, I'm a free man, and I'd make so good a husband as another. Maria did always find I so," he says.'

'Well, the man couldn't have said more.'

'So you'd think. But why don't he say summat now? There, I've a-kept his house an' seen arter his childern for more nor four year. Time's gettin' on, ye know; I bain't so young as I was.'

Mrs Fry began a polite disclaimer, but was overruled by the other.

'I bain't – tisn't in natur' as I could be. I wer' gettin' a bit anxious this year when poor Sibley did seem to be hangin' on so long, so I axed Rector to have 'en prayed for –.'

'A-h-h-h?' ejaculated Martha, as she paused. 'An' that did put the Lard in mind of 'en, I should think.'

'It did put the Lard in mind of 'en,' agreed Mrs Sibley with gusto. 'The Lard see'd he warn't no good to nobody in the 'sylum, as' so he wer' took.'

'An' Foyle have never come forward?' remarked Mrs Fry, after a significant pause.

'He've never made no offer, an' he've never said a single word to show he were thinkin' o' sich a thing. Not *one* word, Mrs Fry. I've given 'en the chance many a time . . . I says to 'en this marnin', "Mr Foyle," I says, "the New Year's a-comin', an I think there ought to be some change in the early part of it for you an' me." "I don't want no changes," he says, "I'm very well satisfied as I be." I'm gettin' desperate, Mrs Fry.'

'Well, 'tis very onconsiderate,' returned Martha, 'very. I'm sure ye've said all ye could an' done all ye could. 'Tis hard, too, for a woman to have to go a-droppin' hints an' a-takin' the lead in such a delicate matter. I'm sure I don't know what to advise, my dear.'

After much deliberation, a plan is agreed. It is Christmas Eve, and before the family is sent to bed Mrs Sibley intimates to Mr Foyle that she proposes to leave the household the next day, and that he will have to find a new 'Auntie' for the children. They all take it rather badly.

'There, don't ye make such a fuss,' she remarked soothingly. 'Father's a bit upset; ye mustn't mind that. Get on with your teas, dears. There, ye may have a bit of jam to it to-night, as it's Christmas Eve; and afterwards we'll stick up some green, and you must all hang up your stockin's and see what you'll find there in the marnin'.'

Cheerfulness was immediately restored; little faces grimed by tears smiled afresh; plates were extended for plentiful helpings of blackberry jam, and soon little tongues were gleefully discussing the morrow's prospects, and particularly the treasures which might be looked for in the stockings . . . As the children retired for the night, Henery paused beside her for a moment.

'You won't truly go to-morrow, Auntie?' he pleaded coaxingly.

Mrs Sibley paused a moment, and in the interval the sound of the sexton's slouching step was heard without, and his hand fumbled at the latch.

'It do all depend on Father, Henery,' said Mrs Sibley, raising her voice slightly. 'He do know very well as I do want a change.'

Mr Foyle entered, looking weary and depressed, and sat down in his customary chair. Mrs Sibley cast a searching glance round the kitchen, and, possessing herself of a pair of spotted china dogs which adorned the mantel-piece, added them to her collection, and retired.

The sexton lit his pipe, and had been smoking in gloomy silence for some time, when Mrs Sibley re-entered. Going to the dresser, and opening a drawer, she abstracted a number of oranges, nuts, crackers, and other such wares, and filled her apron with them.

'What be them for?' inquired the sexton diffidently.

'Why, they be surprises for the childern,' returned she.

'Ah,' rejoined John Foyle, 'surprises, be they?'

'Yes,' said Mrs Sibley, 'they do look for 'em reg'lar, they do. I always fill their stockin's wi' 'em every Christmas.'

'Oh,' said the sexton, 'put their surprises in their stockin's, do 'ee?'

Mrs Sibley nodded and withdrew, leaving John sunk in profound thought.

'This 'ere be a vale o' tears,' he remarked presently, as he knocked the ashes out of his pipe. He rose, went to the table, turned up the lamp a little more, and fetching pen, ink, and paper from the window-sill on which they usually reposed, sat down to indite a letter. It cost him much labour and thought, but, after all, it was a brief enough document. When completed it ran thus: 'If Mrs Sibley will meet Mr Foyle in the churchyard to-morrow morning about nine o'clock when nobody's about she will hear of something to your advantage. Yours truly, John Foyle.'

'I couldn't,' said the sexton to himself, 'put the question in any sort of public way. The childern is in and out, and the neighbours mid pop in. The churchyard is best and most nat'ral.'

He folded the letter, put it in an envelope, and addressed it; then, looking round, descried hanging over a chair-back one of Mrs Sibley's stockings. 'The very thing!' exclaimed John. 'The Christmas surprises do always go in stockin's. It'll be a surprise for she, I d' 'low –– not but what she didn't look for it,' he added with a grim chuckle.

He placed the letter in the stocking, fastened it securely with a loop of string, and, going cautiously upstairs, slung it over Mrs Sibley's door-handle. He paused a moment, winking to himself, and then made his way on tiptoe to his own room.

Next morning, in the churchyard, it is Mrs Sibley's turn to play hard-to-get.

He descried a tall figure in black making its way, not towards him, but towards that portion of the churchyard wherein reposed the mortal remains of the lamented Mr Sibley. After some hesitation the sexton followed, and Mrs Sibley, having deposited a wreath of evergreens on the grave, turned round with a mournful expression.

'At such times as these, Mr Foyle,' she remarked, 'the mind do nat'rally feel m'urnfull.'

'True, true!' agreed the sexton uncomfortably.

'He was a good husband, Mr Foyle,' said the widow in a melancholy tone.

'To be sure,' said John doubtfully.

'I shall never look upon his like again,' resumed Mrs Sibley, shaking her head.

The sexton glanced from her disconsolate face to the wreath of evergreens, and then back again. Mrs Sibley was still shaking her head with an air of gentle resignation.

'I think I'll be goin',' said Mr Foyle with sudden desperation. 'I thought you did step out to this 'ere churchyard with another intention.'

Mrs Sibley glanced at him in mild surprise.

'Ye didn't chance to get no letter this marnin', I s'pose?' continued the sexton with some heat.

'A letter!' repeated Mrs Sibley.

'E-es, the letter what I did put in your stockin' for a surprise,' added John emphatically.

Mrs Sibley's melancholy vanished as by magic; she smiled on the sexton, not only affably, but positively coyly.

'An' it *was* a surprise!' she exclaimed, 'it *was* indeed. E-es, Mr Foyle.'

She paused again, and then, all scruples apparently vanquished by the delicacy of John's attitude, she extended a bony hand from beneath the folds of her black shawl.

    'That's why I'm here,' she said.[1]

Happy endings were not normally to Hardy's taste. He observed (and had experienced first-hand) that smouldering resentments and unseen tensions within families all too often reveal themselves at Christmas, when normal patterns of life are suspended and expectations forlornly aroused. We may feel that this is a peculiarly modern crisis, engendered by the saccharin juggernaut which we inflict on ourselves each winter. But we have only inherited an age-old problem, and Hardy depicted it in this curiously wrought vignette of a flawed marriage, set on Christmas Eve. It is a product of his last, reflective, years, and was published in 1925.

One Who Married Above Him
Thomas Hardy

IS YOU, I think? Back from your week's work, Steve?'
'It is I. Back from work this Christmas Eve.'
'But you seem off again? – in this night-rime?'
'I am off again, and thoroughly off this time.'
'What does that mean?'
'More than may first be seen . . .

Half an hour ago I footed homeward here,
No wife found I, nor child, nor maid, indoors or near.
She has, as always, gone with them to her mother's at the farm,
Where they fare better far than here, and, maybe, meet less harm.
She's left no fire, no light, has cooked me nothing to eat,
Though she had fuel, and money to get some Christmas meat.

1   Francis, M E, *Dorset dear* (1905), 207-21

Christmas with them is grand, she knows, and brings good victual,
Other than how it is here, where it's but lean and little.
But though not much, and rough,
If managed neat there's enough.
She and hers are too highmade for me;
But she's whimmed her once too often, she'll see!
Farmer Bollen's daughter should never have married a man that's poor;
And I can stand it no longer; I'm leaving; you'll see me no more, be sure.'

'But nonsense: you'll be back again ere bedtime, and lighting a fire,
And sizzling your supper, and vexing not that her views of supper are higher.'
'Never for me.'
'Well, we shall see.'

The sceptical neighbour and Stephen then followed their foredesigned ways,
And their steps dimmed into white silence upon the slippery glaze;
And the trees went on with their spitting amid the icicled haze.

The evening whiled, and the wife with the babies came home,
But he was not there, nor all Christmas Day did he come.
Christmastide went, and likewise went the New Year,
But no husband's footfall revived,
And month after month lapsed, graytime to green and to sere,
And other new years arrived,
And the children grew up: one husbanded and one wived. –
She wept and repented,
But Stephen never relented.
And there stands the house, and the sycamore-tree and all,
With its roots forming steps for the passers who care to call,

And there are the mullioned windows, and Ham-Hill door,
Through which Steve's wife was brought out, but which Steve re-
entered no more.[1]

*The Christmases of the First World War were probably the most cheerless
of Hardy's life, because then death and destruction were no longer
ingredients in the novelist's store, but stark everyday truths. In a letter to
a clergyman friend, dated Christmas Day 1914, he wrote: 'A newspaper
editor asked me to send him a Christmas greeting for his readers, and I
told him the puzzle was too hard for me, seeing that present times are an
absolute negation of Christianity.'[2] And in his autobiography he confided
that the war had destroyed all his belief in the gradual ennoblement of
man, or of any 'fundamental ultimate Wisdom' at the back of things.[3]*

*He was not alone in his introspection. Fellow Dorset novelist John
Meade Falkner (author of* Moonfleet), *had corresponded with Hardy
intermittently and shared his pessimism. 'The vanity of life is borne in
upon me strongly and strangely,' he wrote to Hardy in 1911. Falkner
was directly and heavily involved in the war, since in 1915 he became
chairman of the board of Armstrong Whitworth, a major armaments
manufacturer. A visit to Holy Trinity church, Dorchester, perhaps at
Christmas 1917 or 1918, where his father had served as curate during
the 1860s, drew from him this strange poem, of reminiscence, loneliness
and uncertainty.[4]*

1   Hardy, T, *Complete poems* (1979 ed.), no. 709; 'night-rime' is not a misprint for
    'night-time'.
2   Purdy, R L, and Millgate, M (eds.), *The collected letters of Thomas Hardy*, v (1985),
    71-2.
3   Hardy, T, *The life and work of Thomas Hardy* (M Millgate ed., 1984), 398.
4   Warren, K, *John Meade Falkner 1858-1932: a paradoxical life*, 1995 (Studies in
    British History 32), 276-9.

Christmas Day – The Family Sitting
John Meade Falkner

N THE DAYS of Caesar Augustus
There went forth this decree:
Si quis rectus et justus[1]
Liveth in Galilee,
Let him go up to Jerusalem
And pay his scot to me.

There are passed one after the other
Christmases fifty-three,
Since I sat here with my mother
And heard the great decree:
How they went up to Jerusalem
Out of Galilee.

They have passed one after the other;
Father and mother died,
Brother and sister and brother
Taken and sanctified.
I am left alone in the sitting,
With none to sit beside.

On the fly-leaves of these old prayer-books
The childish writings fade,
Which show that once they were their books
In the days when prayer was made

---

1   'If any are upright and just'. I have been unable to source this quotation.

For other kings and princesses,
    William and Adelaide.

The pillars are twisted with holly,
    And the font is wreathed with yew
Christ forgive me for folly,
    Youth's lapses – not a few,
For the hardness of my middle life,
    For age's fretful view.

Cotton-wool letters on scarlet,
    All the ancient lore,
Tell how the chieftains starlit
    To Bethlehem came to adore;
To hail Him King in the manger,
    Wonderful, Counsellor.

The bells ring out in the steeple
    The gladness of erstwhile,
And the children of other people
    Are walking up the aisle;
They brush my elbow in passing,
    Some turn to give me a smile.

Is the almond-blossom bitter?
    Is the grasshopper heavy to bear ?
Christ make me happier, fitter
    To go to my own over there:
Jerusalem the Golden,
    What bliss beyond compare!

My Lord, where I have offended
    Do Thou forgive it me.

That so, when all being ended,
    I hear Thy last decree,
I may go up to Jerusalem
    Out of Galilee.[1]

During the second year of the terrible war, insignificantly at the foot of a column of an inside page of The Times *on Christmas Eve, was first published 'The Oxen', a short poem which has become one of the best known that Hardy ever wrote. It is constructed about the widespread belief that animals at Christmas possessed supernatural powers or assumed human characteristics, which was often coupled with a notion that only certain people had the ability to witness such a miracle.*

A moving example of such a belief, sincerely held, is recorded in the diary of Francis Kilvert in January 1878. Kilvert was an exact contemporary of Hardy – both were born in 1840 – but his literary career took a very different course. In 1878 he had moved from Wiltshire to serve as a clergyman in a remote region of the Welsh borderland, and had only another year of life ahead of him. Those of his diaries which were not destroyed lay undiscovered for a further sixty years, and were

---

1   Falkner, J M, *Poems* (1932); included in Larkin, P (ed.), *Oxford book of twentieth century verse* (1973), 42-3.

not published until long after Hardy's death. So the poet would not have been aware of this version, told to Kilvert by an elderly lady, Priscilla Price, in her cottage on the hill above Bredwardine, near Hay-on-Wye, when he visited her on 'Old' Christmas Eve, 5th January.

Old Christmas Eve
Francis Kilvert

PEAKING OF THE blowing of the Holy Thorn and the kneeling and weeping of the oxen on old Christmas Eve (to-night) Priscilla said, 'I have known old James Meredith forty years and I have never known him far from the truth, and I said to him one day, "James, tell me the truth, did you ever see the oxen kneel on old Christmas Eve at the Weston?" And he said, "No, I never saw them kneel at the Weston but when I was at Hinton at Staunton-on-Wye I saw them. I was watching them on old Christmas Eve and at 12 o'clock the oxen that were standing knelt down upon their knees and those that were lying down rose up on their knees and there they stayed kneeling and moaning, and tears running down their faces."'[1]

A similar belief, of course, existed in Dorset, and Hardy knew of it long before 1915. According to his second wife it was Jemima Hardy, his mother, who had told it to him.[2] In Tess of the d'Urbervilles, *written twenty-five years earlier, he had used it to comic effect.*

---

1 Plomer, W (ed.), *Kilvert's diary* (1960 ed.), iii, 354.
2 Bailey, J O, *The poetry of Thomas Hardy: a handbook and commentary* (1970), 370-1.

'Tis Quite True, Sir
Thomas Hardy

O<small>H YES; THERE</small>'s nothing like a fiddle,' said the dairyman. 'Though I do think that bulls are more moved by a tune than cows – at least that's my experience. Once there was a old aged man over at Mellstock – William Dewy by name – one of the family that used to do a good deal of business as tranters over there, Jonathan, do ye mind ? – I knowed the man by sight as well as I know my own brother, in a manner of speaking. Well, this man was a coming home-along from a wedding where he had been playing his fiddle, one fine moonlight night, and for shortness' sake he took a cut across Forty-acres, a field lying that way, where a bull was out to grass. The bull seed William, and took after him, horns aground, begad; and though William runned his best, and hadn't *much* drink in him (considering 'twas a wedding, and the folks well off), he found he'd never reach the fence and get over in time to save himself. Well, as a last thought, he pulled out his fiddle as he runned, and struck up a jig, turning to the bull, and backing towards the corner. The bull softened down, and stood still, looking hard at William Dewy, who fiddled on and on; till a sort of a smile stole over the bull's face. But no sooner did William stop his playing and turn to get over hedge than the bull would stop his smiling and lower his horns towards the seat of William's breeches. Well, William had to turn about and play on, willy-nilly; and 'twas only three o'clock in the world, and 'a knowed that nobody would come that way for hours, and he so leery and tired that 'a didn't know what to do. When he had scraped till about four o'clock he felt that he verily would have to give over soon, and he said to himself, "There's only this last tune between me and eternal welfare! Heaven save me, or I'm a done man." Well, then he called to mind how he'd seen the cattle kneel o' Christmas Eves in the dead o' night. It was not Christmas Eve then, but it came into his head to play a trick upon the bull. So he broke into the 'Tivity Hymn, just as at Christmas carol-singing; when, lo and behold, down went the bull on his bended knees, in his ignorance, just as if 'twere the true 'Tivity night and hour. As soon as his horned friend were down, William turned, clinked off like a long-dog, and jumped safe over hedge, before the praying bull had got on his feet again to take after him. William used to say that he'd seen a man look a fool a good many times, but never such a fool as that bull looked when he found his pious feelings had been played upon, and 'twas not Christmas Eve ... Yes, William Dewy, that was the man's name; and I can tell you to a foot where's he a-lying in Mellstock Churchyard at this very moment – just between the second yew-tree and the north aisle.'

'It's a curious story; it carries us back to mediaeval times, when faith was a living thing!'

The remark, singular for a dairy-yard, was murmured by the voice behind the dun cow; but as nobody understood the reference no notice was taken, except that the narrator seemed to think it might imply scepticism as to his tale.

'Well, 'tis quite true, sir, whether or no. I knowed the man well.'

'Oh yes; I have no doubt of it,' said the person behind the dun cow.[1]

---

1 Hardy, T, *Tess of the d'Urbervilles* (1974 ed.), 138-9.

Folklore collectors, like Hardy himself, introduced a note of scepticism towards such legends. Henry Moule, who was the curator of the Dorset County Museum in Dorchester, a friend of Hardy and Falkner's teacher, published a variant of the story in 1889, attached to a standing stone overlooking Blackmore Vale in north Dorset. The stone features in Tess, as the spot where the heroine meets Alec d'Urberville and is persuaded to swear on the stone that she will never tempt him. Hardy described the scene as 'something sinister, or solemn, according to mood', and later based his poem 'The Lost Pyx' on its legend.

Cross-in-Hand Stone
Henry Moule

N Batcombe Down, Dorset, is a stone about three feet high, evidently part of a cross, and called Cross Hand Stone. Why should a cross be set up, away there on the down? Well, this 'be teale twold o't'. Back in the middle ages, one dark, wild winter night, Batcombe priest was sent for to take the *viaticum* to a dying man, two or three miles off. Taking pyx and service-book, he sallied out with a brave heart on his dark, lonely way over Batcombe Down, and safely reached the sick man's house. But on getting in, and producing what was needed for his ministration – where was the pyx? It was lost. He had dropped it on the way, and its fall on the turf of Batcombe Down – in the howling wind too! – had not been heard. Back he toiled, into the darkness and the storm, on his almost hopeless quest. Hopeless? The easiest search ever made. Up on Batcombe Down there was a pillar of fire, reaching from heaven to earth, and steadily shining in the storm. What could this be? He struggled on faster and faster, with strange, half-formed hopes. He came near to the spot over which stood the calm beam in the gale. He saw numbers of cattle of various kinds, gathered in a circle – kneeling – kneeling round the pyx.

Well, this seemed to me to be the mediaeval legend, rendering a reason for Batcombe Cross being set up there, away on the down, where, though time-worn, it yet remains. But (*me judice*) [in my opinion] in the last [i.e. 18th] century a rider was added, as follows:

The priest was much astounded at what he saw, yet not so much so but that he observed among the live-stock a black horse, kneeling, indeed, like the rest, but only on one knee. The priest said to this lukewarm beast, 'Why don't you kneel on both knees, like the rest?' 'Wouldn't kneel at all if I could help it.' 'Who, then, are you ?' 'The devil.' 'Why do you take the form of a horse?' 'So that men may steal me and get hung, and I get hold of them. Got three or four already.'[1]

It is strange that Hardy's poem 'The Oxen' should have become such a favourite at church carol services because, like the legend of the lost pyx, the Devil creeps in at the end. The Devil in this case is Hardy's disillusioned agnosticism. By 1915 the war had destroyed his belief in Christmas miracles ('so fair a fancy few believe in these years'), and left him a reluctant unbeliever who can only ponder the naivety of his youth.

The Oxen
Thomas Hardy

 HRISTMAS EVE, AND twelve of the clock.
　　'Now they are all on their knees,'
An elder said as we sat in a flock
　　By the embers in hearthside ease.

We pictured the meek mild creatures where
　　They dwelt in their strawy pen,

1　*Somerset & Dorset Notes & Queries*, i (1889), 247.

Nor did it occur to one of us there
    To doubt they were kneeling then.

So fair a fancy few would weave
    In these years! Yet, I feel,
If someone said on Christmas Eve,
    'Come; see the oxen kneel

'In the lonely barton by yonder coomb
    Our childhood used to know,'
I should go with him in the gloom,
    Hoping it might be so.[1]

Eventually the hope gave way to incredulity that such things could ever have been. Retrospection filled Hardy's last years, and in many of his later poems he wistfully reflected on the rose-tinted memories of youthful celebration. The return of Christmas and the passing of the year increased the pangs of his nostalgia, and teased from him some of his finest and most characteristic poetry.

Yuletide in a Younger World
Thomas Hardy

W E BELIEVED IN highdays then,
    And could glimpse at night
      On Christmas Eve
Imminent oncomings of radiant revel –
Doings of delight: –
Now we have no such sight.

1   Hardy, T, *Complete poems* (1979 ed.), no. 403.

We had eyes for phantoms then,
    And at bridge or stile
      On Christmas Eve
Clear beheld those countless ones who had crossed it
    Cross again in file: –
    Such has ceased longwhile!

We liked divination then,
    And, as they homeward wound
      On Christmas Eve,
We could read men's dreams within them spinning
    Even as wheels spin round: –
    Now we are blinker-bound.

We heard still small voices then,
    And, in the dim serene
      Of Christmas Eve,
Caught the far-time tones of fire-filled prophets
    Long on earth unseen. . .
    – Can such ever have been?[1]

1   Ibid, no. 841.

7
Going the Rounds

HY WOONCE, AT Chris'mas-tide, avore
The wold year wer a-reckon'd out,
The humstrums here did come about,
A-sounden up at ev'ry door.
But now a bow do never screape
    A humstrum, any where all round,
An' zome can't tell a humstrum's sheape,
    An' never heard his jinglen sound,
As *ing-an-ing* did ring the string,
As *ang-an-ang* the wires did clang.

The strings a-tighten'd lik' to crack
Athirt the canister's tin zide,
Did reach, a-glitt'ren, zide by zide,
Above the humstrum's hollow back.
An' there the bwoy, wi' bended stick,
    A-strung wi' heair, to meake a bow,
Did dreve his elbow, light'nen quick,
    Athirt the strings vrom high to low,
As *ing-an-ing* did ring the string,
As *ang-an-ang* the wires did clang.

The mother there did stan' an' hush
Her child, to hear the jinglen sound,
The merry maid, a-scrubben round
Her white-steav'd pail, did stop her brush.
The mis'ess there, vor wold time's seake,
    Had gifts to gi'e, and smiles to show,
An' measter, too, did stan' an' sheake
    His two broad zides, a-chucklen low,
While *ing-an-ing* did ring the string,
While *ang-an-ang* the wires did clang.

The players' pockets wer a-strout,
Wi' wold brown pence, a-rottlen in,
Their zwangen bags did soon begin,
Wi' brocks an' scraps, to plim well out.
The childern all did run an' poke
    Their heads vrom hatch or door, an' shout
A-runnen back to wolder vo'k,
    'Why, here! the humstrums be about!'
As *ing-an-ing* did ring the string,
As *ang-an-ang* the wires did clang.[1]

'The Humstrum' by William Barnes, the Dorset dialect poet greatly admired by Thomas Hardy, describes Christmas musicians with primitive instruments. But before the melancholy and disillusionment

1   Barnes, W, *Poems* (1962 ed.), i, 449-50.

of his old age, it was Hardy who immortalised rustic music-making. The characters of his Mellstock Quire, stalwarts of the parish church west gallery, take centre stage in the early chapters of Under the Greenwood Tree. *They and other bands of village musicians also appear in a number of poems, as we shall see, practising psalms at the beginning of* Two on a Tower, *and in two of the stories known collectively as* A Few Crusted Characters.

Under the Greenwood Tree *begins with the members of the Mellstock Quire making their way on Christmas Eve to the house of the tranter (or carrier), Reuben Dewy, for the essential preliminaries – cider, and in a lesser degree, practice – to the impending night's carolling.*

Going the Rounds
Thomas Hardy

ETTER TRY OVER number seventy-eight before we start, I suppose?' said William, pointing to a heap of old Christmas-carol books on a side table.

'Wi' all my heart,' said the choir generally.

'Number seventy-eight was always a teaser – always. I can mind him ever since I was growing up a hard boy-chap.'

'But he's a good tune, and worth a mint o' practice,' said Michael.

'He is; though I've been mad enough wi' that tune at times to seize en and tear en all to linnit. Ay, he's a splendid carrel – there's no denying that.'

'That first line is well enough,' said Mr Spinks; 'but when you come to "O, thou man," you make a mess o't.'

'We'll have another go into en, and see what we can make of the martel. Half-an-hour's hammering at en will conquer the toughness of en; I'll warn it.'

A little more practice ensues, a good deal more cider, and a diversion into the intriguing shape of the young schoolmistress's shoe (crucial to the plot later on).

Shortly after ten o'clock the singing-boys arrived at the tranter's house, which was invariably the place of meeting, and preparations were made for the start. The older men and musicians wore thick coats, with stiff perpendicular collars, and coloured handkerchiefs wound round and round the neck till the end came to hand, over all which they just showed their ears and noses, like people looking over a wall. The remainder, stalwart ruddy men and boys, were dressed mainly in snow-white smock-frocks, embroidered upon the shoulders and breasts, in ornamental forms of hearts, diamonds, and zig-zags. The cider-mug was emptied for the ninth time, the music-books were arranged, and the pieces finally decided upon. The boys in the meantime put the old horn-lanterns in order, cut candles into short lengths to fit the lanterns; and, a thin fleece of snow having fallen since the early part of the evening, those who had no leggings went to the stable and wound wisps of hay round their ankles to keep the insidious flakes from the interior of their boots.

Mellstock was a parish of considerable acreage, the hamlets composing it lying at a much greater distance from each other than is ordinarily the case. Hence several hours were consumed in playing and singing within hearing of every family, even if but a single air were bestowed on each. There was Lower Mellstock, the main village; half a mile from this were the church and vicarage, and a few other houses, the spot being rather lonely now, though in past centuries it had been the most thickly-populated quarter of the parish. A mile north-east lay the hamlet of Upper Mellstock, where the tranter lived; and at other points knots of cottages, besides solitary farmsteads and dairies.

Old William Dewy, with the violoncello, played the bass; his grandson Dick the treble violin; and Reuben and Michael Mail the tenor and second violins respectively. The singers consisted of four men and seven boys, upon whom devolved the task of carrying and attending to the lanterns, and holding the books open for the players. Directly music was the theme, old William ever and instinctively came to the front.

'Now mind, neighbours,' he said, as they all went out one by one at the door, he himself holding it ajar and regarding them with a critical face as they passed, like a shepherd counting out his sheep. 'You two counter-boys, keep your ears open to Michael's fingering, and don't ye go straying into the treble part along o' Dick and his set, as ye did last year; and mind this especially when we be in "Arise, and hail." Billy Chimlen, don't you sing quite so raving mad as you fain would; and, all o'ye, whatever ye do, keep from making a great scuffle on the ground when we go in at people's gates; but go quietly, so as to strike up all of a sudden, like spirits.'

'Farmer Ledlow's first?'

'Farmer Ledlow's first; the rest as usual.'

'And, Voss,' said the tranter terminatively, 'you keep house here till about half-past two; then heat the metheglin and cider in the warmer you'll find turned up upon the copper; and bring it wi' the victuals to church-hatch, as th'st know.'

At midnight they set out across the snow, and by two o'clock they have visited most of the outlying parts of the parish. As they trudge back they pass their time arguing the merits of various musical instruments.

By this time they were crossing to a gate in the direction of the school, which, standing on a slight eminence at the junction of three ways, now rose in unvarying and dark flatness against the sky. The instruments were retuned, and all the band entered the school enclosure, enjoined by old William to keep upon the grass.

'Number seventy-eight,' he softly gave out as they formed round in a semicircle, the boys opening the lanterns to get a clearer light, and directing their rays on the books.

Then passed forth into the quiet night an ancient and timeworn hymn, embodying a quaint Christianity in words orally transmitted from father to son through several generations down to the present characters, who sang them out right earnestly:

> Remember Adam's fall,
>> O thou Man:
> Remember Adam's fall
>> From Heaven to Hell . . .

Having concluded the last note, they listened for a minute or two, but found that no sound issued from the schoolhouse.

'Four breaths, and then, "O, what unbounded goodness!" number fifty-nine,' said William.

This was duly gone through, and no notice whatever seemed to be taken of the performance.

'Good guide us, surely 'tisn't a' empty house, as befell us in the year thirty-nine and forty-three!' said old Dewy.

'Perhaps she's jist come from some musical city, and sneers at our doings?' the tranter whispered.

"Od rabbit her!' said Mr Penny, with an annihilating look at a corner of the school chimney, 'I don't quite stomach her, if this is it. Your plain music well done is as worthy as your other sort done bad, a' b'lieve, souls; so say I.'

'Four breaths, and then the last,' said the leader authoritatively. '"Rejoice, ye Tenants of the Earth," number sixty-four.'

At the close, waiting yet another minute, he said in a clear loud voice, as he had said in the village at that hour and season for the previous forty years –

'A merry Christmas to ye!'

When the expectant stillness consequent upon the exclamation had nearly died out of them all, an increasing light made itself visible in one of the windows of the upper floor. It came so close to the blind that the exact position of the flame could be perceived from the outside. Remaining steady for an instant, the blind went upward from before it, revealing to thirty concentrated eyes a young girl, framed as a picture by the window architrave, and unconsciously illuminating her countenance to a vivid brightness by a candle she held in her left hand, close to her face, her right hand being extended to the side of the window. She was wrapped in a white robe of some kind, whilst down her shoulders fell a twining profusion of marvellously rich hair, in a wild disorder which proclaimed it to be only during the invisible hours of the night that such a condition was discoverable. Her bright eyes were looking into the grey world outside with an uncertain expression, oscillating between courage and shyness, which, as she recognised the semicircular group of dark forms gathered before her, transformed itself into pleasant resolution.

Opening the window, she said lightly and warmly – 'Thank you, singers, thank you!'

Together went the window quickly and quietly, and the blind started downward on its return to its place. Her fair forehead and eyes vanished; her little mouth; her neck and shoulders; all of her. Then the spot of candlelight shone nebulously as before; then it moved away.

'How pretty! exclaimed Dick Dewy.

'If she'd been rale wexwork she couldn't ha' been comelier,' said Michael Mail.

'As near a thing to a spiritual vision as ever *I* wish to see!' said tranter Dewy.

'O, sich I never, never see!' said Leaf fervently.

All the rest, after clearing their throats and adjusting their hats, agreed that such a sight was worth singing for.

'Now to Farmer Shiner's, and then replenish our insides, father?' said the tranter.

'Wi' all my heart,' said old William, shouldering his bass-viol.

Farmer Shiner's was a queer lump of a house, standing at the corner of a lane that ran into the principal thoroughfare. The upper windows were much wider than they were high, and this feature, together with a broad bay-window where the door might have been expected, gave it by day the aspect of a human countenance turned askance, and wearing a sly and wicked leer. To-night nothing was visible but the outline of the roof upon the sky.

The front of this building was reached, and the preliminaries arranged as usual.

'Four breaths, and number thirty-two, "Behold the Morning Star,"' said old William.

They had reached the end of the second verse, and the fiddlers were doing the up bow-stroke previously to pouring forth the opening chord of the third verse, when, without a light appearing or any signal being given, a roaring voice exclaimed –

'Shut up, woll 'ee! Don't make your blaring row here! A feller wi' a headache enough to split his skull likes a quiet night!'

Slam went the window.

'Hullo, that's a' ugly blow for we!' said the tranter, in a keenly appreciative voice, and turning to his companions.

'Finish the carrel, all who be friends of harmony!' commanded old William; and they continued to the end.

'Four breaths, and number nineteen!' said William firmly. 'Give it him well; the quire can't be insulted in this manner!'

A light now flashed into existence, the window opened, and the farmer stood revealed as one in a terrific passion.

'Drown en! – drown en!' the tranter cried, fiddling frantically. 'Play fortissimy, and drown his spaking!'

'Fortissimy!' said Michael Mail, and the music and singing waxed so loud that it was impossible to know what Mr Shiner had said, was saying, or was about to say; but wildly flinging his arms and body about in the forms of capital Xs and Ys, he appeared to utter enough invectives to consign the whole parish to perdition.

'Very onseemly – very!' said old William, as they retired. 'Never such a dreadful scene in the whole round o' my carrel practice – never!

And he a churchwarden!'

'Only a drap o' drink got into his head,' said the tranter. 'Man's well enough when he's in his religious frame. He's in his worldly frame now. Must ask en to our bit of a party to-morrow night, I suppose, and so put en in humour again. We bear no mortal man ill-will.'

Eventually, after serenading the vicar, and a stop for refreshment, the members of the quire reach their beds, and a somewhat attenuated repose. But their Christmas duties are far from over.

It being Christmas-day, the tranter prepared himself with Sunday particularity. Loud sousing and snorting noises were heard to proceed from a tub in the back quarters of the dwelling, proclaiming that he was there performing his great Sunday wash, lasting half-an-hour, to which his washings on working-day mornings were mere flashes in the pan. Vanishing into the outhouse with a large brown towel, and the above-named bubblings and snortings being carried on for about twenty minutes, the tranter would appear round the edge of the door, smelling like a summer fog, and looking as if he had just narrowly escaped a watery grave with the loss of much of his clothes, having since been weeping bitterly till his eyes were red; a crystal drop of water hanging ornamentally at the bottom of each ear, one at the tip of his nose, and others in the form of spangles about his hair.

Ablutions completed, three generations of the Dewy family set off with their instruments.

At the foot of an incline the church became visible through the north gate, or 'church hatch,' as it was called here. Seven agile figures in a clump were observable beyond, which proved to be the choristers waiting; sitting on an altar-tomb to pass the time, and letting their heels dangle against it. The musicians being now in sight, the youthful party scampered off and rattled up the old wooden stairs of the gallery like a regiment of cavalry, the other boys of the parish waiting outside and observing birds, cats, and other creatures till the vicar entered, when they suddenly subsided into sober churchgoers, and passed down the aisle with echoing heels.

The gallery of Mellstock Church had a status and sentiment of its own. A stranger there was regarded with a feeling altogether differing from that of the congregation below towards him. Banished ftom the nave as an intruder whom no originality could make interesting, he was received above as a curiosity that no unfitness could render dull. The gallery, too, looked down upon and knew the habits of the nave to its remotest peculiarity, and had an extensive stock of exclusive information about it; whilst the nave knew nothing of the gallery folk, as gallery folk, beyond their loud-sounding minims and chest notes. Such topics as that the clerk was always chewing tobacco except at the moment of crying amen; that he had a dust-hole in his pew; that during the sermon certain young daughters of the village had left off caring to read anything so mild as the marriage service for some years, and now regularly studied the one which chronologically follows it; that a pair of lovers touched fingers through a knot-hole between their pews in the manner ordained by their great exemplars, Pyramus and Thisbe; that Mrs Ledlow, the farmer's wife, counted her money and reckoned her week's marketing expenses during the first lesson – all news to those below – were stale subjects here.

Old William sat in the centre of the front row, his violoncello between his knees and two singers on each hand. Behind him, on the left, came the treble singers and Dick; and on the right the tranter and the tenors. Farther back was old Mail with the altos and supernumeraries ...

The music on Christmas mornings was frequently below the standard of church-performances at other times. The boys were sleepy from the heavy exertions of the night; the men were slightly wearied, and now, in addition to these constant reasons, there was a dampness in the atmosphere that still further aggravated the evil. Their strings, from the recent long exposure to the night air, rose whole semitones, and snapped with a loud twang at the most silent moment; which necessitated more retiring than ever to the back of the gallery, and made the gallery throats quite husky with the quantity of coughing and hemming required for tuning in. The vicar looked cross.[1]

1   Hardy, T, *Under the Greenwood Tree* (1974 ed.), 42-61 (abridged).

That passage read aloud to an audience (as I have done many times) produces hilarity and laughter, especially with the appropriate musical accompaniment. It is a fine corrective to the notion that Hardy's characters are all depressives destined for a bad end. Many years later, in 1894, he returned to the humour of the tired choir and the cross vicar in one of a group of short stories, A Few Crusted Characters, *which are introduced by a narrator in dialect.*

Absent-Mindedness in a Parish Choir
Thomas Hardy

HAD QUITE FORGOTTEN the old choir, with their fiddles and bass-viols,' said the home-comer, musingly. 'Are they still going on the same as of old?'

'Bless the man!' said Christopher Twink, the master-thatcher; 'why, they've been done away with these twenty year. A young teetotaler plays the organ in church now, and plays it very well; though 'tis not quite such good music as in old times, because the organ is one of them that go with a winch, and the young teetotaler says he can't always throw the proper feeling into the tune without wellnigh working his arms off.'

'Why did they make the change, then?'

'Well, partly because of fashion, partly because the old musicians got into a sort of scrape. A terrible scrape 'twas too – wasn't it, John? I shall never forget it – never! They lost their character as officers of the church as complete as if they'd never had any character at all.'

'That was very bad for them.'

'Yes.' The master-thatcher attentively regarded past times as if they lay about a mile off, and went on:

'It happened on Sunday after Christmas – the last Sunday ever they played in Longpuddle church gallery, as it turned out, though they didn't know it then. As you may know, sir, the players formed a very good band – almost as good as the Mellstock parish players that were led by the Dewys; and that's saying a great deal. There was Nicholas Puddingcome, the leader, with the first fiddle; there was Timothy Thomas, the bass-viol man; John Biles, the tenor fiddler; Dan'l Hornhead, with the serpent; Robert Dowdle, with the clarionet; and Mr. Nicks, with the oboe – all sound and powerful musicians, and strong-winded men – they that blowed. For that reason they were very much in demand Christmas week for little reels and dancing parties; for they could turn a jig or a hornpipe out of hand as well as ever they could turn out a psalm, and perhaps better, not to speak irreverent. In short, one half-hour they could be playing a Christmas carol in the squire's hall to the ladies and gentlemen, and drinkin' tay and coffee with 'em as modest as saints; and the next, at The Tinker's Arms, blazing away like wild horses with the "Dashing White Sergeant" to nine couple of dancers and more, and swallowing rum-and-cider hot as flame.

'Well, this Christmas they'd been out to one rattling randy after another every night, and had got next to no sleep at all. Then came the Sunday after Christmas, their fatal day. 'Twas so mortal cold that year that they could hardly sit in the gallery; for though the congregation down in the body of the church had a stove to keep off the frost, the players in the gallery had nothing at all. So Nicholas said at morning service, when 'twas freezing an inch an hour, "Please the Lord I won't stand this numbing weather no longer: this afternoon we'll have something in our insides to make us warm, if it cost a king's ransom."

'So he brought a gallon of hot brandy and beer, ready mixed, to church with him in the afternoon, and by keeping the jar well wrapped up in Timothy Thomas's bass-viol bag it kept drinkably warm till they wanted it, which was just a thimbleful in the Absolution, and another after the Creed, and the remainder at the beginning o' the sermon. When they'd had the last pull they felt quite comfortable and warm, and as the sermon went on – most unfortunately for 'em it was a long one that afternoon – they fell asleep, every man jack of 'em; and there they slept on as sound as rocks.

'Twas a very dark afternoon, and by the end of the sermon all you could see of the inside of the church were the pa'son's two candles alongside of him in the pulpit, and his spaking face behind 'em. The sermon being ended at last, the pa'son gie'd out the Evening Hymn. But no quire set about sounding up the tune, and the people began to turn their heads to learn the reason why, and then Levi Limpet, a boy who sat in the gallery, nudged Timothy and Nicholas, and said, "Begin! begin!"

"'Hey? what?" says Nicholas, starting up; and the church being so dark and his head so muddled he thought he was at the party they had played at all the night before, and away he went, bow and fiddle, at "The Devil among the Tailors," the favourite jig of our neighbourhood at that time. The rest of the band, being in the same state of mind and nothing doubting, followed their leader with all their strength, according to custom. They poured out that there tune till the lower bass notes of "The Devil among the Tailors" made the cobwebs in the roof shiver like ghosts; then Nicholas, seeing nobody moved, shouted out as he scraped (in his usual commanding way at dances when the folk didn't know the figures), "Top couples cross hands! And when I make the fiddle squeak at the end, every man kiss his pardner under the mistletoe!"

'The boy Levi was so frightened that he bolted down the gallery stairs and out homeward like lightning. The pa'son's hair fairly stood on end when he heard the evil tune raging through the church, and thinking the quire had gone crazy he held up his hand and said: "Stop, stop, stop! Stop, stop! What's this?" But they didn't hear'n for the noise of their own playing, and the more he called the louder they played.

'Then the folks came out of their pews, wondering down to the ground, and saying: "What do they mean by such wickedness! We shall be consumed like Sodom and Gomorrah!"

'And the squire, too, came out of his pew lined wi' green baize, where lots of lords and ladies visiting at the house were worshipping along with him, and went and stood in front of the gallery, and shook his fist in the musicians' faces, saying, "What! In this reverent edifice! What!"

'And at last they heard'n through their playing, and stopped.

"'Never such an insulting, disgraceful thing – never!" says the squire, who couldn't rule his passion.

"'Never!" says the pa'son, who had come down and stood beside him.

"'Not if the Angels of Heaven," says the squire (he was a wickedish man, the squire was, though now for once he happened to be on the Lord's side), – ' not if the Angels of Heaven come down," he says, "shall one of you villainous players ever sound a note in this church again; for the insult to me, and my family, and my visitors, and the parson, and God Almighty, that you've a-perpetrated this afternoon!"

'Then the unfortunate church band came to their senses, and remembered where they were; and 'twas a sight to see Nicholas Puddingcome and Timothy Thomas and John Biles creep down the gallery stairs with their fiddles under their arms, and poor Dan'l Hornhead with his serpent, and Robert Dowdle with his clarionet, all looking as little as ninepins; and out they went. The pa'son might have forgi'ed 'em when he learned the truth o't, but the squire would not. That very week he sent for a barrel-organ that would play two-and-twenty new psalm-tunes, so exact and particular that, however sinful inclined you was, you could play nothing but psalm-tunes whatsomever. He had a really respectable man to turn the winch, as I said, and the old players played no more.'[1]

The Mellstock Quire, in fact, according to one of Hardy's most intriguing supernatural poems, had made precisely the opposite mistake.

---

1   Hardy, T, *Life's little Ironies and a Changed Man* (1977 ed.), 172-5.

The Paphian Ball
Thomas Hardy

W E WENT OUR Christmas rounds once more,
With quire and viols as theretofore.

Our path was near by Rushy-Pond,
Where Egdon-Heath outstretched beyond.

There stood a figure against the moon,
Tall, spare, and humming a weirdsome tune.

'You tire of Christian carols', he said:
'Come and lute at a ball instead.

'"Tis to your gain, for it ensures
That many guineas will be yours.

'A slight condition hangs on't, true,
But you will scarce say nay thereto:

'That you go blindfold; that anon
The place may not be gossiped on.'

They stood and argued with each other:
'Why sing from one house to another

'These ancient hymns in the freezing night,
And all for nought? 'Tis foolish, quite!'

' – 'Tis serving God, and shunning evil:
Might not elsedoing serve the devil?'

'But grand pay!' . . . They were lured by his call,
Agreeing to go blindfold all.

They walked, he guiding, some new track,
Doubting to find the pathway back.

In a strange hall they found them when
They were unblinded all again.

Gilded alcoves, great chandeliers,
Voluptuous paintings ranged in tiers,

In brief, a mansion large and rare,
With rows of dancers waiting there.

They tuned and played; the couples danced;
Half-naked women tripped, advanced,

With handsome partners footing fast,
Who swore strange oaths, and whirled them past.

And thus and thus the slow hours wore them:
While shone their guineas heaped before them.

Drowsy at length, in lieu of the dance
'*While Shepherds watched. . .*' they bowed by chance;

And in a moment, at a blink,
There flashed a change; ere they could think

The ball-room vanished and all its crew:
Only the well-known heath they view –

The spot of their crossing overnight,
When wheedled by the stranger's sleight.

There, east, the Christmas dawn hung red,
And dark Rainbarrow with its dead

Bulged like a supine negress' breast
Against Clyffe-Clump's faint far-off crest.

Yea; the rare mansion, gorgeous, bright,
The ladies, gallants, gone were quite.

The heaped-up guineas, too, were gone
With the gold table they were on.

'Why did not grasp we what was owed!'
Cried some, as homeward, shamed, they strode.

Now comes the marvel and the warning:
When they had dragged to church next morning,

With downcast heads and scarce a word,
They were astound at what they heard.

Praises from all came forth in showers
For how they'd cheered the midnight hours.

'We've heard you many times', friends said,
'But like *that* never have you played!

'*Rejoice, ye tenants of the earth,*
And celebrate your Saviour's birth,

'Never so thrilled the darkness through,
Or more inspired us so to do!' . . .

– The man who used to tell this tale
Was the tenor-viol, Michael Mail;

Yes; Mail the tenor, now but earth! –
I give it for what it may be worth.[1]

Hardy's portrayal of the musicians was based, not on personal experience, but on the stories told of his grandfather, whom he never knew. They represented a past era, a lost tradition. As a young child he had attended a harvest home celebration, and he reminisced that this was, 'among the last at which the old traditional ballads were sung, the railway having been extended to Dorchester just then, and the orally transmitted ditties of centuries being slain at a stroke by the London comic songs that were introduced.'[2] The passing of all that the musicians stood for is commemorated in this wistful 'then and now' poem. Hardy himself is presumably 'the sad man' who introduces and ends the poem, sighing his phantasies.

1   Hardy, T, *Complete poems* (1979 ed.), no. 796.
2   Hardy, F, *The early life of Thomas Hardy, 1840 -1891* (1928), 25-6.

The Dead Quire
Thomas Hardy

 ESIDE THE MEAD of Memories,
Where Church-way mounts to Moaning Hill,
The sad man sighed his phantasies:
　　He seems to sigh them still.

''Twas the Birth-tide Eve, and the hamleteers
Made merry with ancient Mellstock zest,
But the Mellstock quire of former years
　　Had entered into rest.

'Old Dewy lay by the gaunt yew tree,
And Reuben and Michael a pace behind,
And Bowman with his family
　　By the wall that the ivies bind.

'The singers had followed one by one,
Treble, and tenor, and thorough-bass;
And the worm that wasteth had begun
　　To mine their mouldering place.

'For two-score years, ere Christ-day light,
Mellstock had throbbed to strains from these;
But now there echoed on the night
    No Christmas harmonies.

'Three meadows off, at a dormered inn,
The youth had gathered in high carouse,
And, ranged on settles, some therein
    Had drunk them to a drowse.

'Loud, lively, reckless, some had grown,
Each dandling on his jigging knee
Eliza, Dolly, Nance, or Joan –
    Livers in levity.

'The taper flames and hearthfire shine
Grew smoke-hazed to a lurid light,
And songs on subjects not divine
    Were warbled forth that night.

'Yet many were sons and grandsons here
Of those who, on such eves gone by,
At that still hour had throated clear
    Their anthems to the sky.

'The clock belled midnight; and ere long
One shouted, "Now 'tis Christmas morn;
Here's to our women old and young,
    And to John Barleycorn!"

'They drink the toast and shout again:
The pewter-ware rings back the boom,

And for a breath-while follows then
    A silence in the room.

'When nigh without, as in old days,
The ancient quire of voice and string
Seemed singing words of prayer and praise
    As they had used to sing:

'*While shepherds watch'd their flocks by night,* –
Thus swells the long familiar sound
In many a quaint symphonic flight –
    To, *Glory shone around.*

'The sons defined their fathers' tones,
The widow his whom she had wed,
And others in the minor moans
    The viols of the dead.

'Something supernal has the sound
As verse by verse the strain proceeds,
And stilly starring on the ground
    Each roysterer holds and heeds.

'Towards its chorded closing bar
Plaintively, thinly, waned the hymn,
Yet lingered, like the notes afar
    Of banded seraphim.

'With brows abashed, and reverent tread,
The hearkeners sought the tavern door:
But nothing, save wan moonlight, spread
    The empty highway o'er.

'While on their hearing fixed and tense
The aerial music seemed to sink,
As it were gently moving thence
        Along the river brink.

'Then did the Quick pursue the Dead
By crystal Froom that crinkles there;
And still the viewless quire ahead
        Voiced the old holy air.

'By Bank-walk wicket, brightly bleached,
It passed, and 'twixt the hedges twain,
Dogged by the living; till it reached
        The bottom of Church Lane.

'There, at the turning, it was heard
Drawing to where the churchyard lay:
But when they followed thitherward
        It smalled, and died away.

'Each headstone of the quire, each mound,
Confronted them beneath the moon;
But no more floated therearound
        That ancient Birth-night tune.

'There Dewy lay by the gaunt yew tree,
There Reuben and Michael, a pace behind,
And Bowman with his family
        By the wall that the ivies bind . . .

'As from a dream each sobered son
Awoke, and musing reached his door:

'Twas said that of them all, not one
    Sat in a tavern more.'

– The sad man ceased; and ceased to heed
His listener, and crossed the leaze
From Moaning Hill towards the mead –
    The Mead of Memories.[1]

MICHAEL MAIL.

1   Ibid, no. 213.

8
The True Meaning

HAT CHILD IS this who, laid to rest
On Mary's lap is sleeping?
Whom Angels greet with anthems sweet,
While shepherds watch are keeping?

This, this is Christ the King,
Whom shepherds guard and Angels sing;
Haste, haste, to bring Him laud,
The Babe, the Son of Mary.

Why lies He in such mean estate,
Where ox and ass are feeding?
Good Christians, fear, for sinners here
The silent Word is pleading.

Nails, spear shall pierce Him through,
The cross be borne for me, for you.
Hail, hail the Word made flesh,
The Babe, the Son of Mary.

So bring Him incense, gold and myrrh,
Come peasant, king to own Him;

The King of kings salvation brings,
Let loving hearts enthrone Him.

Raise, raise a song on high,
The virgin sings her lullaby.
Joy, joy for Christ is born,
The Babe, the Son of Mary.

*This charming Victorian carol, written about 1865 and generally sung
to the Tudor English melody 'Greensleeves', was the work of William
Chatterton Dix, author of several familiar hymns – and many more
which have been forgotten. Insurance broker, accountant and later an
income tax assessor, Dix was a Bristolian who retired to Cheddar in
Somerset, where he was buried in St Andrew's churchyard in 1898.
His middle name commemorates the Bristol poet Thomas Chatterton,
whose biography Dix's father had written.*

*Most Victorian hymn writers were clergymen, but Dix wrote
his hymns for the Bristol church choir (St Raphael's) of which he was
a pious and enthusiastic member. Illness in January 1859 prevented
him from attending church, but he made up for his indisposition by
reading the Biblical account of the epiphany ('the three wise men'),
which inspired him to write from his sick-bed one of the most famous
and best-loved of Christmas carols, 'As with gladness men of old'. And
that offers a good starting-point for considering the religious side of
Christmas – an all too familiar theme, but with some idiosyncratic
Wessex variations.[1]*

1 *Oxford DNB*, online version, article by Gordon Giles, accessed 9 Sept. 2010.
   There is some doubt whether the year was 1858 or 1859.

And it Came to Pass . . .

S WITH GLADNESS . . .' was taken up and published in 1861 in the first full edition of that ecclesiastical warhorse of the Anglican church, *Hymns Ancient and Modern*. But there was a problem – a problem of accuracy – and it is the same problem that confronts anyone who attends a carol service in a pedantic frame of mind. In 1875 Dix was asked to change some of the words of his carol 'so as not to contradict scripture', and he did so grudgingly, although he felt, in the words of his biographer, 'that his poetry reflected popular piety of his day, such that biblical accuracy was inconsequential'.[1]

Everything we know, or imagine we know, about the Christmas story stems from the accounts in the gospels attributed to Matthew and Luke. But their accounts differ, and even contradict each other and themselves.[2] Dix had made the mistake of sending the wise men (who only occur in Matthew's gospel) to find Jesus in the manger (which only occurs in Luke): 'As they offered gifts most rare | At that manger rude and bare'. A manger is a trough where horses or cattle feed, but Matthew specifically says that the wise men went into the house (perceived as no place for a manger), and it was in the house that the gifts were presented.[3]

---

1   Ibid.

2   For example, Joseph's father is called Jacob in Matthew 1.16, but Heli in Luke 3.23. In Matthew (2.14-21) Joseph and Mary take Jesus to Egypt, apparently for a considerable time; in Luke 2.22, 2.39 they travel from Bethlehem to Jerusalem, and then to Nazareth. Quirinius (Luke 2.2), according to a reliable source, Josephus, was governor of Syria in 6 AD, but Herod (Matthew 2.1; Luke 1.5) had died in 4 or 5 BC, so Matthew and Luke date the nativity at least ten years apart, and Luke's account is internally inconsistent: see Fox, R L, *The unauthorized version: truth and fiction in the Bible* (1991), 27-30; Brown, R E, *The birth of the Messiah* (new. ed. 1993), 33-7.

3   Matthew 2.11

Most Biblical scholars accept that the gospels of Matthew and Luke were written a decade or so later than that attributed to Mark (which has no nativity story), around eighty years after the events they purport to describe. In their narratives of the birth and early life of Jesus they clearly did not know of (or chose to ignore) each other's work, and one is not derived from the other, although both may have been drawing on the same store of earlier written or oral traditions.[1] Elsewhere in Matthew, Mark and Luke (which are known as the synoptic gospels), and especially when describing the parables, miracles and teachings of Jesus, the same anecdotes or episodes (known to theologians as pericopes) recur in two or all three gospels, but often in slightly different form or context. From this it is deduced that there was a body of oral tradition which circulated after Jesus's death, passed on from preacher to congregation, teacher to student, and that this was only written down decades later.

The nativity stories which begin the gospels of Matthew and Luke are rather different from the later chapters. For one thing, they seem to have been an afterthought. All four gospels, quite logically, begin their accounts of Jesus's ministry with descriptions of his forerunner, John the Baptist. In Mark and John these open their gospels; in Matthew and Luke John the Baptist heads a new beginning, at the start of their respective third chapters. In both cases the nativity has been tagged on to the front. And the reason for this is clear from their content. Both evangelists were anxious to show that the circumstances surrounding the birth of Jesus pointed to his fulfilling the nuggets of Messianic prophecy, as understood by their contemporaries, and found in the Old Testament and elsewhere – thus proving that Jesus was the Messiah and, in Christian terms, the Christ. Their narratives were driven by the need to explain why a preacher from Nazareth must actually have been born in Bethlehem

1   Brown, R E, *The birth of the Messiah* (new. ed. 1993), is probably the fullest modern treatment of the nativity legends, but most reputable Gospel commentaries also tackle these issues and difficulties.

(as foretold by the prophet Micah), but also to have come out of Egypt (Hosea). The story of Mary's virginity is also the fulfilment of a prophecy, by Isaiah, 'Behold a virgin shall conceive, and bear a son . . ', but this is based on a mistranslation of a Hebrew word meaning 'young girl' into a Greek word meaning 'virgin' (which is not necessarily the same thing). The three wise men and their gifts, and the massacre of the innocent children, are also prefigured in obscure Old Testament passages; and Luke's account draws tacit parallels with Old Testament heroes, Daniel, Gideon, Abraham and Sarah, Hannah and Samuel.[1]

Most casual participants in Christmas religion are probably unconcerned with the finer points of biblical criticism, and derive their perception of the nativity from the annual carol service, Handel's *Messiah*, and paintings by old masters reproduced on Christmas cards. We are moving into dark but intriguing territory. And, at the risk of treading on traditionalist toes, there are more illusions to be shattered.

First, the census. There was a census, in 6 AD, under Quirinius (whom Luke refers to), but no record of one under Herod, and certainly not one that involved the whole Roman world. In any case Quirinius only became governor a decade or so after Herod had died. The 6 AD census was for taxation purposes and would have taken property-owners to register in a town where they held property. Even if Joseph had owned property in Bethlehem (which is unlikely as the story tells us that he had nowhere to stay), pregnant Mary need not have accompanied him; and if, as is much more likely, any property owned by Joseph was in Nazareth, where he lived, then he would not have to register or pay tax. Galilee, in which Nazareth lay, was independent of Roman rule at this period, and the census and tax could not have been imposed there.[2]

Next, the inn and the manger. The problem here – apart from the complete absence of a stable, asses, oxen, and farmyard animals

---

1 Warner, M, *Alone of all her sex: the myth and cult of the virgin Mary* (1976), ch.1
2 Fox, R L, *The unauthorized version* (1991), 28-31.

generally (other than sheep) from the biblical account – lies with the meaning of inn. The Greek word *kataluma* translated as 'inn' could mean anything from a temporary shelter such as a tent, to a billet, a lodging house, or – in modern parlance – a function room. The upper room in which the last supper took place was described in Mark's gospel as a *kataluma*.[1] When the compilers of the Authorized Version of the Bible in 1611 translated the word as 'inn' they were perfectly correct, because at that time the English word 'inn' meant a lodging of various kinds. It was a place where one stayed when not at home. If, as is often assumed, registration for the census involved an influx of strangers to Bethlehem, the evangelist was perhaps thinking of a makeshift campsite to accommodate them; any notion of a thatched English village pub serving real ale is probably quite wide of the mark.[2]

The Three Wise Men. These mysterious characters appear only in Matthew's gospel, but there is no indication (other than the three categories of gifts) that there were three of them nor, for that matter, that they were men – the possibility that some were women was acknowledged by the Church of England in 2004.[3] 'Wise men' translates the Greek *magoi*, 'Magi', a priestly caste of middle-eastern astrologers and philosophers (not kings) connected with the Zoroastrian religion, and perhaps with the Essenes, a Jewish sect which came to have links with early Christianity.[4]

Finally in this demolition of the Christmas story, it may come as a surprise to many to realise that there is nothing in the biblical accounts to fix the nativity to December, or even to the winter season. In fact it has long been recognised that winters are too cold

1 Mark 14.14; see Brown, *Birth of the Messiah*, 399-401, 670-1

2 Warner, M, *Alone of all her sex*, 13, although I think it unlikely that the Greek *phatne*, translated as 'manger', can bear the meaning 'crib' in the sense of a cradle. She mistakenly transliterates *kataluma* as *katalemna*, and *phatne* as *thaten*.

3 Clennell, A, *Independent*, 10 Feb. 2004

4 McKenna, S, 'The Magi – a short history', www.farvardyn.com/shelagh.php, accessed 20 Sept. 2010.

in Palestine for shepherds and sheep to abide outdoors in the fields much later than October.[1] The early church, it seems, did not much celebrate birthdays, and throughout the period when the books of the New Testament were written, the later 1st century, attention was focused on the second coming of Christ, which was always believed to be imminent. It was not until Christianity had been incorporated into the Roman imperial administration as the state religion that a festival of Christmas was fixed for 25 December (sometime between 354 and 360 AD). The date was chosen not, as is often claimed, because of the equivalent ancient Roman feast of Saturnalia (although, as we shall see, this bore many similarities to the medieval and modern Christmas), but because it appropriated another midwinter festival. This, the birthday of the unconquered sun, celebrated the winter solstice (placed by the Julian calendar on 25 December), and was the key event in the worship of a rival religious cult adopted by the Roman emperors, the *Deus Sol Invictus*, or 'unconquered sun god'.[2] In this, as in so much else, we see that Christmas is an amalgam of many different strands and beliefs.

All but the most stubborn Christian fundamentalists recognize that the biblical narratives of the nativity are not 'true' in the literal historical sense, and that whatever religious truths are to be garnered from them derive from their symbolism, their traditions and their sheer beauty. To recognize that they fit into a larger tapestry of winter celebration, shared by people of many religions and none, and that their truths have been embroidered and developed in many subtle ways, should itself be cause for celebration, whatever one's own beliefs. In the rest of this section some of these Wessex variations are explored, beginning with Thomas Hardy.

1   This seems to have been recognized by many biblical scholars, from Joseph Mede (1586-1638) onwards.

2   Miller, D, *Unwrapping Christmas* (1993), 8-11.

The last poem published during Hardy's lifetime was devoted to the interplay between Christianity and pagan superstition. He seems to have formulated the idea for 'Christmas in the Elgin Room' while researching material for The Dynasts in the British Museum in 1905. Perhaps significantly this was probably the year when he first met Florence Dugdale, who was to become his second wife, and who at the beginning of their relationship helped him by following up references in the Reading Room. The poem (subtitled 'British Museum: early last century') was completed in 1926 and submitted to The Times for publication on Christmas Eve 1927. By then Hardy was dying, but was pleased when a warm appreciation of the piece arrived from the editor of The Times, and another from an old friend, Sir Edmund Gosse. His reply to Gosse, written on Christmas Day, was the last letter that he wrote.

Christmas in the Elgin Room
Thomas Hardy

HAT IS THE noise that shakes the night,
  And seems to soar to the Pole-star height?'
   – 'Christmas bells,
   The watchman tells
Who walks this hall that blears us captives with its blight.'

  'And what, then, mean such clangs, so clear?'
  '– 'Tis said to have been a day of cheer,
   And source of grace
   To the human race
Long ere their woven sails winged us to exile here.

  'We are those whom Christmas overthrew
  Some centuries after Pheidias knew

How to shape us
And bedrape us
And to set us in Athena's temple for men's view.

'O it is sad now we are sold –
We gods! for Borean people's gold,
    And brought to the gloom
    Of this gaunt room
Which sunlight shuns, and sweet Aurore but enters cold.

'For all these bells, would I were still
Radiant as on Athenai's Hill.'
    – 'And I, and I!'
    The others sigh,
'Before this Christ was known, and we had men's good will.'

Thereat old Helios could but nod,
Throbbed, too, the Ilissus River-god,
    And the torsos there
    Of deities fair,
Whose limbs were shards beneath some Acropolitan clod:

Demeter too, Poseidon hoar,
Persephone, and many more
    Of Zeus' high breed, –
    All loth to heed
What the bells sang that night which shook them to the core.[1]

We may perhaps forgive Hardy his obscurity, since he completed it on his deathbed. The Elgin Room housed artefacts from classical Athens, notably the Elgin marbles from the Parthenon which were purchased

---

1   Hardy, T, *Complete poems* (1979 ed.), no. 917.

by the British government in 1816 (hence the reference to 'early last century' in the subtitle). They included work by the famous 5th-century BC *sculptor Pheidias. The Borean people (people of the north wind) is the name he imagined Greek gods might call the inhabitants of Britain. In fact we were known as the Hyperboreans, 'the people who lived beyond the north wind', and not long after the time of Pheidias a Greek philosopher, Hecataeus of Abdera, had written a description of us. His work is lost, but parts were copied centuries later by the Greek historian Diodorus Siculus into his history. He seems to be referring to a well-known archaeological site in Wiltshire.*

The Renowned Temple
Diodorus Siculus

MONGST THEM THAT have written old stories much like fables, Hecateus and some others say, that there is an island in the ocean over against Gaul, (as big as Sicily) under the arctic pole, where the Hyperboreans inhabit; so called, because they lie beyond the breezes of the north wind. That the soil here is very rich, and very fruitful; and the climate temperate, insomuch as there are two crops in the year.

They say that Latona [Leto, mother of Apollo] was born here, and therefore, that they worship Apollo [the sun god] above all other gods; and because they are daily singing songs in praise of this god, and ascribing to him the highest honours, they say that these inhabitants demean themselves, as if they were Apollo's priests, who has there a stately grove and renowned temple, of a round form, beautified with many rich gifts. That there is a city likewise consecrated to this god, whose citizens are most of them harpers, who, playing on the harp, chant sacred hymns to Apollo in the temple, setting forth his glorious acts. The Hyperboreans use their own natural language; but of long and antient time have had a special kindness for the Grecians, and more especially for the Athenians and them of Delos. And that some of the Grecians passed over to the Hyperboreans, and left behind them divers presents, inscribed with Greek characters; and that Abaris formerly travelled thence into Greece, and renewed the antient league of friendship with the Delians.

They say, moreover, that the moon in this island seems as if it were near to the earth, and represents in the face of it excrescences like spots in the earth. And that Apollo once in nineteen years comes into the island; in which space of time the stars perform their courses, and return to the same point; and therefore the Greeks call the revolution of nineteen years the Great Year. At this time of his appearance (they say) that he plays upon the harps, and sings and dances all the night, from the vernal equinox to the rising of the Pleiades, solacing himself with the praises of his own successful adventures.[1]

The round temple, the worship of the sun god, and the astronomical calculations, all point to Stonehenge, distantly perceived and interpreted within the pantheon of classical Greece – and presided over by a ministry of musical, scientific priests – a Celtic ('Hyperborean') equivalent of the Magi. We seem to be going round in circles.

1   Booth, G, *The historical library of Diodorus the Sicilian* 2 vols 1814, vol. 1, 138-9

Winter Solstice

HEORIES ABOUT THE purpose of Stonehenge are legion, and it would be beyond the scope of this book to add to them. But amid all the astronomical speculation one intended alignment seems to be agreed by all reputable archaeologists who have studied and written about the monument. The axis of Stonehenge, through the central trilithon, the bluestone circle, the surrounding sarsens and the heelstone, corresponds with the midsummer sunrise in one direction, and the midwinter sunset in the opposite direction.[1] Very few people can be unaware that the summer solstice is celebrated annually at Stonehenge. Celebrating the winter solstice on a December afternoon in the middle of Salisbury Plain is a less appealing prospect. And yet there is more to celebrate. The summer solstice represents the sun in splendour, at the height of his power, the point at which the inevitable weakening begins. By contrast the winter census is the time when the dying sun begins his slow recovery. It is a celebration of birth and salvation – just like the Christian Christmas.

Because of this many archaeologists have pointed out that it may be the winter sunset, rather than the summer sunrise, that was the most important date in the Stonehenge calendar. R S Newall, one of the select band of archaeologists who have actually excavated at Stonehenge, wrote in 1953:

> Are we to believe that the worshippers at Stonehenge walked
> up the avenue and in at the entrance and then turned right
> round with their backs to the great trilithon to face the focus

---

1 See Ruggles, C, 'Astronomy and Stonehenge' in Cunliffe, B, and Renfrew, C (eds.), *Science and Stonehenge* (British Academy, 1997), 203-29, for the most authoritative discussion

of their worship? In no temple does this happen: the focus of the building is always opposite the entrance; and so here the winter solstice sunset, the death of the sun at the end of the year, this is the sepulchral connexion; this with all it entails is the main purpose of Stonehenge.[1]

Aubrey Burl, another respected archaeologist who has written extensively about Stonehenge, has suggested that a 'sun-watcher' was stationed at Stonehenge to watch for the day when the sun reached the furthest extremes on its summer and winter journeys, and when it occurred he (or presumably she) summoned everyone to a festival or assembly.[2] Timothy Darvill emphasised that it was the life of the sun that was perhaps the main focus of attention at Stonehenge, and compared the five great sarsen trilithons to the classical pantheon of gods and goddesses. 'At the winter solstice the focus was on endings, the sun rising in the east over Boscombe Down, crossing the sky and then setting over Wilsford Down, at a position framed by the great trilithon and directly in line with the principal axis and the avenue leading back to the underworld.'[3] And Julian Richards, writing for English Heritage, suggested that:

> Perhaps this annual event, the shortest day of the year, would be more significant to these agricultural communities, as it marked the time of year when the days would begin to lengthen. As the hours of daylight increased from this turning point onwards the certainty would grow that the seasons were going to follow their natural order, spring would come after winter, crops would grow and life would go on as before.[4]

1   Newall, R S, 'Stonehenge' (letter), *Man*, liii (1953), 144.
2   Burl, A, *The Stonehenge people* (1987), 202-5.
3   Darvill, T, *Stonehenge: the biography of a landscape* (1996), 144.
4   Richards, J, *English Heritage book of Stonehenge* (1991), 128.

Wessex, as well as providing a likely focus for pagan midwinter ceremony, was also hugely influential in shaping the ways in which the medieval Christian church celebrated its beliefs, including its observance of Christmas. A few miles from Stonehenge stands Old Sarum, where a new cathedral to serve the whole of Dorset, Wiltshire and Berkshire was begun in the year 1075. The body of liturgical observances and rituals which evolved first at Old Sarum and then in the present Salisbury Cathedral was known as the Use of Sarum. During the 13th century it seems to have come into use in churches through the diocese and by 1300 in other dioceses too. In the later middle ages it became the standard Latin service book of the English medieval church. From the first complete English translation of the Sarum Missal. published in 1868, here are three pieces of verse. known as sequences. which were chanted or spoken as part of the special Christmas masses, at midnight. daybreak and morning. They proclaim the Christmas story of Matthew and Luke, embellished with a millennium of Christian tradition and theology.[1]

The Christmas Day Sequence

CHRISTMAS DAY, AT MIDNIGHT
All hosts with one accord
Sing the Incarnate Lord,
With instrument and breath,
Discoursing tidings glad.
This is the hallowed day
On which new happiness
Rose full upon the world;
On this renowned night
Glory was thundered forth,

---

1   For a recent discussion of the antecedents, development and spread of the Use of Sarum, see Pfaff, R W, *Liturgy in medieval England: a history* (2009), 350-87.

By angel voices sung;
Wondrous unwonted lights,
At midnight hour,
Around the Shepherds shone,
Keeping their quiet flocks.
All unexpectedly
God's message they receive.
Who was before the world
Is of a Virgin born;
Glory to God on high
In heaven, and peace on earth.
So doth the heavenly host
Sing praises in the highest,
Let heaven at either pole
Shake with their ringing chant.
On this most holy day
Let glory loudly sung
Through all the earth resound;
Let all mankind proclaim
That God is born on earth.
The foe shall vex mankind
With cruel rule no more;
Peace is restored to earth.
Let all creation joy
In Him Who now is born.
He all upholds alone,
He all did form alone:
May He of His own grace
Loose us from all our sins.

Christmas Day, at Daybreak
Unto the King new born praises sing,
Whose Father by His Word did frame the worlds,

Whose Mother is a Virgin undefiled;
Begotten of the Father, God of God,
Born of His Mother without carnal stain:
Before all worlds begotten of the Father;
When the full time was come His Mother bare Him.
O wonderful, mysterious generation!
O most astonishing Nativity!
O glorious Child! Divinity incarnate!
So Prophets, moved by Thy Holy Spirit,
Spake of Thy coming Birth, Thou Son of God!
So at Thy dawning Angels sing Thee praises,
And to the earth glad tidings bring of peace.
The very elements themselves are glad,
And all the Saints exultingly rejoice,
Crying, All hail! Save us, we pray, O God,
In Persons Trine, one undivided Substance.

Christmas Day, at the Third Mass
This day celestial melody
Was heard by men on earth,
When the Virgin bare a Son
The hosts above sang praise.
What aileth thee, thou world below?
Why joy'st thou not with these?
In pastoral charge the shepherds watch;
Hark! angels' voices clear
Chant forth their strains of holy joy,
Of peace and glory full;
To Christ they render homage due,
To us of grace they sing:
Not unto all such gifts are given,
But to men of good will;
Not irrespectively bestowed,

But measured by dessert;
Affections must be weaned from sin,
So shall that peace on us be shed
Which to the good is promised.
Earthly to heavenly things are joined,
In this respect their praises join,
But by desert they are dissever'd.
Rejoice, O man, when thou dost ponder this;
Rejoice, O flesh, associate with the Word.

His rising by the stars is told
　　With indicating light;
Lo! star-lit chiefs to Bethlehem
　　Follow that planet bright.
The King of Heaven is cradled found
　　Amid the beasts He made,
In a rude manger's narrow bed
　　The Lord of all is laid.
Star of the Sea! Thy Blessed Son
　　The holy Church adores;
That Thou our service wilt accept
　　Devoutly she implores.
Let each redeemed thing the Redeemer's praises sing.[1]

Every Christmas day morning, we are led to believe, the Queen's breakfast table is adorned with sprigs of flowering holy thorn sent from Glastonbury, a tradition now more than eighty years old.[2] But its origin can be traced to a very unholy feud that developed during the 1920s between two double-barrelled Somerset clergy, Revd Lionel Smithett

1　*The Sarum Missal in English*, trans. A H and C B Pearson, 1868
2　Bowman, M, 'The holy thorn ceremony: revival, rivalry and civil religion in Glastonbury,' *Folklore* cxvii, pt. 2 (2006), 123-40, on 124, 128

Lewis, vicar of Glastonbury, and the Very Revd Dr J Armitage Robinson, dean of Wells. On the surface it was a rather one-sided affair – the dean seems not to have acknowledged publicly how hot his subordinate was becoming under the clerical collar.

And Did those Feet?

N 1921 THE Dean, a respected historian and textual scholar, published an erudite and somewhat sceptical analysis of a history of Glastonbury, written by the 12th-century monk William of Malmesbury.[1] He pointed out that, although the manuscript referred to Joseph of Arimathea, Arthur, Lancelot, the Round Table and the Holy Grail, these were not in William's text, but in a later note inserted in the margin. The following year (with an enlarged second edition in 1923) the Vicar produced a booklet which brought together all the early references

1   Robinson, J A, *Somerset historical essays* (1921), 1-25

to Joseph at Glastonbury, and followed it in 1925 with a second publication, *Glastonbury, "the mother of saints": her saints AD 37-1539.* Less concerned with close textual analysis, he firmly believed the legend that Joseph had come to Britain, had settled and evangelized Glastonbury, where he established the oldest church in England, and died and was buried there in 82 AD.[1]

The Dean responded in 1926 with his own careful study of the Arthurian and Joseph legends, and ignored Lewis's work entirely. He did, however, begin with an introductory note, explaining that answering questions about such legends,

> demands a patient research and the critical examination of documents. The task is laborious, but it has a peculiar fascination for those who interest themselves in the process of the medieval mind, who are not content on the one hand to accept traditions as probably true because they were told and believed, or on the other hand to dismiss them at once as what are called monkish tales.'[2]

The Vicar was less subtle. When he produced a new edition of his *Glastonbury . . . her saints*, booklet in 1927, he prefaced it with a ten-page denunciation of the dean's views, which he seems to have interpreted as resulting from the traditional rivalry between Glastonbury and Wells. As his muddle-headed tirade drew to a close he posed the question, 'After all, must we take the Dean too seriously?' (As one of the most senior churchmen in the diocese, and chairman of the executive committee of the Glastonbury Abbey trust, the correct answer was probably 'Yes'). But the Vicar went on to quote a somewhat condescending passage by the Dean about the legends,

1 Lewis, L S, *St Joseph of Arimathea of Glastonbury, or, the apostolic church of Britain* (Glastonbury, 1922); (2nd ed, 1923); *Glastonbury "the mother of saints", her saints ad 37-1539* (Bristol, 1925).

2 Robinson, J A, *Two Glastonbury legends* (1926), v.

and concluded: 'In that sentence the Dean has hanged himself. There he will hang – a man who wrote a book to assassinate two beautiful legends, but does not like to be called an assassin.' And he rounded off his rant by calling the Dean a criminal, and suggesting that he was worthy of 'an interesting psychological study'.[1]

The Dean, who had fought off more significant ecclesiastical predators in the past, ignored the Vicar's call to hang himself, but maintained his position. In two articles, published in 1928 and 1930, he repeated that the references to Joseph were, 'the insertions of a later writer, and need not detain us here'; and that William's history was 'embellished with later legends of which he knew nothing'.[2] Meanwhile the Vicar had adopted a different approach. Appealing to a supposed precedent, and to a relative who was a lady-in-waiting, in December 1929 he sent a sprig of the flowering Glastonbury thorn to Queen Mary. And so a tradition was born.[3]

In its fully developed form the legend tells us that Joseph of Arimathea was a trader who travelled to England, and brought with him Jesus as a child (to whom he was related) to teach him the art of extracting tin. After the crucifixion Joseph returned as a missionary to Britain, and founded the first church in England at Glastonbury. But on his first coming to the town he was faced by a hostile crowd on nearby Werill (Weary-all) Hill, and he struck his hawthorn staff into the ground. Miraculously it took root and blossomed, and as a token of the truth of the Christian message the Glastonbury thorn

1   Lewis, L S, *Glastonbury "the mother of saints", her saints AD 37-1539* (2nd enlarged ed, 1927), ix-xviii, quotes from xviii.

2   Robinson, J A, 'The historical evidence as to the Saxon church at Glastonbury,' *Proc. Somerset Arch Soc.*, lxxiii, (1928), 40-9, quote from 42; 'Note by the Dean of Wells . . ', *Proc. Somerset Arch. Soc.* lxxv, (1930), 31-3, quote from 31.

3   Bowman, M, 'The holy thorn ceremony,' *Folklore* cxvii, pt. 2 (2006), 127-8. The Dean, J A Robinson, died in 1933 after succumbing to dementia: Taylor, T F, *J Armitage Robinson* (1991), 106. The Vicar, L S Lewis, remained at Glastonbury until 1950, when he retired to Farnham (Surrey)and probably died c.1953: *Crockford's Clerical Directory* (1951-2, 1953-4 eds.).

has continued to flower every Christmas Day. Variations of the legend have suggested that the thorn came from the same tree as Jesus's crown of thorns, and that Jesus himself established the first church.[1]

Staffs becoming trees are found elsewhere in Christian tradition, for example at Congresbury in Somerset, Newlyn East in Cornwall, and in Wiltshire, where the village of Bishopstrow ('the bishop's tree') is supposed to derive its name from a legend that St Aldhelm's ashen staff turned into an ash tree while he preached there.[2] These stories, as well as the survival in churchyards of yew trees older than the earliest church on the site, suggest that in such places Christianity supplanted a pagan observance which included the veneration of trees. But the Christmas flowering seems to have originated at Glastonbury. The tradition existed by 1520, when a poem recounting the life of Joseph of Arimathea was published.[3] Here is the relevant part.

> Great meruaylles men may se at Glastenbury
> One of a walnot tree that there dooth stande
> In the holy grounde called the semetory
> Harde by the place where kynge Arthur was founde
> South fro Iosephs chapell it is walled in rounde
> It bereth no leaues tyll the day of saynt Barnabe [11th June]
> And than that tree, that standeth in the grounde
> Spredeth his leaues as fayre as any other tree
>
> Thre hawthornes also that groweth in werall [Weary-all]
> Do burge and bete grene leaues at Christmas
> As fresshe as other in May, whan the nightyngale

1 Carley, J P, *Glastonbury abbey: the holy house at the head of the moors adventurous* (1988), 181-5; Vickery, A R, *Holy thorn of Glastonbury* (West Country Folklore 12, 1979).

2 Vickery, A R, *Holy thorn of Glastonbury* (1979), 13; Chandler, J, *Church in Wiltshire* (2006), 8-9.

3 Skeat, W W, *Joseph of Arimathea . . .* (Early English Text Society, 1871), 49.

Wrestes out her notes musycall as pure as glas
Of all wodes and forestes she is the chefe chauntres
In wynter to synge yf it were her nature
In werall she myght haue a playne place
On those hawthornes to shewe her notes clere

Lo, lordes, what Ihesu dooth in Ianuary
Whan the great colde cometh to grounde
He maketh the hauthorne to sprynge full fresshely
Where as it pleaseth hym his grace is founde
He may loose all thing that is bounde
Thankes be gyuen to hym that in heuen sytteth
That floryssheth his werkes so on the grounde
And in Glastenbury, *Quia mirabilia fecit* ['because he performs wonders']

The Glastonbury thorn recurs quite frequently in 16th and 17th century literature. In 1722, perhaps for the first time in print, the thorn was associated with Joseph's staff, and by then scions of the 'original' thorn were thriving at various sites in and around the town.[1] Botanically it has been identified with a variant of the common hawthorn (*Crataegus monogyna* var. *praecox*) which flourishes in southern Europe and flowers much earlier than the native British species; the Glastonbury thorn may in fact have been brought back by someone from the Mediterranean, as the legend implies.[2] It was credited with such precision in recognizing Christmas Day that a reform to the calendar in 1752 flummoxed it.

The leap year is a device to correct the discrepancy between the calendar and solar years. But for the sake of precision the leap year must be omitted once a century. Until the sixteenth century this

1 Vickery, A R, *Holy thorn of Glastonbury* (1979), 4-9
2 Ibid. 8-9; Grigson, G, *The Englishman's flora* (1955), 170.

was not properly understood, and by then there was some ten clays' divergence. In Great Britain this was tolerated until 1752, in which year eleven days (3rd to 13th September) were entirely omitted from the calendar, so that the 2nd September was followed immediately by the 14th. This synchronized the calendar and solar years, but was resisted by many people, who thought that the government was trying to shorten their lives by eleven days. Fairs and feast days tended to honour the 'old style' dates, as they were known, by taking place eleven (or sometimes twelve) days later than the 'new style' would suggest they should. Consequently either 5th or 6th January, eleven or twelve days after 25th December, was regarded as the real Christmas Day, and was known as 'Old Christmas Day'. This note appeared in the *Western Flying Post* in January 1753, the first Christmas after the alteration of the calendar.

> By a letter from Glastonbury we hear that a vast concourse of people attended the thorn on Christmas Eve, new stile; but to their great disappointment, there was no appearance of its blowing, which made them watch it narrowly the fifth of January, the Christmas day, old stile, when it blowed as usual and in one day's time was as white as a sheet, to the great mortification of many families in that neighbourhood, who had tapp'd their ale eleven days too soon.

People continued to observe thorns on 'Old' Christmas day until the early 20th century, occasionally destroying an uncooperative specimen in their frustration. This is what happened near Crewkerne in January 1878:

> Immense crowds gathered at a cottage between Hewish and Woolmingstone to witness the supposed blooming of a 'Holy' thorn at midnight on Saturday. The weather was unfavourable and the visitors were impatient. There were buds on the plant,

but they did not burst into flower as they were said to have done the previous year. The crowd started singing and then it degenerated into a quarrel and stones were thrown. The occupier of the cottage, seeing how matters stood, pulled up the thorn and took it inside, receiving a blow on the head from a stone for his pains. A free fight ensued and more will be heard of the affair in the Magistrates' Court.[1]

At Glastonbury since 1929, when the Vicar, the Revd Smithett Lewis first sent his sprig to the queen, the affair has been conducted in a more orderly fashion, and has become a civic occasion. The usual ritual is for the cutting ceremony to be held outside St John's parish church a week or two before Christmas, where the oldest child at St John's infants school is supervised in clipping sprigs from the thorn tree growing in the churchyard. Clergy, the mayor and town councillors, parents and the local press all attend, and the legend of Joseph is recounted, including the children's song:

> There is a very special tree
> We call the Holy Thorn,
> That flowers in December
> The month that Christ was born.
>
> We're told this very special tree
> Grew from a staff or thorn,
> Brought by a man called Joseph
> From the land where Christ was born.
>
> It now is our tradition
> To send a sprig of thorn,

---

1   Vickery, A R, *Holy thorn of Glastonbury* (1979), 10-11, quoting *Pulman's Weekly News*, 10 Jan. 1878.

To greet Her Gracious Majesty
On the day that Christ was born.

The sprigs are then sent with a message by the vicar to the Queen, one of whose ladies-in-waiting generally replies on her behalf, and the thank-you letter is pinned on the church notice-board. In 1986 the Queen and the Glastonbury thorn enjoyed a special juxtaposition, when they appeared together on the Christmas postage stamp.[1]

Putting to one side clerical arguments, spurious traditions and loyal ceremony, it fell to an agnostic poet (here writing prose) to express his belief in the true miracle of the Glastonbury thorn. Edward Thomas, four years before he was killed at the battle of Arras in 1917, visited Glastonbury at Easter 1913.

At first I thought I should not see more of the abbey than can be seen from the road – the circular abbot's kitchen with pointed cap, and the broken ranges of majestic tall arches that guide the eye to the shops and dwellings of Glastonbury. While I was buying a postcard the woman of the shop reminded me of Joseph of Arimathea's thorn, and how it blossomed at Christmas. 'Did you ever see it blossoming at Christmas?' I asked. 'Once,' she said, and she told me how the first winter she spent at Glastonbury was a very mild one, and she went out with her brothers for a walk on Christmas day in the afternoon. She remembered that they wore no coats. And they saw blossom on the holy thorn. After all, I did go through the turnstile to see the abbey. The high pointed arches were magnificent, the turf under them perfect. The elms stood among the ruins like noble savages among Greeks. The orchards hard by made me wish that they were blossoming. But excavations had been going on;

---

1 Ibid. 12; Bowman, M, 'The holy thorn ceremony,' *Folklore* cxvii, pt. 2 (2006), 123-4, 128-9, 138.

clay was piled up and cracking in the sun, and there were tin sheds and scaffolding. I am not an archaeologist, and I left it. As I was approaching the turnstile an old hawthorn within a few yards of it, against a south wall drew my attention. For it was covered with young green leaves and with bright crimson berries almost as numerous. Going up to look more closely, I saw what was more wonderful – Blossom. Not one flower, nor one spray only, but several sprays. I had not up till now seen even blackthorn flowers, though towards the end of February I had heard of hawthorn flowering near Bradford. As this had not been picked, I conceitedly drew the conclusion that it had not been observed. Perhaps its conspicuousness had saved it. It was Lady Day. I had found the Spring in that bush of green, white, and crimson. So warm and bright was the sun, and so blue the sky, and so white the clouds, that not for a moment did the possibility of Winter returning cross my mind.[1]

The Christmas flowering of the thorn as a pledge of the return of spring falls very much in the pagan winter solstice tradition of the unconquered sun beginning its journey again. But at Glastonbury in the fifteenth century the developing legend of Joseph of Arimathea was employed to forge another link between winter and spring, Christmas and Easter.

1   Thomas, E, *In pursuit of spring* (1914), 252-3.

Here the experiences of the two Saint Josephs, the husband of Mary, and the Arimathean, are compared. This carol was found in a manuscript commonplace book compiled in Glastonbury around 1450, and the original metrical Latin has been rendered into English prose.

The Two Josephs

ELCOME, FATHER, YOU who were betrothed to the
mother of Christ,
And who witnessed his birth,
Saint Joseph the elder.
Welcome, Father, you who sought from Pilate Christ's body,
Which you took down from the cross,
Saint Joseph the younger

Greeting, old man, you whom the shepherds discovered
By the sweeter flowers of Behlehem
Mother and Child.
Greetings, young man, you who anointed the body of Jesus,
And which you took for burial in your own tomb
With his mother's help.

Rejoice, old man, you who through the star
Witnessed the Magi as they worshipped Christ
And your maiden spouse so tender.
Rejoice, young man, you who saw the face of the risen Jesus
Whom you loved so much
The next day after you had mourned for him.

Be joyful, old man, as you stand dumbstruck
By the force of Symeon's words,

Predicting the sword of your bride's suffering.
Be joyful, young man, you who have protected
The mother of Christ whom you loved,
And here at last you preached the joy of them both.

Farewell, old man, you who, with saddened heart,
With Mary sought Jesus, and then found him
In the temple with the scholars.
Farewell, young man, you who looked for England,
And then came to Glastonbury, where you founded here
This church, the first in all these lands.

Old man, young man, rejoice together.
Keep us in your memory, and in the Lord be strong now,
Joseph, Joseph, equals.
We plead that you will pray for us, as here we stand
So that when we die we shall be strong
To live for all eternity.[1]

Glastonbury can boast one more adaptation (perversion, some would say) of the Christmas story.

The Waning of Bethlehem's Star

 HREE DAYS AFTER Christmas in 1915, at the Crispin Hall in Street, the first performance took place of a musical nativity play, which was subsequently published, adopted by amateur choral societies, and performed around the world. Its title was *Bethlehem*, and it was the work of a composer now

---

1 The Latin poem is printed in Rigg, A G, *A Glastonbury miscellany of the fifteenth century* (1968), 120-2.

for the most part forgotten, but famous for a few years in the 1920s. His name was Rutland Boughton.

Bethlehem is very decidedly a Somerset nativity play. The three shepherds, whose names are Jem, Dave and Sym, have broad West-Country accents, and, when the first of the wise men enters, his song is derived from a Somerset folk tune. The keynote to the drama's success is its simplicity. It is based on the well-known Coventry mystery plays, with Arthurian overtones, and includes several popular carols which, at the original performances, the audience was encouraged to join the performers in singing. The score is tuneful, and much of it sounds like folksong (although only the one genuine folk melody is used); it is not too difficult for amateurs to sing, and there are plenty of homely touches – the gifts which the shepherds bring for the infant Jesus are a whistle, a hat and a pair of mittens. Contemporary events are alluded to, for example when Herod describes himself as 'the mightiest lord and Kaiser that ever walked on ground'.

To explain the significance of the play's links with Somerset, including its first performance here, we have to go back a year, to 1914, and the first of the Glastonbury Festivals. Rutland Boughton was an idealist, whose dream during the years before the war had been to establish a native British opera (he preferred the description 'music drama') based on Celtic and Arthurian legends, just as Wagner had used Teutonic legends to create German opera. Part of the plan was to find an appropriate venue where the works could be performed, and where a kind of 'co-operative' of artists and musicians could live together to experiment and create. Nowadays the term to describe such an endeavour would be a 'workshop'. Surrey woodland near Hindhead was considered, and Letchworth Garden City, but in 1913 Glastonbury was agreed upon, and after a few setbacks (including the declaration of war the same day) the first Glastonbury Festival began on 5 August 1914 – and the Assembly Rooms, down an alleyway behind the High Street, became England's answer to Wagner's Bayreuth.

Supported by the Clark family of Street and other well-wishers, including George Bernard Shaw, the festival overcame its difficulties, and Boughton's dream became a reality. By 1922 he could boast that the Glastonbury Festival Movement had to date staged 266 performances of operas, plays and ballets, 54 concerts and over 500 classes in singing, dancing and similar subjects. What is more, one of the music dramas, *The Immortal Hour*, in that year transferred to the London stage, where it was to achieve a run of 216 consecutive performances – a world record for serious opera that has never been broken. Rutland Boughton became the toast of the musical establishment.

It was a bewildering and unsettling time for the composer. A man of strong socialist and musical principles, he felt uncomfortable in the West End. Matters came to a head in 1926. For the Christmas season he staged a revival of *Bethlehem*, but because of his disgust at the General Strike, and the treatment meted out to the miners, he decided (without consulting his Glastonbury colleagues) to dispense with the traditional trappings of the nativity play, and to set the drama in a miner's cottage, with the characters in modern dress. Herod became a decadent capitalist, and his courtiers included policemen and soldiers.

The religious establishment of the day, which understandably felt a certain possessiveness about the nativity and the way in which it was portrayed, voiced its objections, Boughton fell out with his fellow directors, the production made a loss, and the whole enterprise was effectively bankrupted. The local Glastonbury newspaper, the *Central Somerset Gazette*, announced the following July that the festival would not be held that year. An emergency meeting of the festival company had been held, and had decided to go into voluntary liquidation. Mr Boughton, the principal creditor (he was owed £400), told the newspaper that he would carry on the work of producing English operas himself.

And so the celebrated composer found that his career had gone from rags to riches to rags again, and he retired to a smallholding near Newent in Gloucestershire, from where, indeed, he did make occasional attempts to restart his English opera festival movement. He died in 1960 and, apart from one song from *The Immortal Hour*, his life and work have been largely forgotten. Until the last decade, that is, for perhaps now the tide is turning. There are commercial recordings available of *Bethlehem*, *The Immortal Hour* and *The Queen of Cornwall*, and of some of his orchestral and chamber music. Perhaps, as the qualities of Boughton's music become appreciated again, before long Somerset people will again be able to enjoy live performances of their own nativity play.[1]

If to his contemporaries Rutland Boughton appeared to be 'off message' so far as the true meaning of Christmas was concerned, the Dorset essayist Llewellyn Powys had strayed much further. This is his Christmas story, published in 1935.

A Christmas Tale
Llewelyn Powys

NO MUSIC IN the world is more beautiful than the ringing of church bells heard from a distance over an open country. At Christmas especially does this music move the spirit, so deeply associated is it with the pathos of human imaginings, the pathos of human existence. In the past the Christmas bells of Bindon Abbey must have been audible from Merly Wood to Moigne Down whenever the north-east wind blew over the waters of Poole.

---

1   This piece draws on the following: Hurd, M, *Rutland Boughton and the Glastonbury festivals* (1993); Littlewood, S R, *Somerset and the drama* (Somerset Folk Series 7), 102-3; Hurd, M, liner notes to *Bethlehem* (Hyperion CDA66690); *Central Somerset Gazette*, 22 July 1927, 5.

It is not difficult to understand the indignation of the lay brothers and rustic farmhands who, for so long, had worked upon Abbey grounds when, at the time of the Dissolution of the Monasteries, the famous set of Bindon Bells they had heard ringing so often were distributed amongst the belfries of neighbouring parish churches. This local Catholic resentment has been eloquently preserved in the following rhyme:

> Wool streams,
> Coombe Wells,
> Fordington cuckolds
> Have a' stole
> Bindon Bells.

It was in mediaeval times, when Bindon Abbey was still prosperously established, that the following strange events occurred. A regular priest of the Abbey, known as Father de Brian, had interested himself in the welfare of a certain rook-boy who was employed sometimes in herding swine, and sometimes in scaring birds from the village common-field, each strip of which was divided so precisely by balks of grass. The boy was ruddy and comely to look upon, but generally thought to be one of God's innocents. His simplicity appealed to the elderly churchman who for upwards of three years gave much time to teaching the lad to read Latin from the illuminated manuscripts that were kept chained, each in its place, on the old oak reading-desks that belonged to the Abbey Library.

The monk's judgement was fully justified, and the rook-boy idiot proved an apt and industrious scholar. Not only was he taught letters, but he was also instructed in the mysteries of the Christian religion, as they were understood within the sacred walls of the Cistercian Abbey whose ruins we now look upon.

All might have gone well had not Lubberlu, for so the boy was called by the villein crofters, one May morning wandered down to the

Frome. The cuckoo was bawling from the trees behind Blacknoll, and the excited river-fowl were calling to each other with amorous clucks across the floating levels of water-buttercups, that, flat and white as hail, were lying upon the surface of the clear shining stream. Then he saw a girl peering at him out of a bed of tall rushes. She was unknown to him, a maiden dressed in a coarse gown of woven flax girded with a green girdle. The two made friends. She was beautiful, but there was something fairy about her, and her voice had the shrill quality of a snipe suddenly flushed.

The two became playmates and before long lovers. It was the girl's eyes that especially bewitched the rook-boy scholar, wide-open liquid eyes that would gaze at him from under arched eyebrows. She would never tell him from what village she came, downland or heath, but always on sunshine mornings when he drove his hogs to water he would find her hidden by the swift-flowing river.

They would play together in bulrush jungles or on the open cowslip banks of the meadows, laughing to see the trout rise; and often the girl, in no Christian mood, would weave with slender fingers the field rushes into meshed cages expert to imprison a hipfrog or a dancing grasshopper.

The blue sky and the blue flowing river, the green willows and the green water-flags, together with this wild shy creature, now obsessed the whole being of Lubberlu. His listlessness became manifest. When he should have been tracing the outlines of the initial letters, bright as butterflies in the illuminated scripts of the Abbey, he would be looking out of the narrow lancet window in the direction of the water meadows. For many weeks the old priest held his peace, but as the summer grew towards its close and the last loads of the yellow harvest had been stored in the great ivy-covered Grange, he pressed the boy to make his confession. When he had finished the old man stood up, and with tears running down his cheeks made the sign of the blessed cross over the straw-coloured head of his conjured pupil. He suspected this wanton daughter of the river of belonging to a family outside of Middle Earth–at best a river nymph owning no mortal soul.

After the evening of his confession Lubberlu was never able to find his darling again. All through the autumn in the dusk of late afternoons he would trace the banks of the Frome in its winter desolation, calling and calling from Wool Bridge to Moreton Ford.

At Christmas it fell out that it was the old Priest's turn to officiate at early morning Mass in the small chapel at Ringstead. To reach the village at the appointed hour it was necessary to arouse the porter while it was still night. Lubberlu was to act as acolyte and was already blowing on his fingers outside the gateway of the Abbey. The two started away under the bright stars – the priest on a grey mule, the boy walking at his side. The hedge grass was crisp with hoar-frost. They left the wide, white drove above Belhuish and struck across by Dagger's Gate to the Roman Road that runs above the cliffs. On the downs, in the lew of the furzen, they came upon a flock of sheep, the peaceful animals with frosted backs of wool lying on the stiff turf about the Merlin thorn in an enchanted circle. The venerable clerk did not fail to remind the boy of the scene on the hills of Bethlehem and of the blinding vision that had come to the chatting shepherds.

The homestead dwellers of Ringstead had always been obstinate sons of Belial. Was it for this reason that they and their dwellings were so soon to be destroyed by pirates? They gained a scant livelihood by fishing and it may be that their hours under the stars sharpened their wits to ask awkward questions. How did it come about that Norman priests, like stags in the pride of their grease, knew so much more than ordinary churls? Had they ever spoken with a dead man risen out of the grave?

These jolly libertine lobster catchers had spent their Christmas Eve feasting and love-making behind the doors of their thatched mud houses, that windowless and chimneyless resembled so many beehives set in rows each side of the stream, the very stream that still flows through Ringstead Wood. Much brawn of tusked swine they had devoured, swilling it down with draughts of strong mead. The sound of the small chapel bell, of the Gabriel bell, echoed through the wood, sharp as the tinkling of an icicle in the morning air. The fisher folk snored on in their darkened hovels. None came to the small church, the chancel arch of which is to be seen to-day built about by the wall of the woodland cottage. With my own fingers I have traced its mouldings, the very mouldings which that morning received upon their surfaces the flickering light from the altar candles, a yellow light shining between the beech-trees, visible beyond the seaweed rocks.

The rest of the ancient Ringstead legend is best told in the form of the Christmas ballad which has preserved the sequel of the story in a kind of antiphonal chant talking place between the holy priest and this love-lost son of the earth:

Boy: Green were her eyes
– yellow were her eyes
– Her eyes were like withered sedge!

Priest: This is holy Mass and the hour flies
And there is red in the churchyard hedge,
Raise me aloft my taper's flame,
Light me my candles three,
For I must call on the Baby's name
Who is born to young Mary.

Boy: – O father, I see a blood-red streak
In the reeds where first I caught her
– And I hear a cry makes my heart weak
– And turns my bones to water.
The marsh-bittern and lone curlew,
That cry comes not from them.

Priest: Bring me bread and wine, my Lubberlu
And hold my vestment's hem!
The candles burn – the oxen kneel.
Boy, bring me my holy book
Born is the King of Israel!

Boy: Oh, father, my father, look!
She is pressing her face 'gainst the window-pane,
Where the saints stare in a row,
And her lips are red with the morning's stain,
And her cheeks are white like snow!

*Priest:*Tis Christmas morn and the Mass unsung
For the Baby of young Mary!

But the idiot boy from his side had sprung.
At the window prone was he.
And the oxen knelt in their frozen shed
And the sheep in the hurdled pen;
But Lubberlu lay stark and dead,
He never will come again.

They sign his breast and they sign his brow
With the cross to which they pray
– But two lost souls are flying now
Over the reeds and over the snow,
Over the hills and away.[1]

To end this round-up of thoughtful and thought-provoking Wessex variations on the nativity theme, here is what might be described as a 'green' carol, a reverent celebration of nature. Like Edward Thomas, its

1   Powys, L, *Dorset essays* (1935), 90-4.

author was a casualty of World War One. Charles Hamilton Sorley had scarcely left Marlborough College when he was killed on the Western Front in 1915, and so his poetic genius had no time to reach maturity. Many of his best poems, which were first published in 1916, were written as a schoolboy at Marlborough, and inspired, like this one, by the downs and woods around the town. It is dated 1 December 1913. which means that it was written at the end of Sorley's last term at the college.

The Other Wise Man
Charles Hamilton Sorley

 CENE: A VALLEY with a wood on one side and a road running up to a distant hill: as it might be, the valley to the east of West Woods, that runs up to Oare Hill. only much larger. Time: Autumn. Four wise men are marching hillward along the road.

One Wise Man
I wonder where the valley ends?
On, comrades, on.

Another Wise Man
The rain-red road,
Still shining sinuously, bends
Leagues upwards.

A Third Wise Man
To the hills, O friends,
To seek the star that once has glowed
Before us; turning not to right
Nor left, nor backward once looking.
Till we have clomb – and with the night
We see the King.

All the Wise Men
The King! The King!

The Third Wise Man
Long is the road but –

A Fourth Wise Man
Brother, see,
There, to the left, a very aisle
Composed of every sort of tree –

The First Wise Man
Still onward –

The Fourth Wise Man
Oak and beech and birch,
Like a church, but homelier than church,
The black trunks for its walls of tile;
Its roof, old leaves; its floor, beech nuts;
The squirrels its congregation –

The Second Wise Man
Tuts!
For still we journey –

The Fourth Wise Man
But the sun weaves
A water-web across the grass,
Binding their tops. You must not pass
The water cobweb.

The Third Wise Man
Hush! I say.
Onward and upward till the day –

The Fourth Wise Man
Brother, that tree has crimson leaves.
You'll never see its like again.
Don't miss it. Look, it's bright with rain –

The First Wise Man
O prating tongue. On, on.

The Fourth Wise Man
And there
A toad-stool, nay, a goblin stool.
No toad sat on a thing so fair.
Wait, while I pluck – and there's – and here's
A whole ring . . . what? . . . berries:'

(The Fourth Wise Man drops behind. botanizing)

The Wisest of the Remaining Three Wise Men
O fool!
Fool, fallen in this vale of tears.
His hand had touched the plough: his eyes
Looked back: no more with us, his peers,
He'll climb the hill and front the skies
And see the Star, the King, the Prize.
But we, the seekers, we who see
Beyond the mists of transiency –
Our feet down in the valley still
Are set, our eyes are on the hill.
Last night the star of God has shone,
And so we journey, up and on,
With courage clad, with swiftness shod,
All thoughts of earth behind us cast,
Until we see the lights of God,
– And what will be the crown at last?

All Three Wise Men
On, on.

(They pass on: it is already evening when the Other Wise Man limps along the road, still botanizing.)

The Other Wise Man
A vale of tears they said!
A valley made of woes and fears,
To be passed by with muffled head
Quickly. I have not seen the tears,
Unless they take the rain for tears,
And certainly the place is wet.
Rain-laden leaves are ever licking
Your cheeks and hands . . . I can't get on.

There's a toad-stool that wants picking.
There, just there, a little up,
What strange things to look upon
With pink hood and orange cup!
And there are acorns, yellow – green
They said the King was at the end.
They must have been
Wrong. For here, here, I intend
To search for him, for surely here
Are all the wares of the old year,
And all the beauty and bright prize,
And all God's colours meetly showed,
Green for the grass, blue for the skies,
Red for the rain upon the road;
And anything you like for trees,
But chiefly yellow, brown and gold,
Because the year is growing old
And loves to paint her children these.
I tried to follow . . . but, what do you think?
The mushrooms here are pink!
And there's old clover with black polls,
Black-headed clover, black as coals,
And toad-stools, sleek as ink!
And there are such heaps of little turns
Off the road, wet with old rain:
Each little vegetable lane
Of moss and old decaying ferns,
Beautiful in decay,
Snatching a beauty from whatever may
Be their lot, dark-red and luscious: till there pass'd
Over the many-coloured earth a grey
Film. It was evening coming down at last.
And all things hid their faces, covering up

Their peak or hood or bonnet or bright cup
In greyness, and the beauty faded fast,
With all the many-coloured coat of day.
Then I looked up, and lo! the sunset sky
Had taken the beauty from the autumn earth.
Such colour, O such colour, could not die.
The trees stood black against such revelry
Of lemon-gold and purple and crimson dye.
And even as the trees, so I
Stood still and worshipped, though by evening's birth
I should have capped the hills and seen the King.
The King? The King?
I must be miles away from my journey's end;
The others must be now nearing
The summit, glad. By now they wend
Their way far, far, ahead, no doubt.
I wonder if they've reached the end.
If they have, I have not heard them shout.[1]

---

1   Wilson, J M (ed.), *Collected poems of Charles Hamilton Sorley*, (1985), 56-61 [first published in 1916].

9
The Groaning Board

T CHRISTMAS IT is such a rare jolly time,
With eating and drinking, while yet in our prime;
If I was made king, to my subjects I'll swear,
That Christmas should last for the whole of the year.
There's another good reason why Christmas should last,
Such a season for feasting should never be past;
In mirth and in good fellowship I take great delight up
With singing and music for to keep the night up
I'll now give you an account of our Grand-Master's dinner,
It is true what I say, although I'm a sinner.
How brought on the table, on last Christmas Day,
And how it went off, I am going to say.
But first I should rather say how it came on,
A turbot at top, which was very well done;
Boiled turkey at bottom, with rich oyster sauce,
And forcemeat balls round it all fried to a toss.
A chine was placed near, t'other end was a ham,
And a piece of roast beef, on which you might cram.
Chickens roasted and boiled, at the sides in array,
Such nice ones you'll be sure could not hope for fair play.
There was also a tongue, and hash calves-heads and brains,
But to mention each dish I need take no more pains.
Suffice there was plenty, and that of the best,

Then a haunch of fat venison, to crown all the rest.
The set to then began, with great skill from the first of it,
The meat was cut up, and of course had the worst of it.
The turkey and fowls of their limbs were bereft
And the venison and beef cut in right and left.
Not the meats, but the men, who attacked it were tough,
And the battle long lasted, e'er one cried enough.
Such eating and drinking there was on that day,
Each took what he liked, and drank his own way.
Now the cloth being drawn, soon the wine glasses rattle,
Which succeeded the noise of the knife and fork battle.
All drank what they liked, whether old port or sherry,
And toasted away, until all was quite merry.
A bumper filled and all ready, then up rose the host,
And proposed to his friends he saw round him, a toast
With three cheers, which he knew would make the room ring
With a hearty good will,
'Twas Great George our King.

Salisbury's answer to William McGonagall, there describing 'The Grand Master's Dinner', was Michael Burrough, a banker who was city mayor in 1790, bankrupt in 1810 and dead in 1831. His carnivorous extravaganza, which survives in a manuscript volume now in the Wiltshire & Swindon Archives,[1] introduces us to a perennial feature of Christmas, the excess consumption of food and drink.

Foreshadowed by the pagan Roman celebration of Saturnalia, which also took place in late December, Christmas for a medieval English villager was a time of enforced holiday, when wet or frosty weather precluded most outdoor work, when the sowing of winter corn was finished and spring sowing had not yet begun. G C Homans, social historian of English villages in the 13th century, described it thus:

1   WSA 473/381

Christmas was the time of greatest community good feeling. Cattle, sheep and swine had just been slaughtered. The harvest was in. Of this plenty the husbandman feasted, without giving a thought to the lean times which might be to come. And the height of this feasting was the dinner which on any proper manor on Christmas Day the lord gave in his hall to all his tenants.[1]

If anywhere in Wessex can claim to have preserved the medieval manorial feast at Christmas it is the village of North Curry, on Sedgemoor between Taunton and Langport. With its neighbours West Hatch and Stoke St Gregory, it appears to have maintained a Christmas 'Reeve's Feast' from the middle ages, and perhaps earlier, until 1865. Traditionally the feast was associated with King John, who reigned at the beginning of the thirteenth century, although Somerset antiquarians

1   Homans, G C, *English villages of the thirteenth century* (1941), 357.

writing about it a century or so ago speculated that it had originated in Anglo-Saxon arrangements of land tenure. It is certainly true that North Curry was a royal manor before the Norman conquest and until the late 12th century, although by King John's time it had been sold to the Bishop of Bath and Wells. In 1850, when the custom was in danger of dying out, a local landowner had a tablet inscribed and placed in the church vestry giving full details of the arrangements for the feast. By then, in the words of a later vicar, 'the character of the celebration seems to have degenerated somewhat,' consisting as it did of everyone drinking ale for as long as it took two large candles, one after the other, to burn down. The Victorian hierarchy did not much approve of that sort of thing, and saw to it that in 1868 it was turned into a charity approved by the Charity Commissioners, and the money previously spent on it was distributed in kind. The last time it was held in the 19th century was in 1865, although in recent years it has been revived. Here is a transcript of the salient details from the tablet in the church.[1]

North Curry Reeve's Feast

 HE Reeve provides the feast and in order to enable him to do so – The lords of the manor allowing the lords rent of the Feast Tenement in respect of which he is appointed to the office, an annual allowance of two pounds by the name of Leaze Fees a payment of two pounds under the name of Cane Wood and four Pounds and five shillings under the name of Beef and Pork.

The Reeve is also allowed by the occupier of the lay rectory 36 bushels of good marketable wheat and 48 shillings in money to be rendered on demand at any time within a month before Christmas

---

1   The transcript is taken from Olivey, H P, *Notes on the ancestral manor and hundred of North Curry* (1902), 11-20, abridged; see also Pring, D J, 'North Curry Feast', *Somerset & Dorset Notes & Queries*, xxi (1934), 209-11.

annually and likewise by the holders of the undermentioned estates the quantity of wheat set opposite the names of their tenements respectively to be rendered within the like period [Eleven contributors are named, mostly of two bushels each].

The custom of preparing for and holding the feast is for the Reeve to provide three fat heifers and put them in the manor Pound adjoining North Curry churchyard the Sunday before Christmas day, if Christmas happen to be on any other day than Monday or Tuesday, but if it falls on Monday or Tuesday then the Sunday week before Christmas day for the inspection of the persons entitled to the feast, who may insist on having them changed if good ones are not provided. Then these are killed by a butcher appointed by the Reeve, and the day before Christmas day delivered with a good half pig to two tenants of the manor of North Curry called dealers, who continue for many years but are annually summoned to their duty by the Reeve and have their vacancies filled up by him.

The dealers are to attend on the day before Christmas day except that day be on a Sunday, and then the day preceding, at the Reeve's with a clerk to cut or deal or dole out the beef and pork to the persons entitled to receive it, and they have provided for them by the Reeve beef stakes [sic] and onions for breakfast, top but of beef and three marrow bones boiled with the marrow taken out and spread on toasted bread for dinner, and a feast each of two loaves of bread, eight pennyworth of beef and twopence in money, and one pound of beef suet to be sent home to their houses for their trouble. The dealers serve out two ribs of beef, two ribs of pork, two loaves of bread and twopence in money to each of the holders of the following freehold manors [seven names follow].

They also serve out to the occupiers of two tenements a feast and half, namely three loaves of bread, one shilling's worth of beef and threepence in money. They also serve to the occupiers of the following tenements two loaves of bread, eight pennyworth of beef and twopence in money [140 named tenements follow. Various other

measures are allotted to sixteen other tenants]. Each of which loaves
of bread is to be made of good white flour. To be well baked and to
weigh after baking five pounds, and the beef is to be valued at the
price for which beef of the like quality is then currently selling.

To the Reeve of West Hatch within the said manor the dealers
serve half a bullock and the hind quarter of half a pig for the use of the
tenants of that manor on his paying five shillings for it to the Reeve of
North Curry. But before he is allowed to enter the Reeve's house he is
to sing the following song:

> King John he was a noble knight
> I'm come to demand my right
> Open the door and let me in
> Else I'll carry away my money again.

The dealers serve out these feasts to the persons entitled to them,
who are to send for them between sunrise and sunset the day before
Christmas day, unless it happen to be on a Sunday, and then the day
preceding, and the dealers also serve out for the Reeve a chine, round
and rump of beef for mince meat, and the belly part of the fore quarter
of the half of pig for a feast to be provided the day after Christmas
day except it be a Sunday, and then the day following, by the Reeve
for the lords of the manor of Knapp and Slough, who are called the
'Jacks of Knapp and Slough', and have the feast for themselves and
their attendants after mentioned. Besides the chief feasts of beef etc
in common with the holders of the other five freehold manors they or
their deputies arrive at the Reeve's house the feast day about 1 o'clock.
The Jack of Knapp or his deputy attended by three men and a boy.
And the Jack of Slough or his deputy by two men and a boy.

When the Jack of Knapp or his deputy arrives, the key of the
Reeve's cellar (in which there is to be provided a half a hogshead at
least of good ale for the feast) is given to one of his attendants. The
Jack or deputy proceeds to divide the offal or inferior parts of the

bullocks and half pig, not distributed by the dealers to the holders of tenements, into portions to be given away in the afternoon to the second poor. The Jack of Slough or deputy divides six dozen of bread weighing five Pounds each loaf when well baked provided by the Reeve for the like purpose.

The Jacks and their attendants then sit down to a dinner provided by the Reeve consisting of the chine of beef roasted and the rump and round boiled, the belly piece of the fore quarter of the half pig rolled up and made into a collar of brawn scalded and served up with a sprig of rosemary and powdered with flour, a hen with the head and tail on but the rest of the feathers except the tail plucked off a little boiled and served up on sops of bread, proper vegetables, a large mince pie with an effigy of King John in paste properly painted to represent a king stuck up in the middle of it. Bread and ale and cheese after. When they sit down to dinner two candles weighing a pound each are lighted, and until they are burnt out the Jacks and their attendants have a right to sit drinking ale. After dinner the regular toasts are:

To the immortal memory of King John.
The Real Jack of Knapp.
The Real Jack of Slough.

Afterwards other toasts are given.

The Jacks give away the bread and the offal beef and pork to the second poor. When they have drunk as much as they like, they depart. The Jack of Slough or deputy holding the stirrup of the Jack of Knapp or deputy for him to mount, and receiving a shilling as his fee.

The undersigned declare the above to be the immemorial customs of the feast held annually in the manor of North Curry, and as contributors thereto or partakers thereof they make this recognition for better preserving and keeping up the same [28 signatories].

Despite the tablet in the church declaring these to be the immemorial customs of the feast, they had in fact changed over time, and possibly had been abandoned and then resuscitated in a half-remembered form. The evidence for this is found in the Liber Albus *or 'white book' in Wells Cathedral Library, which describes, among many other things, the possessions of the medieval bishops.[1] This records the customs of North Curry in about 1314. Much is recognisable from the later account – the candles, the reeve, the bread and beef – and John de Knapp and John de la Sloo [Slough] are listed there as real individuals. There is no mention of King John, however, nor of his pie, which seems to have arrived via a different tradition. But a strange and unexplained game was played: each tenant 'will have for himself and his neighbours one wastel loaf, cut into three parts, to play the ancient Christmas games with the said wastel loaf'. It also emerges that there were two classes of tenants on the manor, and that their provisions for the feast were subtly different.[2]*

However much its details may have changed over time, the North Curry tradition, with its reeves, lords of the manor and tenants, was a rare survival of the feudal system which, as manorial ties loosened, was

---

1 HMC *Report on the MSS of Wells Cathedral*, pt 1 (1885). There are in fact two *Libri Albi*.

2 Stokes, J (ed.), *Records of the Early English Drama: Somerset* (1996), 177-84 (text), 808-15 (translation), 915-18 (notes).

abandoned elsewhere. *The half-hearted observance of another feast, and then its demise, is recorded in the parish registers by the rectors of Everleigh, a small Wiltshire village on Salisbury Plain. This tradition, however, was based not on the manor, but on the church.*

Everleigh Christmas Ale

HEN I CAME first to this parish, being now about eleaven or twelve yeares past, it was said there had been a custome longe before of making the neighbourhood eate (only bread and cheese) and drinke at the parsonage house on Christmas day after eveninge prayer, which custome out of neighbourlie kindness, or out of weaknesse (for I misliked it) I continued accordingelie till the gunpowder treason 1605. After which tyme wee agreed both I and the parishioners (except one or two) that that drinkeinge should be on the fifth of November, in remembrance of the deliverance, which continued some few yeares, but after they desyred to have it on their old day, and so had it. This present 9th of September 1610. – John Barnstone.

I never required and claymed of my neighbours a custome from them in lieu of this custome, as both reason and example of other parishes persuaded mee; but they either know it not, or conceale it. – JB.

The survival of this Christmas Ale, as it must have been, continued to upset Mr Barnstone's successors:

I continued (invita Minerva *'against my better judgement'*) to avoyd the clamours of the under sort of the parish, who flock to it as to a Christmas pastime; I could never learne how this heathenish custome had its first birth originall. Sure I am it is of evil report, and no man can imagine into what rudeness in tract of time it may degenerate. It were to be wish'd, that it were layd in the dust, and utterly forgotten. Thomas Ernle rector, Anno Dom. 1667, December 25.[1]

But clerical disapproval had no effect:

Memorandum. When I came to this living I found two very bad customs for which no reason can be assigned. One is the entertainment of bread and cheese and ale on Christmas Day; but on the alteration of the style [the change to the calendar made in 1752] I removed it to the 5th of Jany . . . This 16th May 1755, A Le Moine.

That is the last we hear of an ancient custom. The tradition of feasting at Christmas continued (and continues of course) in all strata of society, and is often described with that regretful tinge of nostalgia, so common in Christmas writing, that things are 'not like the old days'. In the following extract these regrets are expressed from the point of view of the Victorian farmer, who has adopted a Scrooge-like posture at the expense of it all. The author is Richard Jefferies, and it was first published in 1877, a time of severe depression in English agriculture. Doubtless based on his

1   WSA 651/1; these passages have recently been published in Hobbs, S (ed.), *Gleanings from Wiltshire parish registers* (Wilts Record Soc 63, 2010), 99–101.

experience of farming and farmers in north Wiltshire, Jefferies makes a
serious point, about the loss of self-sufficiency in the countryside and the
growth of a consumer society. Here, as elsewhere throughout this book,
a changing Christmas reflects a changing society.

Christmas: Then and Now
Richard Jefferies

IFTY YEARS SINCE the approach of Christmas in that substantial farm-house, with between four and five hundred acres freehold attached, would have been marked by extensive preparations, not only for the festival itself, but for the winter generally. At least one ox would have been slaughtered upon the place, and the major portion salted down for use at home. After drawing the plough, and so working out its keep, this animal could be placed in a stall, and fattened; now you cannot precisely fatten and dine on a steamplough, and possibly the contrast did not seem altogether pleasing to the farmer as he ruminated by the fire. That fire itself was of coal, with a few chunks to make a good blaze; then it would have been entirely of logs, and upon the hearth instead of a grate. These huge hearth fires had one advantage, they gave almost as much light as heat, and in the evening greatly assisted the old dip-candles which were formerly frequently manufactured upon the premises. The petroleum or paraffin lamp has long superseded them; and the coal itself comes by railway, whereas in comparatively quite recent times many farmers, who had large teams of horses standing idle just about that season, used to send a couple of waggons forty or even sixty miles away to the mouth of the nearest pit. This was done in many of the western counties, when the farmstead was within that distance of the Somerset pits, or of the Forest in Gloucestershire. Such a journey was an event to the carters and their lads.

The salt beef was principally for the use of the family itself, but occasionally to vary the bacon served out to the labourers living in the house – a custom which survived in attenuated form till very lately; in the last twenty years many instances might have been found. To this day, in some dairy districts, a fogger or milker or two, sleeps in the back premises, on account of the early hour at which the milking – when there is a herd of sixty or seventy head – must be begun. But they no longer take their meals with the master, or in any way disturb his privacy. The chimneys, built on purpose, used to be hung with sides of bacon put up to smoke; when altered for a grate, the vast size of these shafts causes considerable difficulty before the draught can be properly adjusted. The crane for swinging the pot over the embers has to be removed, to the intense disgust of the housekeeper, who can never quite assimilate herself to the modern range. Our friend, moreover, in the arm-chair, will tell you with extreme emphasis that a joint cooked by that range, with all its scientific arrangement, never tastes so sweet as when roasted, as of yore, before a pile of logs. The invisible effluvia from the coal can never be entirely prevented; and in this epicurean idea he is in a measure right. But wood grows scarcer every year, even in the most outlying districts, from the fashion of cutting, grubbing, and trimming hedges to the smallest dimensions, and from the enormous demands of large provincial towns. The price paid tempts those who still have wood to sell it, and thus the enormous wood-stacks or piles, as they are invariably called in different localities, are now becoming rare.

While thus comfortably reclining he hears the butcher call with his cart for orders, a practice now almost universal, and recollects when it was utterly unknown, and the idea of a farmer purchasing meat would have been scouted as absurd. Then comes the baker to deliver bread, another innovation; the housewife used to bake the whole of the bread required, and proud, indeed, was she of her loaves. When the loaves were done, as the great oven must still be some time ere cooling, she slipped in a dozen or so of small pies and cakes, and such trifles which now come from the confectioners in the nearest town, which also, perhaps, actually supplies the mincemeat already chopped up for the Christmas mince-pies! For oh, for oh, the oven as well as the 'hobby-horse is forgot', and is no more heated with the roughest of the faggots or bush trimmings, or the furze which used to be saved for that purpose, and is now made into a bonfire to get it out of the way, and for the ashes as manure. Even the cottagers no longer bake at home; the baker comes round to the humblest hut. The farmer is a valuable customer in the eyes of the tradesman in the country town, sending there for everything now, while, even fifteen years since, in some localities, all the weekly goods so purchased could be brought home by a labourer on foot with a great wallet slung over his shoulder. Half the rising generation have never seen a real old-fashioned wallet, which had a great capacity, and distributed the weight pretty evenly.

These things appear trifles, but they amount in the aggregate to a serious change; in this way, they require ready money, hard cash. Under the old system of salting beef at home, curing bacon (the pigs, if there are any, go to the bacon factory now), baking bread, brewing beer, and so on, everything seemed to come, as it were, out of the soil, without absolute purchase. Now the farmer imports all his household necessities, and of course has to pay for them; and it is astonishing how this influx of petty cash mounts up. He recollects as he drinks from his quart mug – detesting glass, as all old-fashioned men do – how he used, when young, to rise at four, and sometimes half-past three, and fodder the cattle by the pale light of the winter stars – when 'Charles's wain was over the chimney'. A cold job, my masters! – to step up the ladder on to the hay-rick, each rung coated with frozen rime, and, if there had been any sleet, the windward side of the rick all matted together with icicles, like a wall of ice. A slip with the huge triangular hay-knife in the hand might mean a dangerous cut. Then, with the hay-fork taking the bundle on his back – tightly bound up with the horse-hair 'band' and its wooden loop – he had to cross the swampy meadow, his weight crushing through the ice on the water in the furrows, and unless the boots were well greased, penetrating through the thick leather. Waking the echoes with their mooing the herd comes after him; for in those days the cattle for the most part – except those that were fattening – remained in the field through the winter, roughing it under the shelter of the great hawthorn bushes, now so ruthlessly felled. After breakfast, at six, he had to put on his 'owl-catchers', strong leathern gloves able to resist like gauntlets the thrust of a fierce thorn, and work at hedge-cutting; in which labour, rude as it is, there is an art, nevertheless, so to cut the wood that it shall grow well again, so to bind the branches as to lead them to shoot into a firm compact fence, and to spare and save any promising young ash-sapling or oak, or maybe a stray apple planted by the birds. These gloves were called owl-catchers because an owl often rears her young in a hollow tree, and to put the hand into the hollow and draw them out – unless well protected by leather – is a trifle risky considering the power of claw they possess. Giving the fire a poke with the tip of his nailed boots, he remembers having to pay the sweep last week; with the old open chimney, if the soot accumulated, why, they used to make a heap of straw, and fire it purposely, and so burn the soot out. Or if the chimney at an ordinary time took fire, then stand right inside it with a gun and shoot up it, and the shot and the concussion of the air effectually brought the soot down. You cannot shoot up a chimney with those close ranges filling up all the space at the bottom.

And there's the piano going now in the parlour, from which the stone flags with which it was originally paved have been taken up, and board-flooring put down, for the ladies of the period object to cold feet. His daughters, home for the holidays from boarding-school, are practising the Lancers for the dance which has been arranged for the evening. This brings him back again to the subject of hard cash and its constant outgoing, education included, for the girls must learn music, French, and drawing, and will not touch the cheese-tub, so he must either sell it (the good wife, you see, getting a little less active, as she well may after forty years of honest labour) or pay a kind of lady dairy-maid, which goes much against the grain. John, too, won't take to farming, having aspirations, and a precious expense he has been; and even Robert, who professes to look after the farm, actually insists upon having a morning paper! not to mention 'runs' up to London now and then, when the hunting is slack. Add to this, the voluntary, sarcastically so-called, school-rate (that the parish may escape a school board) and the scarcity of ploughboys and bird-keepers who are imbibing Euclid and the use of the globes instead of learning the business of life; add these together, and the old gentleman grunts to himself as he hears the notes of the merry quadrille. Not but what he loves his boys and girls, not that he grudges the ploughboy the light of knowledge; but business is business, money is money, and with wheat down so low, and dread of foreign disease, and the American cheese import, and so on, why, it is excusable if square-toes feels a little grumpy. He cannot but look with pride upon the two tall, strapping fellows who come in by-and-by, with a couple of rabbits, a hare, and two or three moor-hens – very sweet picking, too, is a plump moorhen. The land being his own, they shoot as they please; but out of true old-fashioned respect for the county family, whose mansion is hidden in the woods yonder, he religiously preserves the partridges and pheasants for the squire and his friends, and the foxes for the hunt. With them walk in two gentlemen from the adjacent town, an auctioneer's son perhaps, or even the local banker's, by no means despising a farmer known to be 'warm' in pocket, and some young corn-dealer, may be. Now, they are quite welcome, and more besides; but why does one of the daintily-dressed visitors lispingly decline anything to eat, because he has just had 'a glath of shewwy and merryfought of a fowl'? When men cannot eat there must be a terrible falling-off somewhere in British manhood. As, however, it is barely half an hour to dinner there is good and reasonable excuse. Meantime, instead of a chat over the prospect of agricultural affairs, they adjourn to the parlour, where there is more congenial society, and soon the latest new songs are heard. For the rising generation somehow never can be got to feel that absorbed interest in corn and cattle characteristic of the old school, amongst whom it was a maxim that no man was fit to be a farmer unless he could contentedly lean against a gate, and watch his sheep for a couple of hours.

After dinner the girls dress – and they do dress now, as 'the governor's' pocket knows well, and in company with their brothers and visitors, proceed to the village church, where a large party presently assembles to decorate it for Christmas. These church-decorating 'bees'! as the Americans would say, have grown quite the rural fashion, and afford plentiful opportunities for chat and flirtation, while twining the evergreen wreaths about the columns, fastening the festoons, snipping, and trimming, and arranging rice and bay-leaves into texts, etc. This occupies the time till evening – and an animated scene it is – then home to tea, and presently a dance. 'The governor' grunts at the church decorators, and the first time it was done refused to go to service at all; there used to be nothing but a little ivy employed, rather in out-of-the-way corners and suggestively than in these glaring, fulsome combinations of holly and so forth, which he stoutly declares to be pagan emblems. Of course he yields and goes to church in the end; but never will praise the prettiest design, which is very unkind, the girls think, 'but just like him, you know, so obstinate!'

Another day, if there has been a good frost, and the water-meadows afford a fine sheet of ice, they go skating, in which the girls are adepts; while the boys go among the dams and hatches in the brook, so as to flood it just in the right way, and not too much every night, thereby ensuring a smooth and glassy surface to their rink. Here also a large party assemble, and when tired of simply wheeling to and fro, a furious game of hockey on the ice begins, and lasts till it is too dusky to see the ball. 'The governor' leans on his ashen stick, and watches, remarking to a friend of the same age, 'None of this in our time – eh? We used to strike out a slide years ago, and be satisfied with that, or, at the most, push ourselves along with a pole armed with a spike to hold the ice, pecking it in between our feet. No skates then – never saw such a thing. Nothing like it used to be; and there's the afternoon express' – as a distant railway whistle comes faintly echoing over the fields, and both farmers instantly take out their watches to set their time by it. 'Christmas is quite upside down to what it was. However, we mean to have a snapdragon tonight in memory of old times; look in and try your luck!'[1]

Jefferies was a skilful reporter who could convey in vivid prose the atmosphere of an occasion without becoming too subjectively involved – opinions are reserved for his characters. A less sophisticated, but more common, approach to this real or imagined change for the worse in Christmas observance, is the sentimental moan. The moaner here is a Crewkerne journalist, Willis Watson, and he is writing in 1919 about the good old days celebrating in a farmhouse fifty years earlier. So he looked back with rose-tinted nostalgic pleasure to precisely the period and circumstance which Jefferies treated with such disdain.

Not Like the Old Days
W G Willis Watson

HRISTMAS DAY! WHAT memories it recalls – the bells ringing in the church tower before morning had well dawned, the bursting stockings hanging at the foot of the bed which Santa Claus had stuffed to bursting point

---

1   Jefferies, R, *Field and farm* (1957), 29-34 (originally published in 1877).

during the night, the Christmas cards bringing old friends nearer to one at the very threshold of the great festival; the 'Happy Christmas' from father and mother, brothers and sisters, the red holly and the pearly berried mistletoe, the decorated church and the singing of the Christmas hymns, the turkey at the head of the dinner table, the plum pudding flying the Union Jack, the games afterwards, the iced cake at tea on which was perched Robin Redbreast, then more games, another look at the presents, followed by snap-dragon, then the loving 'Good-night', the snow-white bed, and sweet sleep.

What happy Christmas Days were those we youngsters in our dear old Somerset enjoyed years ago. They are not the same today; they cannot be. The wheels of time have travelled on and change has succeeded change. The things which gave the greatest possible delight to the children of years ago would be scorned by the superior children of today. But are the latter any happier? Are they as happy as when they made their own enjoyments, made their own Christmas decorations, when mothers made their own Christmas puddings, when father made the arrangement by which the Christmas tree revolved?

This latter incident has recalled to my wife, sitting by my side, a real native of Somerset, the Christmas parties of her youth, some fifty years ago, when she and the other members of the family regularly visited a fine old Tudor farmhouse in the neighbourhood of Chard. Here resided a good farmer and his wife and family – a son and a daughter. They, too, were of the Somerset breed – with hearts as true as gold, full of hospitality, and especially happy when others were also happy. Theirs was a lovely old home, with mullioned windows, and a great water wheel at the side used to drive the mill.

The children were fetched in a dog-cart, and on arrival were warmly welcomed. What a dinner was provided – real old-fashioned fare of roast goose and Christmas pudding. The great kitchen was gaily decorated with holly, mistletoe, and evergreens. Then, later on, they wended their way to the dining hall to revel in the delights of the Christmas tree. The youngest member of the party drew aside a hanging curtain very slowly, and what a sight met their gaze! There was a great Christmas tree, lighted by coloured candles. From the branches depended the most beautiful articles. Hours had been spent in its decoration. There were little figures of Father Christmas, old men and women and children, dangling at the end of elastic, bobbed, and winked at the merry youngsters, as if to welcome them, silver and gold tinsel made the little parcels which contained the most delightful prizes sparkle in the light, and as the tree revolved a veritable fairy scene met the view of the children. Their wonder found expression in various ways, and shouts of delight volleyed and thundered around the walls of the room upon which days had been spent in making it a veritable Christmas picture.

For weeks the good hostess and her friends had been busily engaged in threading holly berries, which now formed all kinds of designs and spelt out words of seasonable welcome. The excitement of the youngsters increased when the time came for stripping the tree. Bags containing numbers corresponding with numbers attached to the articles on the tree were passed round, and each little visitor drew one. What prizes were won amid shouts of delight! All had as many as they could carry. One little maid received from the tree a robin standing on a log of wood, and inside the log was a bottle of scent. She loves robins to this day; another a cloth hedgehog, with its back stuck full of pins; yet another, an egg on a rustic stand, from underneath which a mouse was peeping; others had boxes of bricks. A gun fell to the lot of a bonny boy, and 'thousands of cats' he shot with it in the days which followed. What a chatter, what laughter, what joy. These were happy days.

Then there were games of forfeits, crackers were exploded, and the little ones adorned their pretty little selves with aprons, caps, and jewellery, which were found in the innermost recesses of the crackers. And how lovely were the sugared almonds; there are none like them today. And how the little figures danced on the glass covering the large musical box. Everyone was merry, the hostess perhaps most of all, for she was delighted when entertaining children. Then tea, then games, then oranges and muscatels, everything to make their young hearts glad. And Father Christmas looked down at them from the top of the tree and veritably smiled, for is he not the god of the children? And the robins among the sparkling frosted holly leaves seemed to chirrup with delight.

And, of course, there were Christmas cards, and one which came from this dear old farmhouse was carefully treasured for many years. It bore a picture of a little girl dressed in a blue frock, a white coat, and ermine muff, and a pale blue hat with a band of fur, a crown of red velvet, and a blue feather. The little fairy was walking down the steps of a house carrying a bunch of holly and mistletoe. After fifty years that card is still remembered, still treasured in memory. Perhaps the dear old hostess, still alive, may have forgotten this card, bur the recipient has not.

What a number of things there were to do on this Christmas Day besides stripping the Christmas tree. The blue roan pony, Daniel, had to be visited in his stall, the turkeys and geese inspected, the water wheel visited, and the birds had to have their Christmas dinner. The old squire has passed away, but the old dame still lives, and those children who are left of that merry party still bear in fond remembrance the happy times spent in the old Tudor house. Never a Christmas comes round but the merry scenes are recalled – the happiest Christmas festivals of their lives. It may be today there are far grander presents, far grander parties, but the spirit of hospitality shown by the old folks has never been finer, for they had hearts of gold. How delightful to recall the old days in dear old Somerset, the days of one's childhood, the days when merry Christmas was a real children's festival.[1]

---

1 Watson, W G Willis, *Calendar of customs, superstitions, weather-lore . . . connected with the county of Somerset* (1920), 459-62.

In memory the farmer has become confused with the squire, and Christmas trees and cards have become regarded as old traditions, whereas in fact they were both recent arrivals at the time Willis Watson was recalling. Even more anachronistically he seems to be pushing back into the 1860s the American import of a Santa Claus who filled stockings, which did not become commonplace in England until after 1880, and was not identified with Father Christmas until the 1890s.[1]

The truth seems to be that most groups in society by the 1860s had retreated from the communal feast of earlier times into the 'family' Christmas championed by their role model, Queen Victoria. Louisa Colfox, for instance, chatelaine of Rax house, the seat of Bridport's leading gentry family, for Christmas dinner 1867 prepared a lengthy toast to all her family members, present and absent – no mention of any tenants sharing in the festivities.

Louisa Colfox's Toast

HOUGH SMALL THE number meeting here
Each has the one to them most dear
And health to eat our Christmas cheer
And hope to greet the coming year

---

1   Pimlott, J A R, *The Englishman's Christmas: a social history* (1978), 113-19.

Love and a hearty welcome to you all
Welcome dear Mother, welcome Minnie Small
Welcome Tom's brother, welcome sister Anna
Welcome Miss Carter, in the kindest manner

Alfred of all the dear and hopeful heir
And Alice welcome hearth and home to share
Friends to our daughter from her birth
May ye all cheer each other whilst on earth

Now Father Christmas swift winged thought pray aid
Till we have many a kindly visit paid
First then to Sambourne, venerated Mother
A kiss to you, dear Ellen, your [sic] another

To Knapton House, Arthur and sister Blanche
Kind love to you, and each young olive branch
To Bognor next and here bowed down with years
Kind Uncle William – then good Kate appears.

Heigh presto! Now we cross Atlantic Ocean
Dear Uncle George! to you love and devotion!
Of wife and children health and home bereft
The peace, that passeth understanding thou hast left.

Now back again good Christmas! back to Plush
There sits Aunt Miller, silence now oh hush
In her best gown, and dignified white hair
The hour she sats [sic], in her nice easy chair.

In Grafton St. in London now we go
Forget Aunt Mary Anne, oh no, no, no

And then by taking just a little dodge
We'll drop in on our friends at Tulse Hill Lodge

And at the Davis's we would appear
And wish them happy Christmas and new year
At Mrs Battiscombe we'll take a peep
And solitary Kate we'll take a peep.

Now back to Rax good Christmas thus it ends
With health to all absent and present friends.[1]

It was a similar story at the rectory, in this case West Stafford Rectory, near Dorchester, in 1866. Mother and daughter, Emily and Alice Smith, both recorded Christmas day in their diaries. Mother first:

Christmas in the Rectory

UR DARLING ALICE'S 18th Birthday [on Christmas Day]. We gave her as the joint gift of Parents and brothers and sisters a 50s. gold chain for her watch – and I added a Book of the Communion – May God give her His blessed Spirit and root and ground her in the truth and make

1   DHC D/COL/F23.

her a true disciple of the Saviour. We heard from darling Boz himself who spoke of Mrs Jardine's refusing to let him travel yesterday for fear of consequences – and that he felt so sad to be absent for the first time on Christmas day. Flora wrote also so nicely and sensibly, and both hope to come tomorrow. God grant he may run no risk, and be strengthened to come with real benefit! I played the Harmonium twice and had 3 Hymns at each service. We had a nice address [by] Jn Reggy before the Lord's Supper. Henry, Walter, and Alice rec'd it with me, and Jack helped Papa – Reggy preached on the Saviour's Birthday in the afternoon, 2d Luke – I sat with G' Floyer. We had the usual Xtmas Dinner at 6 – and 'Buz' after. I felt very tired and had a doze and after Tea sang.

And here is what Alice chose to record:

. . . Various bands of singers passed by house in evening [Christmas Eve]. Began W. Irving's Christmas story after Wicked Robber [a game referred to earlier]. The hall nicely decorated. In morning [Christmas Day] Mamie gave me a card case of mother-of-pearl. Heard from Mary M. Miss Bucanon sent photo of herself. Georgie Thomas and Miss Bushnan wrote and sent me an ivory bracelet. All the rest gave me a gold watch chain, and Mama a book for Communion. We gave Reggy [presumably their curate] a Xmas stocking, and stood round dining room table while he pulled the things out. Brats gave presents to the babies. I, Jag and Toby then went round to give our presents to servants. I gave collars and cuffs. Church nicely decorated. Papa made a short sermon, stayed to sacrament, Then lunched off soup, etc. Played with Eva in the garden before 2nd church. Rather gloomy day. Bos rather better. Rainy after church. Sat with Josey and Baby. Had Xmas dinner at 6, turkey, flaming plum pudding, snapdragon, champagne, etc, etc. Reggy came down to half of it. Played Buz and Personal game after. Mama not very well. Bos wrote and seemed anxious about himself. Mrs Floyer came and saw the children.[1]

Of course, for a child, or even for a grown man imagining himself back into childhood, it was the food that mattered. Here is Edward Slow of Wilton, dialect rhymer, with one of his most popular pieces – the opening lines were even incorporated into the Shrewton mummers' play.

Figgetty Pooden
Edward Slow

AH, WEN I wur a girt hard bwoy,
We appetite nar mossel coy,
Tha baste thing out ta gie I joy
    Wur a girt big figgetty pooden.

Tha very neam ow'un zeem'd anuff
An ta smill un, ow did meak I puff,
An lor, ow I did vill an stuff,
    When mother mead a pooden.

1   DHC D500/4, 6.

Hache birthday she wur sure ta meak,
A girt plum pooden, an a keak,
An ax a vew vrens to parteak,
      Of her nice figgetty pooden.

Tho mother adden much ta spend
She mead un good ya may depend,
An purty quick ther wur a end,
      A thick ar birthday pooden.

Na vear a any on't getten stale,
If I wur handy an wur hale,
Me appetite hood never wail,
      As long as ther wur pooden.

Not that I wur a girt big glutton
Like thic chap, as ate a laig a mutton,
Tho me waiscut oft I did unbutton
      When twur a extry girt un.

When I wur in tha village choir,
An a veast wur gied ess be tha Squire,
Tha us'd ta com in ael a vire,
      An as black mwoast as me hat.

An twur rare vun to zee em smoke,
Var in wine an brandy they did zoak,
An pon me zong it wur no joke,
      Aten much a that ar pooden.

Var mezelf I'd zooner av em plain,
Zo's you can cut an com again,
Wieout tha dread a gien ee pain,

Like tha there brandy poodens.

Wen in ta Zalsbry oft I went,
Var measter on a errant zent,
I warn, mwoast ael me brass wur spent,
    In buyin zim figgetty pooden.

I used ta knaa a leetle shop,
In Brown Street, wur I off did pop,
An well vill up me ungry crop,
    We nice sweet figgetty pooden.

Tha used ta beak em in a tin.
An tha ooman she did offen grin,
Ta zee ow zoon I did ate in
    Her nice hot figgetty pooden.

Times on times we vun she've cried,
An wur ablidged ta hould her zide,
Ta zee ow zoon away I'd hide,
    That ar dree penneth a pooden.

It done her good she did declare,
Ta zee I ate me pooden there,
An she aelways gied I mwourn me shear,
    Cos I wur vond a pooden.

Ah, oft I thinks apon tha time,
When Crismis bells merry da chime,
What a girt pooden, nice an prime,
    Mother did meak var we.

A used ta come in steamin hot,

Nearly as big's a waishen pot.
Wie vigs an currands zich a lot,
     In thick ar Crismis pooden.

Lore, ow me young eyes glissen'd at un,
An fiather he did zay, 'Odd drat 'un,'
I do believe while I wur chatten,
     Thic bwoy ud ate thic pooden.

Dree sorrens on't I aelwys had,
An fiather he did look like mad,
Bit mother she wur aelwys glad,
     An zay 'Lar let'n av his pooden.'

A coose, I diden av much mate,
Nar gierden stuff apon me plate,
An pooden aelwys wur a trate,
     Specily thick one at Crismis.

Tho I own, I did av mworn me wack,
Me lips var mwore did offen smack,
An me waistcut offen wur main slack,
     Wen tha pooden wur ael gone.

His mother once mead a girt pooden,
Thinkin she'd gie her bwoy a dooin;
Atter aten till na mwore a cooden,
     Cry'd, cos a adden vinish'd un.

Wen I grow'd up a biggish bwoy,
Wat thay calls a hobbledehoy,
Tha chaps did try I to annoy
     Be caalin out 'Figgetty pooden.'

Bit there I diden use ta keer,
Var ael ther chaff, an joke, an sneer,
I diden stop it, never vear,
      Wen ther wur any pooden.

A contented bwoy I aelways wur,
An diden cry an meak a stur,
Wen he wur gone cos there wurnt mwore,
      Like a bwoy I knaas who did.

If ever I da av a wife,
Ta liv wie I ael drop thease life,
I'll tell her, if she dwoant want strife,
      Ta meak I plenty a poodens.

Begar, I hooden mind betten a crown,
That if a chap is mainly down,
Nuthen ull cure un I'll be bown,
      Like a girt big figgetty pooden.

A zeems ta drave ael keer away,
An meak yer heart veel light an gay,
That you'll zeem merry ael tha day
      Atter aten figgetty pooden.

Zoo teak thease hint ael labourers wives
If you da wish var happy lives,
You'll av em zure, if you contrives
      Ta get lots a figgetty poodens.

If ya caant avoord much butcher's mate,
Ta putt apon yer husbin's plate,

Putt avore un then, what he can ate,
    A nice girt figgetty pooden.

His health an straingth it will zustain,
An vlesh he's zartin zure to gain,
An a unger never he'll complain,
    If ya gets un lots a pooden.

Meself, ael things I hood gie up,
Even do wieout me pipe an cup,
Var I cud dinner, tay, an zup,
    On a nice girt figgetty pooden.[1]

Naturally you'll be wanting the recipe for this gastronomic treat. In another of Slow's efforts, a rather banal short story, he supplies us with the ingredients and the method – but still in thick Wiltshire dialect.

One Crismiss, Tom's wife had a leetle bit a money laved her be a woold uncle; zoo she promised her bwoys that shood av a downright good trate a figgetty pooden Crismis day. Zoo a day ar two avore, there wur zich a ta do in Tom's cottage, meaken an stirri up tha batter var that poodens; there wur a gallin an haaf a baste vlower, poun an haaf a brade crumbs, vower poun a beef zuet, zix poun a vigs, zix poun a currands, two poun a zultannys, poun a orange peel, haaf poun a hoss

1   Slow, E, *The Wiltshire Moonrakers edition of West Countrie Rhymes* (1903), 123-7.

- 324 -

spice, a dozen haigs, an haaf a pint a brandy, twer ael put into a girt washen pan, an Tom, he's wife, and bwoys ael had a good goo in at that stirren on it up; when trur done and mead up, there wur zeven nice girt big figgetty poodens; zoo thay wur ael tied up in cloths and bwiled var zix howers in that girt washen copper. Now mind, zays ther mother, we shill av two var Crismis an one every Zundy atterwards till thame gone, an be that time ael o'ee ull be about zick a figgetty poodens I specs. Zoo two on em wur duly got rid of at Crismis, an tha raste on em put in beasins ael in a row on tha top shelf a tha kitchen cupboard.[1]

Something of the spirit of Christmas benevolence to one's social inferiors still lingered in the minds of the Victorian gentry, and this often took the form of paying for a special meal or 'treat'. Scan the last December issue of any local newspaper, and you will find a page or more of reports similar to the following, from Devizes and Calne at Christmas 1892 and 1890 respectively.

Christmas Treats

REAT TO SCHOOL CHILDREN: The Mayor (Mr G.H. Mead) on Friday evening entertained the children attending the [Devizes] British Schools to a tea, in the Corn Exchange.

There were three long rows of tables extending the whole length of the hall and each was crowded. There were over 500 children present. The tea was supplied by Mr Stevens and Mr Ellen, and a number of ladies and gentlemen, including the Mayor and the Mayoress and the teachers waited. For more than an hour the children, with children's

---

1   Slow, E, *Humourous West Countrie Tales*, undated pamphlet [c.1905], 3-4. Note that this story, entitled 'Tha Bran Figgetty Pooden', is not included in the 1899 collection of tales.

appetites, kept their attendants exceedingly busy. Plenty of bread and butter and cake was supplied, and was put away with astonishing celerity to the accompaniment of a band in the gallery and a babel of voices below. After a long time the unrestrained prompting to satisfy the demands of autocratic stomachs became less active and on the other hand vociferation became more loud and insuppressible. In due time all were satisfied, and then the tables were removed and games of various kinds were indulged in and were superintended by the Mayor, Mayoress, teachers, and other friends of the school. After an evening's fun, which will be remembered for a long time, the children separated, not without cheers loud and prolonged for the Mayor and Mayoress, who had so thoughtfully remembered the little ones and contributed to their happiness in the season of good-will.[1]

CHRISTMAS AT CALNE WORKHOUSE: Great pains were taken to brighten the lot of the 84 inmates on Christmas day. In the morning each inmate was presented with a Christmas card and letter, generously provided by Miss Wickham, of Bournemouth. The dining-hall and wards were very prettily decorated for the occasion. The dinner consisted of roast beef and plum pudding, of which there was a liberal supply; one pint of ale was served to each adult, and in addition one ounce of tobacco was distributed to each man, and half an ounce of snuff to the women, the children and those in the sick wards receiving oranges and sweets. Mr T. Harris sent a present of one shilling each to the men, ninepence to the women, and sixpence to the children. Mr and Mrs E.R. Henly, Mr and Mrs T. Harris, together with several ladies and gentlemen of the neighbourhood, were present in the dining-hall. In addition to the above Lord Henry Bruce, MP, sent a liberal supply of tobacco for the men; a quarter of a pound of tea, one pound of lump sugar, and half an ounce of snuff for each woman; and plum cake, oranges and sweets for the children. After tea, the master,

1   *Devizes & Wiltshire Gazette*, 22 Dec. 1892.

matron, porter and nurse, together with the inmates, assembled in the dining-hall, where the children sang several Christmas carols, and a number of well-rendered songs and recitations were given, a very pleasant and enjoyable evening being brought to a close by the singing of the National Anthem. Cheers were given in very hearty fashion for the guardians, Lord Henry Bruce, Mr T. Harris, and the master and matron, after which the inmates retired to their respective rooms, apparently happy and contented, and grateful for the kindness that had been bestowed upon them.[1]

Such events, as reported in the local press, generally passed off with due decorum and respect – unless, that is, strong liquor was taken in excess. Then things might go awry. Our trawl through the Christmas menu concludes with a cautionary tale, from the pen of the essayist and novelist Maurice Hewlett, of Broad Chalke close to the Wiltshire-Dorset border. He was writing in 1922.

Mead
Maurice Hewlett

ND FOR OUR drink, it will be mead. Metheglin, if you will have it; I prefer the monosyllable. It is a noble liquor, but asks, even demands, moderation. Personally I take it in a liqueur glass, like cherry brandy, which, however, it does not at all resemble. There is nothing sweet about good mead; nothing sticky or viscid. It is a thin, clear, amber-coloured bever, slightly aromatic, very insidious, ruthless to those who exceed. And to explain how ruthless, to what exceeding bitter end, I cannot do better than wind up my essay with the story of Farmer Hackbush, Farmer Norton and Farmer Gell, who met at the house of a friend

---

1   *Marlborough Times*, 3 Jan. 1891.

on the border of this shire last Boxing Day, and revelled, not wisely, upon mead. They revelled long and deeply, until they were conveyed somehow to the station and heaved into the milk-train of the small hours, consigned to the guard; all for the same destination and, as it turned out, destiny. For at their wayside station, where they were duly heaved out into the breathless, dewy dark – that intense dark of the hours before dawn – they were conveyed into the three tax-carts and slumbering boys which awaited them. They were heaved in – Farmer Hackbush, Farmer Norton, Farmer Gell; mechanically they took and shook the reins, and murmured Cooorroop! And each of them, thanks to a sober, instructed cob, reached a house, an open front door, and an awaiting matron in a dressing-gown. But none reached his own front door. For Farmer Hackbush was heaved into the front door and arms of Mrs Gell, and Farmer Gell into those of Mrs Norton, and Farmer Norton into those of Mrs Hackbush. All at 5 am. And what happened next, in each or any case, I don't know.[1]

---

1   Hewlett, M, *Extemporary essays* (1922), 174-5.

10
Misrule, Mischief, Mishap, Mistletoe: The Christmas Party

RIDAY DECEMBER 17TH was the date chosen by Mrs Comfort to hold her Junior Party – only boys under twelve years of age being invited. As the hall clock chimed six, small boys in Eton collars and Sunday suits were to be seen shyly wending their way to the drawing room, where Mrs Comfort was waiting to receive them.

Previously a number of small objects had been cleverly hidden about the room, so each boy was provided with a pencil and card on which to write the names of the things he found. After searching carefully for about ten minutes the small competitors were seen to be anxiously comparing their number of successes, another five minutes and all the cards were collected and given to Mr Comfort for correction.

Later on, games were played in the dining hall. It was great fun to see the boys trying to balance themselves in a basket hung on a brush handle resting on two chairs. They were given a stick with which to steady themselves sufficiently to knock off the pennies on the chairs without overbalancing. This looked an easy task and many a boy confidently waited his turn – but, alas! he shared the fate of his predecessors! 'Basket on top, boy underneath!'

If one can judge by the amount of laughing and singing which accompanied the game of 'Musical Chairs', it certainly should be voted one of the favourites of the evening. As the number of players decreased so the excitement increased, until at last only two boys were left – then another few bars of music, which suddenly stopped, left the proud victor seated on the remaining chair.

Various other games were played until eight o'clock, when supper was served in the library. Seven of the tallest boys were chosen by Mr Comfort to help him look after the ladies and younger guests.

The supper table was very artistically arranged. In the centre, surrounded by gaily lighted candles, was a tall trifle shaped like a tower, containing a variety of charms. After justice had been paid to sandwiches, sausage-rolls, mince pies, cakes and jellies, the trifle was served. For a while everyone was very quiet, then there was a general chorus of, 'Look what I've found!' or, 'I've found a lucky shoe!' or, 'Here's Pip, Squeak or Wilfred!'

When supper was over the boys returned to the drawing room, where Mrs Comfort distributed small prizes to the winners of the different games. The lights were then turned out and the room was transformed into a veritable Fairy-land by the stars that showered from the 'sparklers' held by the boys.

The ringing of the front door bell announced the arrival of parents and friends, so after the boys had said goodnight to Mrs Comfort, and thanked her for such a pleasant evening, the party broke up.

A mild introduction to the world of the Christmas party, where everything goes to plan and a good time is had by all. It had to, of course, because this was the report written up in the school magazine for parents (and prospective parents) to read. The year was 1927, and the rather genteel establishment for boys was Lewisham School in Landemann Circus, Weston super Mare, which was supervised by the headmaster and his wife, Mr and Mrs Comfort.[1] *Typical of hundreds of similar celebrations, such parties were the sanitised descendants of much more rumbustious affairs. Usually such occasions passed off happily, though chaos or even tragedy might ensue.*

William Barnes took his partying seriously, and made sure that everyone enjoyed themselves. He was a fine poet, and any difficulties in grasping his meaning are amply repaid by the quality of his images. Hardy held his work in such esteem that in 1908 he edited and published a selection of Barnes's best poems (in which he included 'Chris'mas Invitation'). In this and its sequel, 'Keepen up o' Chris'mas', a whole catalogue of amusements and customs is presented for us to chew over and join in.

Chris'mas Invitation and Keepen up o' Chris'mas
William Barnes

CHRIS'MAS INVITATION

Come down to-morrow night; an' mind,
Don't leave thy fiddle-bag behind;

---

1   *Lewisham Newsletter*, Easter 1928, 14-15 (copy in Weston super Mare Local Studies Library).

We'll sheake a lag, an' drink a cup
O' eale, to keep wold Chris'mas up.

An' let thy sister teake thy earm,
The walk won't do her any harm;
There's noo dirt now to spweil her frock,
The ground's a-vroze so hard's a rock.

You won't meet any stranger's feace,
But only naighbours o' the pleace,
An' Stowe, an' Combe; an' two or dree
Vrom uncle's up at Rookery.

An' thou wu'lt vind a rwosy feace,
An' peair ov eyes so black as sloos,
The prettiest woones in all the pleace, –
I'm sure I needen tell thee whose.

We got a back-bran', dree girt logs
So much as dree ov us can car;
We'll put em up athirt the dogs,
An' meake a vier to the bar.

An' ev'ry woone shall tell his teale,
An' ev'ry woone shall zing his zong,
An' ev'ry woone wull drink his eale
To love an' frien'ship all night long.

We'll snap the tongs, we'll have a ball,
We'll sheake the house, we'll lift the ruf,
We'll romp an' meake the maidens squall,
A-catchen o'm at blind-man's buff.

Zoo come to-morrow night; an' mind,
Don't leave thy fiddle-bag behind;
We'll sheake a lag, an' drink a cup
O' eale, to keep wold Chris'mas up.

EEPEN UP O' CHRIS'MAS

An' zoo you didden come athirt,
To have zome fun last night: how wer't?
Vor we'd a-workd wi' all our might
To scour the iron things up bright,
An' brush'd an' scrubb'd the house all drough;
An' brought in vor a brand, a plock
O' wood so big's an uppen-stock,
An' hung a bough o' misseltoo,
An' ax'd a merry friend or two,
      To keepen up o' Chris'mas.

An' there wer wold an' young; an' Bill,
Soon after dark, stalk'd up vrom mill.
An' when he wer a-comen near,
He whissled loud vor me to hear;
Then roun' my head my frock I roll'd,
An' stood in orcha'd like a post,
To meake en think I wer a ghost.
But he wer up to't, an' did scwold
To vind me stannen in the cwold,
      A-keepen up o' Chris'mas.

We play'd at forfeits, an' we spun
The trencher roun', an' meade such fun!
An' had a geame o' dree-ceard loo,
An' then begun to hunt the shoe.

An' all the wold vo'k zitten near,
A-chatten roun' the vier pleace,
Did smile in woone another's feace,
An'sheake right hands wi' hearty cheer,
An' let their left hands spill their beer,
    A-keepen up o' Chrismas.[1]

William Barnes was a clergyman as well as a poet, and his work was admired not only by Hardy, but also by another man of the cloth who was not afraid to let his hair down, Francis Kilvert. In his diary Kilvert records at length a trip he made in 1874 to visit the Dorset bard.[2] But after Christmas 1872 he had other pleasures to report.

A Curate goes Wild
Francis Kilvert

T 8 O'CLOCK Fanny, Dora and I went to a jolly party at Sir John Awdrys at Notton House [near Lacock, north Wiltshire]. Almost everybody in the neighbourhood was there. There had been a children's party with a Christmas

1   Barnes, W, *Poems* (1962 ed.), i, 176-7
2   Plomer, W (ed.), *Kilvert's diary* (1960 ed.), ii, 437-44.

Tree at 5 o'clock, but when we drove up the harp and the fiddles were going. 'Bang went the drum, the ball opened immediately, and I knew not which dancer most to admire,' but I think it was – Francie Rooke. Dear little Francie Rooke. The dining room was turned into the ball room, beautifully lighted overhead, and the smooth polished oaken floor went magnificently, just like glass, but not a bit too slippery, though Eliza Stiles came down with a crash full on her back in Sir Roger de Coverley, and there was a roar of laughter which, combined with Eliza's fall, shook the room.

I danced a Lancers with Harriet Awdry of Draycot Rectory, a quadrille with Sissy Awdry of Seagry Vicarage, a Lancers with Louise Awdry of Draycot Rectory, a Lancers with Mary Rooke of the Ivy, and Sir Roger with dear little Francie Rooke of the Ivy. How bright and pretty she looked, so merry, happy and full of fun. It was a grand Sir Roger. I never danced such a one. The room was quite full, two sets and such long lines, but the crush was all the more fun. 'Here,' said Francie Rooke to me quietly, with a wild, merry sparkle in her eye, and her face brilliant with excitement, 'let us go into the other set.' There was more fun going on there, Eliza Stiles had just fallen prostrate. There were screams of laughter and the dance was growing quite wild. There was a struggle for the corners and everyone wanted to be at the top. In a few minutes all order was lost, and everyone was dancing wildly and promiscuously with whoever came to hand. The dance grew wilder and wilder. 'The pipers loud and louder blew, the dancers quick and quicker flew.' Madder and madder screamed the flying fiddle bows. Sir Roger became a wild romp till the fiddles suddenly stopped dead and there was a scream of laughter. Oh, it was such fun and Francie Rooke was brilliant. When shall I have another such partner as Francie Rooke?

An excellent supper and we got home about one o'clock, on a fine moonlit night.[1]

1 Ibid., 305-6.

Thomas Hardy's earliest portrayal of Christmas among his Dorset neighbours supplied the opening to his first novel, The Poor Man and the Lady, *which he wrote in 1868, when he was 28 and working as an architect's assistant. It was never published, and the manuscript has not survived. But from it he appears to have rescued the Christmas episode, and adapted it for* Under the Greenwood Tree, *so that it has become one of the best-loved evocations of country merry-making in English literature.*

The Tranter's Party
Thomas Hardy

HE GUESTS HAD all assembled, and the tranter's party had reached that degree of development which accords with ten o'clock P.M. in rural assemblies. At that hour the sound of a fiddle in process of tuning was heard from the inner pantry.

'That's Dick,' said the tranter. 'That lad's crazy for a jig.'

'Dick! Now I cannot – really, I cannot have any dancing at all till Christmas-day is out,' said old William emphatically. 'When the clock ha' done striking twelve, dance as much as ye like.'

'Well, I must say there's reason in that, William,' said Mrs. Penny. 'If you do have a party on Christmas-night, 'tis only fair and honourable to the sky-folk to have it a sit-still party. Jigging parties be all very well on the Devil's holidays; but a jigging party looks suspicious now. O yes; stop till the clock strikes, young folk – so say I.'

It happened that some warm mead accidentally got into Mr. Spinks's head about this time.

'Dancing,' he said, 'is a most strengthening, livening, and courting movement, 'specially with a little beverage added! And dancing is good. But why disturb what is ordained, Richard and Reuben, and the company ghinerally? Why, I ask, as far as that do go?'

'Then nothing till after twelve,' said William.

Though Reuben and his wife ruled on social points, religious questions were mostly disposed of by the old man, whose firmness on this head quite counterbalanced a certain weakness in his handling of domestic matters. The hopes of the younger members of the household were therefore relegated to a distance of one hour and three-quarters – a result that took visible shape in them by a remote and listless look about the eyes – the singing of songs being permitted in the interim.

At five minutes to twelve the soft tuning was again heard in the back quarters; and when at length the clock had whizzed forth the last stroke, Dick appeared ready primed, and the instruments were boldly handled; old William very readily taking the bass-viol from its accustomed nail, and touching the strings as irreligiously as could be desired.

The country-dance called the 'Triumph, or Follow my Lover,' was the figure with which they opened. The tranter took for his partner Mrs. Penny, and Mrs. Dewy was chosen by Mr. Penny, who made so much of his limited height by a judicious carriage of the head, straightening of the back, and important flashes of his spectacle-glasses, that he seemed almost as tall as the tranter. Mr. Shiner, age about thirty-five, farmer and church-warden, a character principally composed of a crimson stare, vigorous breath, and a watch-chain, with a mouth hanging on a dark smile but never smiling, had come quite willingly to the party, and showed a wondrous obliviousness of all his antics on the previous night. But the comely, slender, prettily-dressed prize Fancy Day fell to Dick's lot, in spite of some private machinations of the farmer, for the reason that Mr. Shiner, as a richer man, had shown too much assurance in asking the favour, whilst Dick had been duly courteous.

We gain a good view of our heroine as she advances to her place in the ladies' line. She belonged to the taller division of middle height. Flexibility was her first characteristic, by which she appeared to enjoy the most easeful rest when she was in gliding motion. Her dark eyes

– arched by brows of so keen, slender, and soft a curve, that they resembled nothing so much as two slurs in music – showed primarily a bright sparkle each. This was softened by a frequent thoughtfulness, yet not so frequent as to do away, for more than a few minutes at a time, with a certain coquettishness; which in its turn was never so decided as to banish honesty. Her lips imitated her brows in their clearly-cut outline and softness of bend; and her nose was well shaped – which is saying a great deal, when it is remembered that there are a hundred pretty mouths and eyes for one pretty nose. Add to this, plentiful knots of dark– brown hair, a gauzy dress of white, with blue facings; and the slightest idea may be gained of the young maiden who showed, amidst the rest of the dancing-ladies, like a flower among vegetables. And so the dance proceeded. Mr. Shiner, according to the interesting rule laid down, deserted his own partner, and made off down the middle with this fair one of Dick's – the pair appearing from the top of the room like two persons tripping down a lane to be married. Dick trotted behind with what was intended to be a look of composure, but which was, in fact, a rather silly expression of feature – implying, with too much earnestness, that such an elopement could not be tolerated. Then they turned and came back, when Dick grew more rigid around his mouth, and blushed with ingenuous ardour as he joined hands with the rival and formed the arch over his lady's head; which presumably gave the figure its name; relinquishing her again at setting to partners, when Mr. Shiner's new chain quivered in every link, and all the loose flesh upon the tranter – who here came into action again – shook like jelly. Mrs. Penny, being always rather concerned for her personal safety when she danced with the tranter, fixed her face to a chronic smile of timidity the whole time it lasted – a peculiarity which filled her features with wrinkles, and reduced her eyes to little straight lines like hyphens, as she jigged up and down opposite him; repeating in her own person not only his proper movements, but also the minor flourishes which the richness of the tranter's imagination led him to introduce from time to time –

an imitation which had about it something of slavish obedience, not unmixed with fear.

The ear-rings of the ladies now flung themselves wildly about, turning violent summersaults, banging this way and that, and then swinging quietly against the ears sustaining them. Mrs. Crumpler – a heavy woman, who, for some reason which nobody ever thought worth inquiry, danced in a clean apron – moved so smoothly through the figure that her feet were never seen; conveying to imaginative minds the idea that she rolled on castors.

Minute after minute glided by, and the party reached the period when ladies' back-hair begins to look forgotten and dissipated; when a perceptible dampness makes itself apparent upon the faces even of delicate girls – a ghastly dew having for some time rained from the features of their masculine partners; when skirts begin to be torn out of their gathers; when elderly people, who have stood up to please their juniors, begin to feel sundry small tremblings in the region of the knees, and to wish the interminable dance was at Jericho; when (at country parties of the thorough sort) waistcoats begin to be unbuttoned, and when the fiddlers' chairs have been wriggled, by the frantic bowing of their occupiers, to a distance of about two feet from where they originally stood.

There is a brief respite, and then the dancers prepare for that most delightful of country-dances, in Hardy's opinion, the six-hands-round.

'Before we begin,' said the tranter, 'my proposal is, that 'twould be a right and proper plan for every mortal man in the dance to pull off his jacket, considering the heat.'

'Such low notions as you have, Reuben! Nothing but strip will go down with you when you are a-dancing. Such a hot man as he is!'

'Well, now, look here, my sonnies,' he argued to his wife, whom he often addressed in the plural masculine for economy of epithet merely; 'I don't see that. You dance and get hot as fire; therefore you lighten your clothes. Isn't that nature and reason for gentle and simple? If I strip by myself and not necessary, 'tis rather pot-housey I own; but if we stout chaps strip one and all, why, 'tis the native manners of the country, which no man can gainsay? Hey – what did you say, my sonnies?'

'Strip we will!' said the three other heavy men who were in the dance; and their coats were accordingly taken off and hung in the passage, whence the four sufferers from heat soon reappeared, marching in close column, with flapping shirt-sleeves, and having, as common to them all, a general glance of being now a match for any man or dancer in England or Ireland. Dick, fearing to lose ground in Fancy's good opinion, retained his coat like the rest of the thinner men; and Mr. Shiner did the same from superior knowledge.

And now a further phase of revelry had disclosed itself. It was the time of night when a guest may write his name in the dust upon the tables and chairs, and a bluish mist pervades the atmosphere, becoming a distinct halo round the candles; when people's nostrils, wrinkles, and crevices in general, seem to be getting gradually plastered up; when the very fiddlers as well as the dancers get red in the face, the dancers having advanced further still towards incandescence, and entered the cadaverous phase; the fiddlers no longer sit down, but kick back their chairs and saw madly at the strings, with legs firmly spread and eyes closed, regardless of the visible world. Again and again did Dick share his Love's hand with another man, and wheel round; then, more delightfully, promenade in a circle with her all to himself, his arm holding her waist more firmly each time, and his elbow getting further and further behind her back, till the distance reached was rather noticeable; and, most blissful, swinging to places shoulder to shoulder, her breath curling round his neck like a summer zephyr that had strayed from its proper date. Threading the couples one by one they reached the bottom, when there arose in Dick's mind a minor misery lest the tune should end before they could work their way to the top again, and have anew the same exciting run down through. Dick's feelings on actually reaching the top in spite of his doubts were supplemented by a mortal fear that the fiddling might even stop at this supreme moment; which prompted him to convey a stealthy whisper to the far– gone musicians, to the effect that they were not to leave off till he and his partner had reached the bottom of the dance once more, which remark was replied to by the nearest of those convulsed and quivering men by a private nod to the anxious young man between two semiquavers of the tune, and a simultaneous 'All right, ay, ay,' without opening the eyes. Fancy was now held so closely that Dick and she were practically one person. The room became to Dick like a picture in a dream; all that he could remember of it afterwards being the look of the fiddlers going to sleep, as humming-tops sleep, by increasing their motion and hum, together with the figures of grandfather James and old Simon Crumpler sitting by the chimney–corner, talking and nodding in dumb-show, and beating the air to their emphatic sentences like people near a threshing machine.

The dance ended. 'Piph-h-h-h!' said tranter Dewy, blowing out his breath in the very finest stream of vapour that a man's lips could form. 'A regular tightener, that one, sonnies!' He wiped his forehead, and went to the cider and ale mugs on the table.[1]

The quickening pace of life in Victorian England, the shrinking of horizons as the railways linked country to town, and the mass migration

1 Hardy, T, *Under the Greenwood Tree* (1974 ed.), 65-71 (abridged).

of impoverished village families to sprawling cities, all threatened to erode rural traditions, and to destroy patterns of life that had evolved over centuries. In consequence there grew among the reading public a feeling of nostalgia for the world that was embedded in nearly everyone's past, but was being forgotten. Hardy's novels caught this mood, and helped to foster it.

The customs and folklore which he described were also being studied, in a more scholarly way, by the late Victorian antiquaries. In Dorset the leading folklorist of the period Hardy counted as a friend, John Symonds Udal. He pursued a long and eminent career as a barrister, judge, and colonial administrator, which took him to Fiji, and ultimately to the Leeward Islands, where he held the post of Chief Justice. In 1911 he retired and began to write up his folklore notes. His book was eventually published in 1922, three years before his death. It incorporated many pieces which he had written for journals years before, including notes on 'Christmas in Dorsetshire'. Here are Udal's remarks about one of the popular Christmas games played at the party described by William Barnes.

Playing Forfeits
John Symonds Udal

LAYING FORFEITS WAS a very favourite amusement with Dorset folk during the long winter evenings, and more particularly at Christmas-tide, when the family circle had generally more than its usual complement. There should be, if possible, twenty or thirty present to play forfeits properly, who arrange themselves round the room as conveniently as possible, and should be careful to be provided with some trifling article wherewith to pay the forfeits should any be incurred.

In some places the players sit in two lines opposite each other, each holding in his or her hand a piece of paper, or pencil, or thimble, or some such slight article, wherewith to pay their forfeit in case they should make a mistake in answering.

A common form of playing forfeits was that of a game which involved a question and answer. Two persons sat in front of the party, one of whom says as follows: 'Here's a poor old sailor just come from the sea, pray what have you got to give him ?' Whoever is called upon to answer the question must be careful not to mention the word 'red', 'white', 'blue' or 'black', or even, sometimes, give the name of any colour at all; and must not say 'yes' or 'no', – in default of which she or he will have to pay a forfeit. The questioner then passes on to the next one, and says: 'Here's a poor old sailor just come from sea, pray what have you got to give him ? ' The one questioned must be careful only to answer, 'Nothing at all.' The other replies, 'Nothing at all!' and with an insinuating attempt to obtain an answer that will subject the speaker to a forfeit will add, 'Not a red coat?' or 'Not a blue hat?' On the person interrogated persisting in replying 'Nothing at all', the other moves on, in the hope of getting a more favourable response out of another player; and so on, until the questioner has gone all round. After this has been done, any forfeits that may have been obtained have to be redeemed by those persons who have been so unfortunate as to incur them.

Another form of playing forfeits was called 'Yes, No, Black, and White', these being the four words which must not be mentioned in the answer. In this game any kind of question was permitted.

This was sometimes called 'The old soldier', when each of the party in turn must take a poker in the right hand and knock, and, passing it to his neighbour with the left, say: 'An old soldier is come to town, what will you please to give him? You may answer whatever you like, except 'yes', 'no', 'white', or 'black'. The object is to induce the person interrogated to use one or other of these words, when a forfeit occurs.

Another form the game would sometimes take was that of a 'word puzzle', when an outlandish single word, or a curiously involved sentence had to be repeated several times (seven or nine was the usual number) without a mistake; on failure of which a forfeit was exacted.

The following is a specimen of such a word: 'Aldibirondi-fosdiforniosdikos'; and this of a sentence: 'Of all the saws I ever saw saw, I never saw a saw saw as that saw saws.'

Here is another of a slightly different character in a versified form:

A twister of twist once twisted a twist,
And the twist that he twisted was a three-twisted twist;
But in twisting the twist one twist came untwisted,
And the twist that untwisted untwisted the twist.

There is another one, which I can give but imperfectly, for I can only remember up to twelve, though I fancy there are eighteen or more ; and an old Dorsetshire lady from whom I have heard it has now (in her ninetieth year) forgotten it. It is as follows, and each rhyme is to be repeated backwards as in the last:

A gaping, wide-mouthed, waddling frog,
Two pudding-ends won't choke a dog;
Three monkeys tied to a log
Four mares stuck in a bog;
Five puppy-dogs and our dog Ball
Loudly for their breakfast call;
Six beetles on a wall,
Close to an old woman's apple-stall;
Seven lobsters in a dish,
As good as any heart can wish;
Eight cobblers, cobblers all,
Working with their tools and awl;
Nine comets in the sky,
Some are low and some are high;

Ten peacocks in the air,
I wonder how they all got there –
You don't know and I don't care;
Eleven ships sailing on the main,
Some bound for France and some for Spain,
I wish them all safe back again;
Twelve hunters, hares, and hounds,
Hunting over other men's grounds."

The redemption of the forfeits takes place in the following way. Two persons, as before, remain in front of the others, the one sitting in a chair facing the party, the other kneeling down and laying his or her head in the lap of the other, with the face downwards. The person sitting in the chair will hold the forfeited article that is about to be redeemed over the bent head of the person kneeling in front of her, and will say as follows: 'Here's a thing, and a very pretty thing! What must the owner of this pretty thing do to redeem it again?' Or, 'What must the owner do to receive it again?' Whatever the person who has his or her head in the other's lap (and who, of course, cannot see what or whose is the article held up) says the owner of that article must do, or the forfeit cannot be redeemed, let it never be so much prized. The penalties of redemption sometimes oblige the ordeal of crawling up the chimney, or, at least, attempting to do so; or giving a sweetheart's name; or she or he may be told to 'run the gauntlet', or 'to go through purgatory', both of which have specific penalties attached to them by Dorset players; or to sing in one comer of the room, cry in another, laugh in another, and dance in another.

Sometimes the task imposed is either something which is apparently impossible to perform, such as being told 'to bite an inch off the poker', or 'to put yourself through the key-hole'; or else it is designed to make the victim ridiculous.

There are many other ways and means suggested by which the forfeits may be redeemed, and much amusement is frequently caused before the articles can be reclaimed. The game is often kept up with spirit for hours.[1]

As the old word-games were being forgotten, and only sketchily recorded for posterity, another Christmas party 'tradition' was invented, the cracker. The brainwave of an importer of bon-bons, Tom Smith, he discovered in 1846 that his sweets went with a bang, literally and figuratively, at Christmas if enclosed in a wrapper which, when opened, detonated a small explosion. Small gifts and paper hats were substituted for sweets by 1871, and at some stage a printed joke was added.[2] Local newspapers had for some years employed jokes and witticisms as fillers at the ends of columns, and so around Christmas such pleasantries could be described as crackers. This 1894 selection is from the Weston super Mare Gazette.

Christmas Crackers

 HEN MAY A thief be justly termed a gaol-bird? When he's been a robin.

Why should a baby never be taken into a painter's studio? Because of them easels.

Why is the remainder of a leg of mutton like Windsor? Because it is near eaten (Eton).

---

1   Udal, J S, 'Christmas in Dorsetshire', *Notes & Queries*, 6th series, ii, (1880), 504.

2   Pimlott, J A R, *The Englishman's Christmas: a social history* (1978), 130; Weightman, G, and Humphries, S, *Christmas past* (1987), 43-6.

Why are temperance societies a bar to friendship? Because they prevent shaking hands.

What is the best way to make a thin child fat? Throw it out of the window and it will come down plump.

Why should a clergyman always wear well-fitting clothes? Because he should never be a man of loose habits.

How many young ladies will it take to reach from London to Brighton? Fifty-two, because a miss is as good as a mile.

What is the difference between a bantam cock and a dirty housemaid? One is a domestic fowl, and the other is a foul domestic.

Why are bonfires like grey-headed sinners? Because they scintillate (sin-till-late).

When has a man a right to scold his wife about his coffee? When he has sufficient grounds.

Why is a man seeking the company of conspirators like another going through a field where there are tall trees growing? Because he's going where there's high-trees-on (high treason).

Why is a watch which has been allowed to run down, through carelessness, like the Western Bank? Because, through bad management it has stopped, and consequently gives no more tick, and in order to set matters right, requires to be wound up.

What animal is that which in the morning goes upon four legs; in the afternoon upon two, and in the evening upon three? Man – in the morning of his life upon all-fours; in the afternoon on two; and in the evening with a stick.[1]

Not everyone enjoyed a joke at Christmas. Hardy's brooding nostalgia for the Christmases of his youth was not, it seems, merely a literary conceit. In his later years, instead of enjoying a party, he seems to have wallowed in misery.

---

1   *Weston super Mare Gazette*, 22 Dec. 1894; the last of these 'jokes' is as old as the Oedipus legend of Greek tragedy.

Far From the Christmas Spirit

 ELLIE TITTERINGTON WAS in service as parlour-maid in the Hardy household during the 1920s, and forty years later she was persuaded to record some of her memories of life at Max Gate.[1] Far from placing him on a par with the Almighty, the maids did not see Mr Hardy as a great literary figure, she recalled, but just another man, with no obviously impressive qualities. Christmas was a quiet day without any fuss, and birthdays were not noticeably different from other days. The usual daily routine was followed.

Hardy's two marriages were childless, so that in adult life he rarely, if ever, enjoyed the excitement of a Christmas spent among supercharged children. This may help to account for the attitude he revealed in his correspondence. Writing about Christmas 1896 he told a friend: 'As you will imagine, our Christmas and new year here have been quite uneventful, except by post. But I agree with what Mrs Sheridan was saying to me a day or two ago, that a Christmas which brings no tragedies is upon the whole a thing to be thankful for when

---

1 Titterington, E, 'The domestic life of Thomas Hardy (1921-1928)', *Thomas Hardy Monographs*, iv (1963).

you have passed the time of life for expecting positive joys.'[1] Two days earlier he had written: 'I have been all right in health and have had a Christmas of the dull kind which contents so-called "pessimists" like me – in its freedom from positive sorrows.'[2] The gloom continued. To a correspondent at Christmas 1905 he sent a card which said simply: 'My dear Shorter: Many thanks. The same good wishes for you and Mrs Shorter. We are having a nice dull time here. Truly yours, T.H.'[3] And on Boxing Day 1924 the sentiment was much the same: 'We have been as cheerful as may be this Christmas, and I hope you have also. But I long ago entered the region in a lifetime in which anniversaries are the saddest days of the year.'[4]

Two Christmases were particularly dismal. Florence Dugdale, who was to become Hardy's second wife, was initiated into the Max Gate Christmas in 1910, and recalled the experience ruefully in a letter fifteen years later. 'My mind goes back to a Christmas day – 1910 – when I sat here alone, and vowed that no power on earth would ever induce me to spend another Christmas day at Max Gate. T.H. had gone off to Bockhampton to see his sisters, after a violent quarrel with the first Mrs T.H. because he wanted me to go to see the sisters too, and she said I shouldn't because they would poison my mind against her – and then – oh dear oh dear, *what* a scene – and he went off and she went up to her attic-study to write her memoirs until he came back at 8.30. It was the first Christmas of the kind I had ever spent, having always been with a party of cheerful people before that.'[5]

But worse was to come. Hardy's penultimate Christmas – 1926 – coincided with the demise of Wessex, Florence's dog, who had lived with them all their married life together, and who was peculiarly

1   Purdy, R L, and Millgate, M (eds.) *Collected letters of Thomas Hardy*, ii (1980), 142.

2   Ibid., 141.

3   Ibid., iii (1982), 191.

4   Ibid., vi (1987), 300.

5   Millgate, M (ed.), *The letters of Emma and Florence Hardy* (1996), 234.

affectionate towards them (and violently hostile to everyone else). 'We have had a sad aftering to our Christmas,' wrote Hardy to friends. 'Our devoted (and masterful) dog Wessex died on the 27th, and last night had his bed outside the house under the trees for the first time for 13 years.'[1] Florence was equally devastated: 'Of course he was merely a dog, and not a good dog always,' she wrote, 'but *thousands* (actually thousands) of afternoons and evenings I would have been alone but for him, and had always him to speak to. But I mustn't write about him, and I hope no one will ask me about him or mention his name.'[2]

Max Gate in winter, recalled Nellie Titterington, was a grim, cold house. Once when she stoked up a welcoming fire for the return of Florence and distinguished guests (Siegfried Sassoon, T.E. Lawrence, and E.M. Forster), Hardy – with the excessive thrift which was an impoverished childhood's legacy – carefully removed with tongs all the lumps of coal which were not actually alight. One Christmas his gifts to the staff – a half-crown each left in small envelopes – were rejected as an insult, until Florence quadrupled them.

It is perhaps not surprising, therefore, that Hardy's writing is peppered with unpleasant things happening to people at Christmas. In his poem 'The Rash Bride' a young wife, hearing the carollers, throws herself down a well. In one of his short stories, 'The Grave at the Handpost', a suicide is buried on Christmas Eve. And, most memorably, as Far From the Madding Crowd *reaches its electrifying climax, Mr Boldwood's Christmas party is interrupted by the arrival of a stranger, Sergeant Troy, who has come to clutch his wife, Bathsheba, from his rival's attentions.*

1   Purdy, R L, and Millgate, M (eds.) *Collected letters of Thomas Hardy*, vii (1988), 54.
2   Millgate, M (ed.), *The letters of Emma and Florence Hardy* (1996), 247.

The Stranger at the Party
Thomas Hardy

OLDWOOD WAS AMONG those who did not notice that he was Troy. 'Come in, come in!' he repeated, cheerfully, 'and drain a Christmas beaker with us, stranger!'

Troy next advanced into the middle of the room, took off his cap, turned down his coat-collar, and looked Boldwood in the face. Even then Boldwood did not recognize that the impersonator of Heaven's persistent irony towards him, who had once before broken in upon his bliss, scourged him, and snatched his delight away, had come to do these things a second time. Troy began to laugh a mechanical laugh: Boldwood recognized him now.

Troy turned to Bathsheba. The poor girl's wretchedness at this time was beyond all fancy or narration. She had sunk down on the lowest stair; and there she sat, her mouth blue and dry, and her dark eyes fixed vacantly upon him, as if she wondered whether it were not all a terrible illusion.

Then Troy spoke. 'Bathsheba, I come here for you!'

She made no reply.

'Come home with me: come!'

Bathsheba moved her feet a little, but did not rise. Troy went across to her.

'Come, madam, do you hear what I say?' he said, peremptorily.

A strange voice came from the fireplace – a voice sounding far off and confined, as if from a dungeon. Hardly a soul in the assembly recognized the thin tones to be those of Boldwood. Sudden despair had transformed him.

'Bathsheba, go with your husband!'

Nevertheless, she did not move. The truth was that Bathsheba was beyond the pale of activity – and yet not in a swoon. She was in a state of mental *gutta serena*; her mind was for the minute totally deprived of light at the same time that no obscuration was apparent from without.

Troy stretched out his hand to pull her towards him, when she quickly shrank back. This visible dread of him seemed to irritate Troy, and he seized her arm and pulled it sharply. Whether his grasp pinched her, or whether his mere touch was the cause, was never known, but at the moment of his seizure she writhed, and gave a quick, low scream.

The scream had been heard but a few seconds when it was followed by a sudden deafening report that echoed through the room and stupefied them all. The oak partition shook with the concussion, and the place was filled with grey smoke.

In bewilderment they turned their eyes to Boldwood. At his back, as he stood before the fireplace, was a gun-rack, as is usual in farmhouses, constructed to hold two guns. When Bathsheba had cried out in her husband's grasp, Boldwood's face of gnashing despair had changed. The veins had swollen, and a frenzied look had gleamed in his eye. He had turned quickly, taken one of the guns, cocked it, and at once discharged it at Troy.

Troy fell. The distance apart of the two men was so small that the charge of shot did not spread in the least, but passed like a bullet into his body. He uttered a long guttural sigh – there was a contraction – an extension – then his muscles relaxed, and he lay still.[1]

---

1   Hardy, T, *Far from the madding crowd* (1974 ed.), 377-8.

Death at Christmas, when birth is celebrated, may be seen in Hardy's artistry as a kind of literary oxymoron. But of course in real life too there are Christmas tragedies – none, perhaps, so moving as this sad reversal of the nativity, described by Thomas Crockford, rector of Fisherton Delamere near Wylye in Wiltshire, in his parish register for the year 1617.

LIZABETH PIERSON OR Vargeis the elder, spinster daughter of John Pierson or Vargeis, farmer of Bapton, and his wife Catherine; she suffered from epilepsy and finally died on 16th December, and was buried on the 17th.

George Vargeis, the illegitimate son of Elizabeth Vargeis the younger, daughter of John Vargeis or Pierson, farmer of Bapton, was born on the 17th and baptized on the 19th of December.

Elizabeth Pierson or Vargeis the younger, another daughter of John Pierson or Vargeis, farmer of Bapton, and his wife Catherine. She was a girl deceived by the attentions of a false and good-for-nothing boyfriend, by the name of Durham, who took her virginity after leading her on with the prospect of marriage. It is said that, worn our by the pain of childbirth, she languished repentantly for a little while, and then expired. She died and was buried on Christmas Day, 25th December.

George Pierson or Vargeis, illegitimate son of the foresaid Elizabeth, a very small baby, died and was buried on 31st December.[1]

Here is another Christmas tragedy, possibly with a macabre basis in fact. 'The Missletoe Bough' is a sentimental ballad which enjoyed great popularity among the Victorians. Its author was a native of Bath, who

1   WSA 522/1.

died in 1839, and it was set to music by Henry Bishop, better known as the composer of 'Home, Sweet Home'. Several places have been suggested as the inspiration for the story, including Marwell Hall, near Winchester. But Somerset historians claim that the source is Bawdrip, near Bridgwater, and it is certainly true that the church boasts a monument (inconveniently hidden behind the altar) which tells of Eleanor Lovel. She died in 1681, 'snatched away on her wedding day by a sudden and untimely fate. . .' This, according to the ballad, is what happened to her.

The Missletoe Bough
Thomas Haynes Bayly

HE MISSLETOE HUNG in the castle hall,
The holly branch shone on the old oak wall
And the baron's retainers were blithe and gay
And keeping their Christmas holiday.
The baron beheld with a father's pride
His beautiful child, young Lovell's bride,
While she with her bright eyes seemed to be
The star of that goodly company.
Oh the missletoe bough, oh the missletoe bough.

I'm weary of dancing now she cried
Here tarry a moment, I'll hide, I'll hide,
And Lovell be sure thou'st the first to trace
The clue to my secret lurking place.
Away she ran, and her friends began
Each tower to search, and each nook to scan
And Lovell cried, 'Oh, where dost thou hide?
I'm lonesome without thee, my own dear bride.'
Oh the missletoe bough, Oh the missletoe bough.

They sought her that night, and they sought her next day
And they sought her in vain when a week passed away.
In the highest, the lowest, the loneliest spot
Young Lovell sought wildly, but found her not.
And years flew by, and their grief at last
Was told as a sorrowful tale long past.
And when Lovell appeared, the children cried,
'See the old man weeps for his fairy bride.'
Oh the missletoe bough, Oh the missletoe bough.

At length an oak chest that had long lain hid
Was found in the castle, they raised the lid
And a skeleton form lay mouldering there
In the bridal wreath of the lady fair.
Oh sad was her fate! In sportive jest
She hid from her lord in the old oak chest.
It closed with a spring, and her bridal bloom
Lay withering there in a living tomb.
Oh the missletoe bough, Oh the missletoe bough.[1]

The unexpected, whether it be a sudden change of fortune, or a reversal of normal behaviour, haunts the history of Christmas. It was there at the Saturnalia, the pagan Roman midwinter festival when slaves dressed up in their masters' clothes. It was there in the Christian tradition of a virgin birth. We have seen it enshrined in the mumming plays, the wassail ceremonies, the pantomime and the kneeling oxen. And it manifested itself in the middle ages as a time of misrule, when authority was mocked and overturned, the world made to stand upside-down. For a short period each year the normal rules did not apply.[2]

1   SRO D/P/baw 23/2; Cary, D M, *Some ballad-legends of Somerset* (Somerset Folk Series xiv, 1924), 93-4.
2   Humphrey, C, *The politics of carnival: festive misrule in medieval England* (Manchester UP, 2001); Burke, P, *Popular culture in early modern Europe*, rev.

Sensible rulers have seen the carnival atmosphere of misrule as a safety valve, a regulated release of the social pressures which might otherwise build up and explode into outright rebellion. Less confident authorities have feared misrule, as a cloak for treachery, and from time to time have tried to prohibit it. John Jewel, protestant bishop of Salisbury from 1560 until his death in 1571, ordered his clergy in 1569 to report:

> *whether there have bene any Lordes of misrule, or disguised persons in Christmas, or dauncers, minstrels, or May gamers, at any other time, that have unreverently come into your Church, and there played unseemely parts, with scoffes, jestes, and ribauldrie talke, or daunsing, and namely in time of Common prayer, and what their names be, and the names also of such others as came with them to maintaine such disorder.[1]*

ed. (Ashgate, 1996), esp. 178-204.

1   Bishop John Jewels' visitation Injunctions (STC 10326.5), 24.

Between 1647 and 1660, after their victory in the civil wars, the puritan-dominated commonwealth government formally abolished Christmas altogether, and tried to stop anyone celebrating it.[1] Their dilemma was not new – it had been played out in Salisbury some two centuries earlier.

The Boy Bishop

NE OF THE most popular attractions in Salisbury Cathedral is the medieval clock. Its mysterious workings near the west end of the north aisle are often surrounded by admirers. Behind them as they inspect its crude horology, between two pillars of the nave arcade, there has reposed the stone effigy of a bishop, ever since it was removed there early in the seventeenth century. Nothing remarkable about that, perhaps, except that he is less than three feet tall. The likely explanation, first offered in 1811, is that the sculpture covers not the whole body of a bishop, but the buried heart, entrails or some other portion of his anatomy, and that the rest of him lies elsewhere. But when the monument was first discovered and placed there, possibly in about 1616, this was not realized, and by 1649 a completely different explanation had gained currency. It referred back to a custom, discontinued for a century, of electing each Christmas from among the choristers a 'boy-bishop', who, for a few days each year, was treated with all the respect accorded to, and carried out many of the duties performed by, the real bishop at other times. The tomb, so the story ran, must have commemorated one such boy bishop who died during his brief tenure of office.[2]

This strange custom of the boy bishop, by no means restricted to Salisbury, but practised in many medieval cathedrals and parish

---

1   Durston, C, 'Lords of misrule: the Puritan war on Christmas 1642-60', *History Today*, Dec. 1985, 7-14.

2   Gregory, J, *Episcopus puerorum in die innocentium, or a discovery of an ancient custom in the church of Sarum* (1683: Wing G1915).

churches, was older than Salisbury Cathedral itself, and is reminiscent of the Roman Saturnalia, from which it may have derived. In the Church calendar 28 December is Holy Innocents' Day or Childermas, commemorating Herod's infanticide, and this quite naturally became the feast around which the boy bishop's activities were centred. In some churches his election took place three weeks earlier, on 6 December. This was the feast of St Nicholas (Santa Claus), the patron saint of children, whose cult became extremely popular around 1100. Also around Christmas the Lord of Misrule and the Feast of Fools offered excuses for thinly disguised pagan festivities in the Saturnalian tradition.

The boy bishop was a cathedral chorister, and was elected by his fellow-choristers, who jealously guarded their right to choose him themselves. Special vestments were provided for his use, and with his fellows he took the place of the real bishop and senior clergy at the cathedral services from vespers on 27 December (the feast of St John the Evangelist) until vespers on the following day, Holy Innocents'. During this time the senior clergy took on the role of the choristers, occupying the lower stalls and performing the humbler duties. Although he did not actually officiate at mass on Holy Innocents' Day, the boy bishop did preach the sermon. It would have been written for him to deliver, and generally dealt with the topic of childhood. As his reward for these rather awe-inspiring responsibilities he was allowed to pocket the offerings (known as oblations) made at the high altar on that day; these could amount to a handsome sum by medieval standards, exceeding £5 on at least one occasion.[1]

If from this description you have a picture of angelic choirboys solemnly performing an ancient ritual you would probably be quite wrong.[2] There survive from medieval Salisbury enough prohibitions,

1 Fletcher, J M J, *The boy-bishop at Salisbury and elsewhere* (Salisbury, 1921); Robertson, D, *Sarum Close* (1938), 78-94.

2 A slightly fuller account of this incident and its aftermath is published as Chandler, J, 'The feast of the not so innocent: a Christmas story', *Regional*

and reports of 'manifest unruliness' surrounding the proceedings, to suggest that, in the spirit of Saturnalia, this was a time for letting off steam, mocking all authority, and generally messing about. In 1448:

> A certain vicar of this church, who occupies the bishop's stall and that of the prebend of Potterne, fatally wounded one of a canon's servants in the house of the choristers. This occurred about eight o'clock at night as he was accompanying the choristers from the canon's house to their residence. The cause of this misfortune was the unrestrained behaviour of the boys who were hitting out with sticks, and the fooling around of the vicars.[1]

This somewhat alarming report was entered (in Latin) by the Salisbury Cathedral chapter clerk. It introduces his minutes of a meeting of the dean and chapter held on 28 December 1448 to discuss events of the night before. The dean, precentor and other senior churchmen decided that measures must be taken to prevent a recurrence of this 'cause of injuries and lapses' which they attributed to the unrestrained behaviour of the boy choristers, and the taunting of the vicars and the other staff and servants of the church, who were larking about inside and outside the cathedral during the times of divine service on Innocents' Day. A second meeting was convened in the chapter house two days later, when a series of statutes was drawn up restricting the movements and weaponry of the choristers and vicars, and ordering that the vicars whose turn it was to read, sing or chant during service on the feast of the Holy Innocents should do so reverently, and without introducing any 'scornful, howling or profane songs'. In the course of the meeting reference was made to the vicars'

Historian (UWE, Bristol), forthcoming (Autumn 2010).

1   Salisbury Cathedral Archives, Chapter Act Book: Burgh, 37-8; partially translated in *Wilts. Arch. Mag.* xlviii (1937-9), 211. My thanks to Suzanne Eward, Salisbury Cathedral Librarian, for allowing me to examine the original document.

frequent habit of leaving the close for the city outside the permitted times, and hanging about in taverns and other shameful and dubious places, which had resulted in fights and fatal injuries, to 'the serious lapse of the church of Salisbury'.

The unruly 'vicars' were not the parish priests of modern parlance, but the vicars choral – singing youths and men who were employed by the non-resident canons of medieval secular cathedrals to deputise for them at services.[1] Their capacity for drinking, brawling and lechery was notorious, and cathedral records are full of interesting accounts of their exploits, and the authorities' attempts to curb them. Most recently at Salisbury this had been attempted through a series of statutes drawn up six years earlier, on 21 December 1442 (the date was perhaps significant, as an attempt to forestall trouble over the Christmas period).[2] But such prohibitions serve to underline the fact that, legitimately or not, the vicars had more contact, and more in common with the ordinary citizens of Salisbury than did the canons and senior clergy. The choristers, too, sons of local laymen, might expect sympathy from the city if it seemed that the dean and precentor were treating them unjustly.

The dean and chapter seem not to have been concerned with the death *per se*. Neither the perpetrator nor the victim was named, and no punishment or recompense was discussed. Vicars fighting to the death in taverns were mentioned as if commonplace. Their problem was with the effect on the reputation of the church, the harm to its dignity and the serious lapse which might result from such goings on. 'Lapse' is perhaps an unsatisfactory rendering of the Latin word *scandalum*, which conveys the idea of a stumbling-block causing a

1   Edwards, K, *The English secular cathedrals in the middle ages* (1967), 252-8; those over the age of 30 were generally ordained priests. See also Dobson, B, 'The English vicars choral: an introduction', in Hall, R, and Stocker, D (eds.), *Vicars choral at English cathedrals* (2005), 1-10.

2   Transcribed and translated in Wordsworth, C, and Macleane, D (eds.) *Statutes and customs of Salisbury cathedral* (1915), 320ff.

fall, and thereby a falling into temptation. The carnival atmosphere surrounding the boy-bishop ceremony, which led to the servant's death, was a threat to order, within the close and outside, and the authorities – in particular the precentor, whose responsibility the choristers were – felt they must rein it in.

The precentor, Nicholas Upton, was a distinguished scholar – an authority on heraldry – who had himself enjoyed a colourful past. He had served in the French wars in the retinue of the earl of Salisbury, took part in an abortive crusade and wrote a treatise on military strategy. As a herald granting arms he played practical jokes – gelded oxen for the arms of a man unfortunately injured in the genitals, partridges (symbolizing sodomy) for another gentleman. He owed his clerical preferment to friends in very high places, the dukes of Gloucester and Suffolk, and was therefore associated with the court of Henry VI.[1]

The chapter meeting laid down a series of specific prohibitions designed to prevent a recurrence of the misfortune.[2] Choristers were to go to supper at canons' houses individually, not in groups; and they were not to carry sticks nor disturb the services. The vicars, who earlier in the year had been stopped from playing ball games in their common hall,[3] were now ordered to dress properly, behave in a seemly manner during services, not to steal the candles, and under normal circumstances not to carry offensive weapons.

In December 1449 Upton went further by attempting to prevent a recurrence of the previous year's mishap by vetting the boy-bishop's appointment. Instead of permitting the choristers a free choice he put forward just three names from which they had to elect their 'bishop'. In thus asserting himself he may have been influenced by the

1   *Oxford DNB*, online, accessed 13.10.2010.
2   *Wiltshire Arch. & Nat. Hist. Mag.* xlviii (1937-9), 211-12.
3   Wordsworth, C, and Macleane, D (eds.) *Statutes and customs of Salisbury cathedral* (1915), 332.

practice at St Paul's, London, where he had previously been a canon, and where the senior clergy chose the boy-bishop.[1] Presumably his authority carried the day and they obeyed, but under such protest that a meeting of the chapter took place on 28 December, Innocent's Day, to discuss 'the subject of disagreement which had lately arisen' between the precentor and all the other major clergy. The meeting overruled the precentor and declared that for the future the choristers' ancient custom of electing freely their bishop should prevail.[2]

How are we to interpret this humiliating climbdown? The historian of the choir school saw it as a victory for the choristers: 'The Precentor, vanquished by his own Choristers, found himself in a minority of one.'[3] But it was not the choristers who debated and made decisions in chapter. True, there may have been a certain sympathy among the canons for upholding the ancient topsy-turvydom – Bishop Metford himself, forty years earlier, had paid minstrels and players for entertainments in his presence when spending Christmas at his Potterne residence.[4] Or a feud may have developed between Upton and the other major clergy, who used this issue to embarrass him, or to distance themselves from his unpopularity.

A more likely scenario is that the rapid u-turn was the result of panic among the cathedral clergy at the effect of Upton's attitude on the dangerously deteriorating relationship between the close and the city. Bad enough that a townsman had died at the hands of a churchman the previous Christmas. But then six months later, one evening in June 1449, there had been a serious riot staged by Salisbury citizens against Lord Moleyns, a leading courtier and Wiltshire magistrate, at the George Inn. Precentor Upton and another canon intervened, by fetching 'the body of our lord' (i.e. the host or

---

1   Hutton, R, *Stations of the sun* (1996), 101.
2   SCA Chapter Act Book: Burgh pp 21-2.
3   Robertson, D, *Sarum Close* (1938), 86.
4   Woolgar, C M (ed.), *Household accounts from medieval England* (1992), i, 418-19.

sacrament), and with this talisman led the unfortunate Moleyns to safety in the close.[1] Worse was to come. On 9 December 1449 the former dean of Salisbury, by then bishop of Chichester, applied to go abroad on pilgrimage to escape the hostility of the mob, but was murdered by soldiers at Portsmouth in January 1450.[2] Bishop William Ayscough of Salisbury, like his former dean and his current precentor, was very close to the discredited and deeply unpopular Henry VI, whose perceived maladministration was widely blamed for a collapse in cloth exports.[3] The bishop had embittered the citizens of Salisbury in 1441 and provoked a riot in 1443 by asserting his right of tenure to property in the city;[4] by 1449 his life too was in danger.

If the cathedral authorities felt as Christmas 1449 approached that they were sitting on a tinder-box, they had a stark choice. Either they could continue to rein in the choristers and attempt to subdue the misrule surrounding the boy-bishop, or they could brave out the festive anarchy and hope that the tinder failed to ignite. They appear first to have followed Upton and chosen the former course, wavered and then backtracked. But the pent-up hostility was unstoppable. On 29 June 1450, during Cade's rebellion, Bishop Ayscough was lynched at Edington by a disaffected mob, mostly from the clothing district of west Wiltshire, but also from Salisbury. His residences were looted and the houses of several canons were raided, including Upton's in the close.[5]

1   SCA Chapter Act Book: Burgh p 1. This marginal entry is badly stained, and barely legible. An apparently accurate translation (probably by Christopher Wordsworth) is given in Haskins, C, *The ancient trade guilds and companies of Salisbury* (1912), 292.

2   *Oxford DNB*, online, accessed 13.10.2010.

3   Hare, J N, 'The Wiltshire risings of 1450: political and economic discontent in mid-fifteenth century Wiltshire' *Southern History* iv (1982), 13-31

4   Street, F, 'The relations of the bishops and citizens of Salisbury . . . pt.1' *Wiltshire Arch. & Nat. Hist. Mag.* xxxix, (1915-17), 185-257, on 227, 229.

5   Hare, J N, 'The Wiltshire risings of 1450', *Southern History* iv (1982), 14-15; *Oxford DNB*, online, accessed 13.10.2010.

That was the end of Bishop Ayscough. The ceremony of the boy bishop lasted as long as the Middle Ages, but it could not survive the strictures of the Reformation. In 1541 a royal proclamation forbad all such 'dyvers and many superstitions and chyldysh observances', in which 'children be strangelie decked and apparayled to counterfeit priestes, bishoppes, and women, and so be led with songs and daunces from house to house, blessing the people and gatheryng of money; and boyes do singe masse and preache in the pulpits, with suche other unfittinge and inconvenient usages'.

And so the practice died, and Salisbury forgot all about it until recently (the ceremony has now been revived and is held every Christmas), except for the effigy in the cathedral nave – and that refers to something else altogether.

11
Ring in the New

HIS IS THE last day of the year. And many customs are associated with it. There is, of course, the bell-ringing – 'Ring out the old, Ring in the new'; there are the thousands of good wishes one proffers to the others, there are the merry parties – the seeing of the old year out and the new year in, and the clinking of glasses as the clock in the old church tower tells the midnight hour. Our forefathers knew how to enjoy themselves, and on no night in the year was greater merriment, greater conviviality, and greater good-will expressed than on New Year's Eve. It was on this night that the village inns were scenes of jollity and fun. Old Boniface was then seen at his best – his hospitality was unbounded.

Publicans are the *bêtes noires* of some folk, and the public house is looked upon as a sink of iniquity. But at this season of the year one may reflect that the infant Saviour would probably have been born in an inn if the crowded condition of the house had not forced the Holy Mother to seek shelter in an adjoining stable. And one wonders exceedingly why some professing Christians have such strong feelings against a house which represents the birth-place of Christ. The man who fell among thieves was taken to an inn, and his wounds dressed. Probably that is the reason why today, in country places, especially if one wishes to receive solace, comfort, and hospitality, one usually selects the village hostelry, and is not often disappointed at the reception accorded. But it is at Christmas-tide especially that the inn appeals to one's fancies. A picture which must ever attract the literary character is that of the Holly Tree Inn, drawn by Dickens. Here the guests were expected to join in the general 'convivials', rather than spend the idle hours alone with books.

It was in such a house as this that at Christmas-tide the bowl of punch used to circulate, and it was a liquor described by Dickens as, 'uncommonly good Punch!' Yes, the words bring back happy memories of my native town in Somerset. Then it was genial landlords and landladies were wont to invite their customers on New Year's Eve to gather around the steaming bowl to partake of their hospitality, and, incidentally, to wish the worthy hosts the compliments of the season. The brewing of the punch was quite a ceremonial art. It was not concocted in a twentieth-century hurry, but deliberately each ingredient was carefully measured and mixed, and the brewing jealously guarded from outsiders. Its component parts were kept a family secret, and handed down by father to son, or, by purchase, from landlord to landlord of the inn which had earned a reputation for its punch.

There were many such houses in Somerset; but none stood higher in the county – or perhaps in the whole of England – than the George at Crewkerne, in the days of old Mrs Marsh, whose name and fame, fifty years ago, as a brewer of punch, pervaded the land. It is perpetuated in the pages of *Punch* that there were only two places at which real, genuine punch could be obtained – the one was at the George at Crewkerne; the other at Punch Office, Fleet Street. There are still inns situate in Somerset where the old-time custom of free punch is observed on New Year's Eve. 'Success to old England', was always drunk in a steaming glass of punch, and if ever there were a beverage associated with Britain this is one.

The custom of drinking punch on New Year's Eve only dates back to the latter part of the seventeenth century. But it soon established itself, and was proclaimed the 'King of Drinks', among its devotees being Fox and Sheridan and 'all the statesmen of the Whig party'. Not only was it a beverage with the idle rich, but the humble poor acquired the palate, and a punch bowl was found in the houses of many far beneath the rank and social status of the noble. The bowl often figured in the lists of wedding presents, and formed the gift bestowed upon men who had earned the respect and goodwill of their fellows. Punch accommodates itself to the means of all classes, rich and poor. As Leigh Hunt has said, 'You may have it of the costliest wine or the humblest malt liquor'. In many a hostelry in Somerset one sees the old punch bowl occupying a place of honour in the bar. It remains to be gazed upon all the year round, or until some special event is celebrated or New Year's Eve is honoured. Then it is taken down, carefully dusted, carried behind the scenes into an inner room or the kitchen – at all events away from the eyes of the public – and there the mystic rites are performed, something after the following formula:

> Whene'er a bowl of punch we make,
> Four striking opposites we take
> The strong, the weak, the sour, the sweet,
> Together mixed, most kindly meet;
> And when they happily unite,
> The bowl is pregnant with delight.

Even now the secret is not revealed, for the old published recipes vary in an extraordinary degree, and what ingredient it is which made a certain punch here and there along the countryside in Somerset more famous than the other was ever jealously guarded. There is little doubt that the old bowl of punch on New Year's Eve is a continuation of the custom handed down from our Anglo-Saxon forefathers, who passed the wassail bowl on the vigil of the New Year to those assembled around the glowing hearth to drown every former animosity. Tonight in many an inn in dear old Somerset the punch bowl will be filled and pledges of friendship will be renewed, and a custom which has existed in this country for certainly over fourteen hundred years will be perpetuated.[1]

Christmas may be over, but another celebration follows in its wake. For some, like Willis Watson in 1920 salivating at the memory and prospect of an exquisite beverage, it is another excuse for feasting. His Somerset contemporary, the novelist Walter Raymond, shared the enthusiasm for punch, because he could show off his prowess at making it – even though, according to Watson, he was a week premature. Here we find him, on Christmas Eve 1909 (or a few years earlier), about to take his leave of the couple with whom he had been lodging at 'Sutton' (probably Withypool on Exmoor), when visitors arrive.

Aunt Juke's Bowl
Walter Raymond

N' THAT'S JAPHETH. I do know his step. He do hit one heel harder than t'other on the flagstone. He'll put his head in an' holler to smith, an' they'll be here in ten minutes –'

1 Watson, W G Willis, *Calendar of customs, superstitions, weather-lore . . . connected with the county of Somerset* (1920), 475-8.

'Who will be here, Mrs Heppell?'

'The handbell ringers. They do go about Sutton at Christmas, an', of course, they must come in with the bells, if you didn't mind. An' the book is for the church ringers –'

'Of course, they must come in, Mrs Heppell. Make haste, my good woman. Run for your life. Scald out the washhand basin. Bring up the soup-ladle. Get glasses. Get spoons. Get lemons. Get sugar. Bustle, I tell you, and put on the biggest kettle to your name.'

'What for?' asked Mrs Josiah Heppell, in surprise.

'Because I am an artist, woman. Because I am a genius at it –

'At what?'

'At the brewing of punch.'

'Then my old Aunt Juke's old blue bowl 'ud be better,' said she, 'an' I'll fetch un up from parlour table to once. Hark! There they be, then, by the scuffle. An' that's the tressels dapped down till Heppell do ope the door. I'd better to run –'

She ran.

The handbell ringers came quietly. They set up their board and tressels and arranged their bells in a subdued whisper. And gradually acquaintances who were not ringers slyly found their way into the room, which was large enough indeed to hold the whole parish. At last, it seemed that we were all there. For Uncle Dick went driving past and Heppell stopped him, and Dairyman, having an errand into the village, was pulled in by force. Somebody ran to borrow glasses at the Manor Farm and to ask Mr William Purchase to step across.

The Sutton handbell ringers rang carols on the bells very sweetly and proceeded to 'The Missletoe Bough' and other Christmas ballads. By that time the water boiled. The old room was filled, with the fragrance of lemons and, well, of other things. Old Aunt Juke's old blue bowl was a jewel. Likely enough it had seen orgies in its time. Did the unexpected warmth from the biggest kettle revive old memories,

I wonder? At least it brought goodwill to that little company, and an hour of old-fashioned jollity.[1]

Impromptu celebrations, unless attended by an author, rarely find their way into print. More typical, if more humdrum, is the report in the local newspaper, here describing new year celebration in a Pewsey Vale village in Wiltshire. Accurate, no doubt, but hardly one of Aunt Juke's orgies. The most exciting aspect, not reported, may have been what the children got up to with their new knives while the grown-ups were away having tea.

Wilcot, Pleasant Gatherings

N New Year's Day, Mrs Davidson, of West Stowell, gave the children of the day and Sunday schools, with their teachers and the members of the Girls' Friendly Society, a substantial tea of cake and buns, in the village schoolroom. After tea, a fine Christmas tree was unveiled, laden with pretty toys, work-boxes, knives, and other useful things. Each child was presented with a present from the tree by Colonel and Mrs Davidson. At the close of the proceedings, the children gave ringing cheers for those who had provided them with such a treat, and also for the Misses Smelt and other friends who had waited on them. The National Anthem was then sung, and as the children left the room each received two oranges, a basket of sweets and some crackers.

The next day, January 2nd, being Major Trafford's birthday, that gallant officer gave his usual treat to all the villagers above 16 years of age. At 6 o'clock they assembled at Stowell Park House, where a sumptuous meat tea was provided for them. All present were well entertained by Mrs Trafford, Miss Austin, the Major, Captain Greenwood, Mrs Greenwood, and Mr Austin. After partaking of

1   Raymond, W, *English country life* (1910), 436-43.

the good things, the Major's health was drunk with hearty cheers, all present wishing him many happy returns of the day. He suitably responded, saying it gave him much pleasure to welcome them once more. He was sorry to say there were several old faces missing, but some new ones appeared. Wishing them a happy and prosperous new year, he expressed a hope that they would enjoy themselves. The rest of the evening was spent in songs, recitations, and dancing; 'God save the Queen' being sung at the close of the proceedings, which were most enjoyable throughout.[1]

The social life of another Wiltshire community, Corsley near Warminster, at around the same period was chronicled with great precision. We probably know more about Corsley at the beginning of the 20th century than anywhere else in Wiltshire. But we know rather less about the life and tragic death of our informant. Maud Davies studied at the London School of Economics under Sydney and Beatrice Webb, who suggested that she should investigate the sociology of her own village. The resulting book, Life in an English Village, *was published in 1909. Miss Davies then moved to London, where she studied poverty and became involved in philanthropic causes. But in February 1913 her body was found on a railway line near Kensington and, although an open verdict was*

1   *Marlborough Times*, 10 Jan. 1891.

recorded, she was thought to have taken her own life. She was thirty-seven.[1] Here she describes the community's drinking habits at Christmas.

One Person, Drinking
Maud Davies

OCIAL LIFE IN Corsley centres round the family or household, round clubs for games and recreation, and the public-houses, and round the churches or chapels of the various religious denominations. In a scattered parish, such as Corsley, where many of the houses are situated in lonely lanes, the family is naturally inclined to live a more isolated life than in villages where even on a dark winter's night the street forms a sociable meeting-place; and although Corsley is well provided with public-houses – and it cannot be said that these are unattended – yet most of the married men prefer to have their cask of beer at home, taking a glass after supper with their wives, rather than turn out habitually into the dark muddy lanes which have to be traversed before they reach the haunts of men . . .

But while part of the people appear to be almost puritanical in their lives, it must be admitted that there are some families who regularly frequent the public-house. It is not the custom for sons living at home to pay more than 7s or 8s per week to their parents, unless in exceptional cases. A few sons living with parents consequently get into the habit of working only part time, and thus take to loafing ways, working on odd jobs not more than two or three days a week, much to the distress of the parents. Those young men who, working regularly, occupy their leisure with performance on a musical instrument, or some such hobby, usually save a good deal of money. Others, though spending a considerable part

---

1 Davies, M, *Life in an English village* (1909), new ed., with introduction by Dr Jane Howells forthcoming (Hobnob Press).

of their earnings on beer and tobacco, yet manage to save something. A remaining section spend all they get on food and drink, or dissipation in the neighbouring towns, to the neglect sometimes of their recognised liabilities to relatives. These people, mostly unmarried men, described by a native of Corsley as 'sillylike', thinking, she says, of nothing but what they eat and drink, and going to the public-house in the evening for a 'lark', form the chief clientele of the public-houses. It was not found possible to ascertain the amount of beer consumed in Corsley, for while some keepers of public-houses were good enough to furnish particulars, others declined to do so, and a large amount of beer is also taken direct from the brewers by the cottagers and others. It cannot, however, be doubted that the average consumption per head is somewhat large. At Christmas-time, 1905, notes were made of persons in the six public-houses of Corsley, including one situated a few yards outside the parish, with the following results:

December 25th	Present
1. 9 pm.	8 men, 2 wives.
2. 9.30 pm.	11 men, 4 strange women. Singing.
3. 9.50 pm.	13 men, 1 wife, also 10 strangers, male and female. Gramophone and singing.

December 26th	
1. 7.30 pm.	15 men.
2. 8 pm.	17 men.
3. 8.30 pm.	17 men, with 5 wives or daughters, 4 strangers, male and female. Gramophone.

December 27th	
1. 9 pm.	10 men.
2. 10 pm.	5 men, one with wife and daughter from Frome.
3. 9.30 pm.	14 men. Concertina and tambourine playing.

4.	8.15 pm.	6 persons. Talking of coming election.
5.	9 pm.	4 persons. Talking about Ireland, one of the company being bound there.
6.	7.45 pm.	4 persons. Playing bagatelle.

December 28th

1.	9.30 pm.	8 men
2.	9.30 pm.	8 men
3.	6 pm.	9 men
4.	8 pm	7 persons. Talking of agriculture.
5.	7 pm.	2 persons. Playing darts.
6.	9 pm.	6 persons. Playing bagatelle.

December 29th

4.	9 pm.	5 persons. Playing darts.
5.	9.30 pm.	1 person. Drinking.
6.	9 pm.	6 persons. Playing bagatelle.

December 30th

1.	7 pm.	4 men.
2.	7.30 pm.	2 men. The landlord gave free drinks, 8.30 to 10 pm., to finish up the Christmas holidays.
3.	8 pm.	5 men.

December 31st

1.	9 pm.	8 men.
2.	8 pm.	9 men.
3.	9.40 pm.	6 men.

January Ist

4.	9.30 pm.	3 persons. Playing darts.
5.	8 pm.	8 persons. Playing darts.
6.	8.30 pm.	2 persons. Drinking only.

January 2nd

4.	9 pm.	1 person. Drinking.
5.	9.45 pm.	2 persons. Playing darts.
6.	9.15 pm.	4 persons. Playing bagatelle.

January 3rd

4.	8.45 pm.	10 persons. Talking of the coming election.
5.	8 pm.	4 persons. Playing dominoes.
6.	9.15 pm.	8 persons. Playing bagatelle and talking of the coming election.

January 6th

4.	8.30 pm.	5 persons. Talking of shooting pigeons, there being a shooting match in the village.
5.	8 pm.	10 persons. Playing darts and talking of coming election.
6.	9 pm.	9 persons. Playing bagatelle – some only drinking.

It is not to be supposed that this census, taken at Christmas-time, and when also an election was looming in the near future, is in any way typical of the ordinary attendance, which is probably considerably smaller at a less festive season. Moreover, besides the number of persons noted as 'strangers', many names are included of persons not residing in Corsley, though well known to some of the inhabitants. An investigation at this time, however, showed the kind of amusement which was sought in these houses, games such as 'darts' or bagatelle probably taking an even more prominent place at a season when exceptional entertainments such as gramophones and singing were unprovided. But no doubt, though the number who go merely to 'soak' may not be numerous, a considerable amount of liquor is consumed by the players, or conversationalists, as well as by the less sociable drinkers.[1]

1   Davies, M, *op. cit.* (1909 ed.), 276-84 (abridged).

One has to admire the indomitable Miss Davies for embarking on a twelve days of Christmas pub crawl in the interests of social science. Somewhat less conscientious, one feels, was a friend of her father's, a neighbouring clergyman.[1] George Atwood was rector of Bishopstrow near Warminster from 1883 until his death in 1921, and his unpublished diaries, in a sometimes illegible scrawl, are preserved in the Wiltshire & Swindon Archives.[2] These extracts from Christmas 1913, sum up nicely his character and attitudes. They also focus on the kind of country pursuits that many of his class indulged in between Christmas and New Year.

Fifteen Snipe and a Few Pheasants
George Atwood

MONDAY 22 DECEMBER. Fine, dull. This morning went into Warminster. Saw Wakeman about the girl Legge – she's not feeble-minded but *wicked*. Also saw Ponting about the water at Norton in case the diphtheria case can be traced to it. Then on to the garage and the club. Gave my contribution to the steward and stewardess's Xmas box, and took old

---

1 After Maud's death George Atwood and Byam Davies, her father, took a holiday abroad together, which is described in Atwood's diary.
2 WSA 1229/1.

Cole Hamilton in and made him do the same. Then home to lunch and at 2 o'clock Herbert A'Court took me to Trowbridge – Dick being in London trying on his new dress clothes!!! Call at Assoc'n Office no good the Agent in Warminster. Home to tea at Eastleigh. Also saw Gratney and Harry Laverton. Home to dinner. I am glad to say my remedy of last night quite effective – finest medicine there is!

Tuesday 23 December. Rain all day without ceasing. In the morning went into Warminster. Got some Xmas presents. Went to Wakeman's office about that girl – also up to the Union. Saw Bradbury and the master about Xmas matters. Lunched with the Buttons then muddled about at home until tea time. I should have gone up to the Reformatory but it was really too wet for anything. The Ladies decorated the Church today as it was more convenient than doing it on Wednesday; the real reason being that the hounds meet at Greenhill today and most of them want to be there. I posted numerous cards of Xmas wishes and suchlike rubbish. Went to a choir practice in the evening.

Wednesday 24 December. Fine and frosty. Started at quarter to ten to shoot with Lord B [Bath]. Party was Gratney, Montgomerie, John Thynne, Crutwell, Col. Ruggles-Brice and self. We had quite a good day, about 400 – and several woodcock, six I think. Came home about five. Picked up some things in Warminster. Went in and saw Herbert A'Court. Lord B. gave me two woodcock, one of which I gave to old Wakeman, as I know no man who will enjoy it more. Then dinner and bed. I am still a bit wobbly about the tum-tum, but hope it will wear off.

Thursday 25 December. Fine frosty morning, rain p.m. Service at 8 a.m. 37 communicants; 11 a.m. 26 communicants. Lunched with the Southeys at Eastleigh, and directly after I started off. Went to the Workhouse it poured with rain. Saw or went through all the sick wards, and wished the poor old folk the good wishes of the season.

Very pleased with all I saw, then on to the Reformatory still pouring with rain. And saw all the boys at tea. Said a few words to them then back just in time to dress for dinner at the Bruces. A family dinner party. Bettie and Hazel there with the others I am glad to say.

Friday 26 December. Drizzle and cold. Went at 10.30 to Longbridge Deverill to shoot snipe. Met the guns at Crockerton. Col. Ruggles-Brice, Lord Bath, Lord Weymouth, W. Montgomerie, self. We had an excellent drive out of the big marsh, but no other luck all day. Shot 15 snipe (about) and a few pheasants in the withy bed. But although not a great bag had a pleasant day. Driver Peter. Called on Wakeman on my way back and told him I could not come to the meetings on Saturday. I did this with regret but I have given up so much shooting for business this year I felt justified.

Saturday 27 December. Fine frosty. Shot duck at Shearwater. We distributed ourselves round the lake, Lord B., Gratney and self – the other three guns on the Longleat Ponds. Lionel, Harry and Mabel came out and sat with me during first drive. We got all told between 50 and 60 duck and teal. Dined at the Bruces.

Sunday 28 December. Dull inclined to snow. Services at 11 o'clock and 6. Good congregations considering the day. Bettie and Hazel came to lunch and stayed to tea. Cole Hamilton came to supper.

Monday 29 December. Snow on ground, cold north wind. My birthday and a most uncomfortable day. No breakfast to speak of. All cold and miserable. My sandwiches all wrong and packed in a portmanteau-like parcel. Could not take them to the Board so had to work on an empty stomach until I got home from the Board at 3.30. I then got a cup of luke-warm Bovril, and practically had nothing to eat until tea at 4.30. If I lived as well as the cats I should be a happy man – who at least have their food well and carefully cooked and served hot. I should have thought a husband was of as much importance as a cat, but apparently not. Heard from Toby. (The two people who remembered my birthday were Maria, dear little girl, and Mrs Cochrane)

One man who would not have shown the Revd. Atwood much sympathy was Thomas Hardy. His response to severe winter weather was compassion for the animals and birds who had to fight to survive it. Both he and his first wife Emma staunchly championed causes promoting animal welfare, and found the shooting of gamebirds sickening. In a letter at Christmas 1905 he commented caustically about the seasonable habit of, 'killing a host of harmless animals to eat gluttonously of, . . . by way of upholding the truths of Christianity'.[1] And his moving self-obituary, the poem 'Afterwards', includes the lines: 'When the hedgehog travels furtively over the lawn, One may say, "He strove that such innocent creatures should come to no harm . . .".[2] Snowfall turned his mind to the plight of birds.

Birds at Winter Nightfall
Thomas Hardy

ROUND THE HOUSE the flakes fly faster,
And all the berries now are gone
From holly and cotonea-aster
Around the house. The flakes fly! – faster
Shutting indoors that crumb-outcaster
We used to see upon the lawn
Around the house. The flakes fly faster,
And all the berries now are gone![3]

1   Purdy, R L, and Millgate, M (eds.) *Collected letters of Thomas Hardy*, iii (1982), 189.
2   Hardy, T, *Complete poems* (1979 ed.), no. 511.
3   Ibid., no. 115.

The stark contrast between the cheery world indoors, and the suffering outside the window, pricked his conscience.

The Reminder
Thomas Hardy

HILE I WATCH the Christmas blaze
Paint the room with ruddy rays,
Something makes my vision glide
To the frosty scene outside.

There, to reach a rotting berry,
Toils a thrush, – constrained to very
Dregs of food by sharp distress,
Taking such with thankfulness.

Why, O starving bird, when I
One day's joy would justify,
And put misery out of view,
Do you make me notice you![1]

During the final year of the nineteenth century – 1900, not 1899 – the naturalist W H Hudson published Nature in Downland, *which is still admired as one of his most successful country books. In it he described with typical enthusiasm the life-cycle of the missel-thrush.*

1 Ibid., no. 220.

A Glorious Bird
W H Hudson

HERE IS ONE thing to make a lover of bird-music happy in the darkest weather in January in this maritime district. Mid-winter is the season of the missel-thrush. The song-thrush has been heard since the end of November, but he is not the true winter singer. He is heard often enough – a bird here and a bird there – when the sun shines, and in cloudy or in wet weather too, if it be mild. But when it is too gloomy for even his fine temper, when there is no gleam of light anywhere and no change in that darkness of immense ever-moving cloud above; and the south-west raves all day and all night, and day after day, then the storm-cock sings his loudest from a tree-top and has no rival. A glorious bird! . . .

When all the most luscious of the wild fruits have been eaten, and frosts and winds make the open downs impossible to live on, the missel-thrushes break up their flocks and every bird goes back to his lowland home. There is then not an orchard, nor copse, nor grove, without a pair of the big thrushes; and on the flat-wooded country on the north of the downs these birds are, I think, just as numerous. Home again from his long outing, the missel-thrush soon begins to sing; and if you should observe him in rough or gloomy weather, perched on an elm-top, swayed about this way and that by the gusts, singing his best, you must believe that this dark aspect of things delights him; that his pleasure in life, expressed with such sounds and in such circumstances, must greatly exceed in degree the contentment and bliss that is ours, even when we are most free from pain or care, and our whole beings most perfectly in tune with nature.

As to the song; although we probably value it most for its associations, and because it is often heard when other bird-voices are silent, it is also beautiful in itself. The sound is beautiful in quality, but the singer has no art, and flings out his notes anyhow; the song is an outburst, a cry of happiness, and is over in a moment, and after a moment of silence he repeats it, and so on for ten or twenty minutes or longer. In its quality the sound is most like the blackbird's; and when, in early spring, the blackbird, perched on a tree-top, first tries his long disused voice, the short confused phrases he blurts out are so like the song of the missel-thrush that any one may be easily deceived by them. The difference in the voices of the two birds is that the missel-thrush is not so full and mellow, and is slightly metallic or bell-like; and it is probably due to this quality that the song carries much further than that of the blackbird.[1]

It is Hudson's power of meticulous observation, allied to his total empathy with the creature he describes, which distinguishes his work. If Hardy had discovered this passage when it first appeared in print – as surely he must – he would have been struck by those words: 'you must believe that this dark aspect of things delights him'. It was precisely the image which he took up for his famous poem about the turn of the century.

'The Darkling Thrush' bears the date 31st December 1900, and we are intended to read it as if written at the last nightfall of the century.

1   Hudson, W H, *Nature in downland* (1900), 248-53.

In fact it had been published in a magazine two days' earlier, and was originally entitled, 'By the Century's Deathbed'.[1] The new title was skilfully chosen, as commentators have observed, since the unusual word 'darkling' had been used twice before in poems about birdsong: by Milton in Paradise Lost, *and by Keats in 'Ode to a Nightingale'. More significantly, Matthew Arnold referred to the upheaval of belief which the nineteenth century had brought, as 'a darkling plain', in his influential poem 'Dover Beach', published in 1867.[2] For Hardy the onset of the new century signified his maturity towards an uncertain old age (he celebrated his sixtieth birthday in 1900), the reluctant jettisoning of religious belief, and a distressingly faltering marriage. And yet, and yet – the missel-thrush delights in the dark aspect of things.*

The Darkling Thrush
Thomas Hardy

 LEANT UPON A coppice gate
    When Frost was spectre-gray,
And Winter's dregs made desolate
    The weakening eye of day.
The tangled bine-stems scored the sky
    Like strings of broken lyres,
And all mankind that haunted nigh
    Had sought their household fires.

The land's sharp features seemed to be
    The Century's corpse outleant,
His crypt the cloudy canopy,

1   Hardy, T, *Complete poems* (1979 ed.), no. 119, note on p.150.

2   Bailey, J O, *The poetry of Thomas Hardy: a handbook and commentary* (1970), 166-8; cf William Barnes's poem, *A Winter Night*, included above, p. 128.

The wind his death-lament.
The ancient pulse of germ and birth
    Was shrunken hard and dry,
And every spirit upon earth
    Seemed fervourless as I.

At once a voice arose among
    The bleak twigs overhead
In a full-hearted evensong
    Of joy illimited;
An aged thrush, frail, gaunt, and small,
    In blast-beruffled plume,
Had chosen thus to fling his soul
    Upon the growing gloom.

So little cause for carolings
    Of such ecstatic sound
Was written on terrestrial things
    Afar or nigh around,
That I could think there trembled through
    His happy good-night air
Some blessed Hope, whereof he knew
    And I was unaware.[1]

The last day of the century, for which 'The Darkling Thrush' *was written, spurred writers of every rank to attempt excellence. The reporter for the* Dorset County Chronicle, *Hardy's local newspaper, clearly took enormous pains to report the night's events at Dorchester in what he considered an appropriate way. He even invoked poetry (Cowper, not Hardy, alas!).*[2]

1   Hardy, T, *Complete poems* (1979 ed.), no. 119.
2   This is understandable, as Hardy had then only just begun publishing his poetry.

A Fine Moonlight Evening

XIT THE NINETEENTH CENTURY – ENTER THE TWENTIETH. The solemnity always associated with the close of a year was this year intensified – possibly ought to have been intensified a hundredfold – by the fact that the end of 1900 was also the end of the Nineteenth Century. With the vigil of watchnight services, with the requiem of muffled bell-peals, and also with the revelry of a wake, the old century was ushered to its rest, to be numbered with that ever-growing portion of eternity which we call the past. It departed laden with all the multitudinous joys and sorrows, hopes and fears, laughter and tears, successes and failures, of the most eventful and epoch-making hundred years of the whole world's history. Much matter did its departure afford for reflection to the contemplative mind; and in Dorchester, as in every other town throughout the land, special aids were offered to reflection, such as services at the churches and that throbbing bell-music which so stirs mind and heart and intensifies feeling.

> With easy force it opens all the cells
> Where memory sleeps.

But men differ from one another in few things more than in the attitude they assume at such times. Silence and solemnity with some find their counterpart in riot and revelry with others. Possibly this phenomenon is of the necessity of things, and illustrates that rebound, that back-swing of the pendulum, which finds philosophic expression in the axiom, 'every action has its reaction'.

But the province of the news paragraphist is to chronicle events, not to soliloquise on abstruse speculations. At all the churches of the town but St Peter's, where a watchnight service was held, special services began at the reasonable hour of eight o'clock, when the streets were as yet quiet, and the congregations coming out of church had not to thread their way through a crowd of midnight wassailers. The services generally took the form of thanksgiving for the past and supplication for the future, and earnest, thought-stimulating addresses were delivered by the respective incumbents.

It was a fine moonlight evening, exceptionally exhilarating in such a season as we have been having. The wild tearing winds of the day had sunk to rest, leaving the roads dry and smooth and the air crisp; yet there was an aqueous aureole around the moon promising – or portending – more rain. This came to pass in the early morning. But on such a night it was a pleasure to be out of doors, and the promenaders and churchgoers were more than usually numerous. Muffled peals and changes were rung at intervals on the bells, both of St Peter's Church and of Fordington St George, and the Volunteer Band, under Bandmaster J. Stevens, played in the streets. Shortly before eleven the lights shining in St Peter's Church reminded the passers-by of the watchnight service about to begin. . .

After the hour of midnight had struck, and the church bells had solemnly knelled the departure of the old year, they burst out into cheery peals to welcome in the new – peals in which every note of melancholy was swallowed up in full-hearted joy. It was a case of 'L'an est mort. Vive l'an!' The sweet, mellow tones of Fordington St George bells vied with those of St Peter's. Then the Volunteer Band started playing in Cornhill, and kept it up until after one o'clock. The programme of course included 'Auld Lang Syne' and 'God Save the Queen'. There was singing and cheering among the populace, encouraged by occasional supplication to 'liquid comfort'. Sundry libations were poured to Bacchus in the neighbourhood of the Town Pump, which seemed to be taken for an altar or pillar erected to that bibulous deity. At last, slowly but truly, came blessed silence, followed by sleep and oblivion. And thus the New Year had been ushered in.[1]

Contemporaries recognised that the last night of the 19th century was an auspicious occasion. Despite half the world, one imagines, singing 'God save the Queen' on New Year's Eve, she died three weeks later (an irony perhaps not lost on religious sceptics) and an era closed. The fall of a stone at Stonehenge on the same New Year's Eve may have seemed to some a remarkable portent of disaster, the apocalypse even.[2] Such fears have in fact been expressed as several new years approached, when the world might literally be turned upside-down – 1691, 1881, 1961.[3] In Wimborne Minster there is the tomb of a barrister, Anthony Ettrick, built into a recess in the minster wall. Its unusual position, half inside and half outside the church, has been explained as the result of a vow made by Ettrick, when he fell out with the church authorities, that he would never be buried within the minster or without it. But a further eccentricity was suggested by a Dorset historian, Richard Grosvenor Bartelot, in 1938.

Ettrick like many others felt sure that the end of the world was to come in 1691 because those figures are the same when turned upside down. . . So he prepared his coffin and dated it

1 *Dorset County Chronicle*, 3 Jan. 1901.
2 Chippindale, C, *Stonehenge complete* (rev. ed. 1994), 164.
3 Such fears may now be dismissed for a long time – the next 'upside-down' year will be 6009.

1691 and placed it in the wall so that he might hear the sound of the last trump. Afterwards he lived on until 1703, and his executor just painted 1703 in inferior paint over the date 1691 as you see it today.[1]

On several occasions it must have seemed that the old year was not going to give up without a fight. In north Wiltshire at the close of 1859 a tornado was witnessed by the learned vicar of Yatesbury, near Calne, the Revd. Alfred Smith. He collected reports from all his neighbours and wrote up an exhilarating account of its progress across the countryside.

The Great Storm of 1859
Alfred Smith

HE CLOSE OF the year 1859 will long be remembered by the inhabitants of some of the villages of north Wilts. as the period of 'the Great Storm'. It occurred at about half-past one p.m. on Friday, December 30th, and beginning its devastations about a mile to the south of Calne, and coming up from the west, it shaped its course for E.N.E., and took nearly a straight line in that direction for about thirteen miles, its breadth varying from 250 to about 400 yards: at what velocity it rushed over this course it is

---

1   Curtis, C D, 'Monmouth rebellion. Anthony Ettrick', *Somerset & Dorset Notes & Queries* xxii (1936-8), 203-6.

impossible to conjecture, but it seems to be universally allowed that from two to three minutes was the time occupied in passing over any given spot; and during these few moments, it swept a clear and most perceptible path in its onward progress, tearing up by the roots and snapping short off the huge trunks of some of the largest elms and other trees, unroofing houses, stacks, and cottages, and hurling men and cattle to the ground, and dashing them furiously to and fro, and rolling them over and over in its rough embrace.

The first intimation we have of its assuming any great force is on the property of the Marquis of Lansdowne, near the Devizes road, about a mile south of Calne, where it broke off the large branch of an oak tree within the precincts of Bowood Park; thence, steering eastwards, it partially tore off the thatch of a cottage; blew down three trees at Stock Street, the property of Mr Robert Henley; and passed on to the Rookery Farm, where it also prostrated several fine elms and decapitated others. Thence to Quemerford Villa, astonishing the inmates by bursting in the door and windows: and so on to Mr Slade's Mill. Here it scattered far and wide the stone tiles of the roofing of the stables and other buildings, in addition to other damage. And now hurling down several trees on its way, it reached Blacklands Park, hitherto renowned for its magnificent timber. First it partially unroofed the new lodge, and snapped off many of the firs which formed a shelter at its back, then rushing forth into the Park, swept down no less than 148 trees, some of great size and beauty, tearing up some by the roots, and snapping off other large trunks, as if they had been twigs; so that to the inmates of the house, who were looking from the windows, and who were slightly removed from the main line of the storm, it appeared as if all the trees in the Park were simultaneously, and in an instant dashed headlong to the earth.

But the work of desolation goes on apace now, and away goes the storm, leaving Blacklands far behind, along the Bath road. Here it seems to have rushed up the gully, along which the greater part of the village of Cherhill is built. A few of the most prominent particulars in this locality may exemplify its violence: and first Cherhill Mill deserves especial mention, no less than fifty trees having been thrown down within a very small space; and yet Mr Reynolds the miller (who in passing to the mill could not reach it before the storm was upon him, and clung to a rail of the orchard during its entire passage) assures me that he neither heard nor saw a single tree fall, so awful and bewildering was the effect of its sudden tremendous and deafening attack. Again, in another instance, the roof of a cottage was lifted off in a mass and deposited in the road.

And now 'Excelsior' was the battle cry of the hurricane, and with a shriek of victory and a roar of exultation it rushed up the narrow ravine at the extreme east end of Cherhill, and on and away for the open down; and chancing to fall in with a wheat rick which stood in its path, it carried the greater part along with it, hurling whole sheaves several hundred yards, threshing out the corn all over the field, and whirling large quantities of straw above a mile. Spying six large trees standing out on the exposed plain, it hurled five of them to the ground like ninepins, and then on it dashed towards Yatesbury, which was to be the principal scene of its triumph. And first, singling out here and there a fir tree in some long plantations and belts on my glebe, it snapped them off or tore them up, to the number of forty, with most fantastic partiality, as if sending out a whiff for the purpose, as the main body of the storm hurried by, and leaving the surrounding trees apparently unruffled by the breeze. Thence, abstaining from the slightest injury to the Church, and scarcely removing a tile from the School, it began a furious onslaught on the timber all around, uprooting one of the large yews on my glebe, but sparing the pride of our churchyard, (which without partiality I believe to be the finest and best grown yew tree in the county) and overturning right and left, on either side of the church, the large trees which were the ornament of that portion of the parish.

Then straight away for Mr John Tanner's and the south end of the village, where it did more damage than in any other spot on its whole course: for first it entirely unroofed several cottages, ricks and barns: then threw down chimneys and outhouses: lifted off in a mass the entire roof of a long cattle-shed: smashed in the windows on the south front of the house: laid flat the east and west walls of the kitchen garden: prostrated two barns: and uprooted or broke off almost all the fine elms round the house: in addition to the playful freaks of throwing a cow into a pond, hurling one of the large cart horses from one end of the yard to the other, and dashing him at length against the shed at the extreme end; and as a climax, taking up a heavy broad-wheeled waggon weighing 22 cwt., and lifting it over a high hedge, depositing it on its side a dozen yards or more from where it stood. After these eccentric manoeuvres and wondrous feats of strength, away goes the hurricane for Winterbourne Monkton, coursing again for two miles over open country, and only marking its path here and there by overthrowing the few trees which stood in its way.

Most mercifully not a single life was lost, nor did any serious accident occur to either man or beast. Hair-breadth escapes indeed there were in abundance: for instance, several men and boys were buried under the ruins of fallen barns both at Yatesbury and Monkton, and how they all escaped the heavy beams and rafters which fell all around them, seems perfectly miraculous, but they were all extricated from their perilous position with no worse result than sundry bruises and an exceeding terror. Still more remarkable are some of the instances of narrow escape of destruction among the cattle. At the extreme west of Cherhill, near Mr Maundrell's farm, lies a narrow strip of meadow of about half an acre in extent, Surrounded with elms, no less than 23 of which were swept down in an instant, and appeared completely to choke up the field; yet it will hardly be believed that a donkey belonging to the carpenter, Charles Aland, who dwells hard by, and which had been turned into this meadow, was found unhurt amidst the prostrate timber, though there appeared scarcely a vacant space wherein it could stand. Nor was this the only animal bearing a charmed life which the worthy carpenter possessed, for a large tree fell across his pig-sty, crushing it to the earth, but the pig crept out uninjured, and was found standing by its ruined home perfectly untouched. I have already remarked on the overthrow of Mr Tanner's cart horse and cow at Yatesbury; but when the storm was gone by, they seem to have emerged, the one from the shed into which he was whirled, the other out of the pond into which she was cast, none the worse for their temporary discomfiture. Indeed the only creatures which seem to have lost their lives in the hurricane, were sundry hares and partridges, three or four of the former having been picked up dead, immediately after the storm, and I myself having chanced to ride by some of the latter, which I found almost entirely denuded of feathers, doubtless the effect of their being repeatedly dashed with violence on the earth.

I come now to speak of the hail-stones which accompanied the storm in large quantities, and which from their enormous size and peculiar shapes were almost as extraordinary as the tornado itself. moreover, their forms seem to have varied in different localities; thus Mr Spenser of Bowood saw some more resembling flat pieces of ice than hail: they were nearly half an inch in thickness, and from two to three inches in diameter, star-shaped, with rays ranging from four to seven in number, and the rays of different sizes. Others again were wedge-shaped and about three inches in length, and in some cases several of these were frozen together. At Yatesbury the hailstones were of an entirely different shape, for they had now lost their wedge-like character, and resembled rough irregular stones of about two inches in diameter, and this form may perhaps have been produced by their being whirled about and retarded in their fall, when the storm was at its greatest violence. At Cherhill there was little or no hail, but to the north on the hill above they fell freely, and I have a graphic description of their shape from Mr Neate's shepherd, who likened them to the middle of a waggon wheel, with the spokes all broken off. At Monkton no hail was seen, though there was an abundance of rain, but at Berwick Bassett the hailstones fell in large quantities, and for their enormous size I am happy to be able to adduce the testimony of the Rev R. Mead and Mr Viveash, who measured some and found them to be 4¾ inches, and others again, measured accurately with compasses, proved to be no less than 5½ inches, and some even to have exceeded 6 inches in circumference, with a diameter of half an inch.

I regret that I have no means of ascertaining the precise amount of rain which fell during the hurricane, but that a very copious discharge then took place is certain, and by way of obtaining the nearest information on this head within my reach, I have instituted enquiries at all the mills near which it passed, and from one and all I derive the same reply, that the rise of the water was both greater and more sudden than was ever remembered on any former occasion of other heavy rains: this is the unanimous opinion of the millers at Cherhill, Quemerford, and Blacklands Mills, where, though within a mile of the source of the stream which turned them, it was found necessary to draw the hatches and stop the works for a time, on account of the rush of water which bore down with irresistible fury immediately after the storm had passed by.

I should add that the day of our hurricane was marked throughout by sudden and violent gusts of wind, accompanied with hail and rain in heavy showers; those who were hunting with the Duke of Beaufort at Bremhill on that day will not readily forget the hail-stones, which descended with such force as to cut their hands till their knuckles bled, and to make their horses kick and plunge from the pain inflicted by them. Still more will the day be remembered in England as the disastrous day of storm, which cost her the life of one of her best officers, the gallant Captain Harrison of the Great Eastern. While those of the inhabitants of North Wilts. who live within its limits, will never forget to the last day of their lives 'the great Wiltshire storm of December 30th, 1859'.[1]

1   Smith, A C, 'The great Wiltshire storm of 1859', *Wilts. Arch. Mag.* vi (1860), 365-

Forty-four years later, to the day, Somerset was shaken by an earthquake.

A Passing Animal

 WELL-MARKED SHOCK OF earthquake was felt on the northern side of the Mendip Valley on Saturday night, Dec 30, 1893. The circumstances seem rather peculiar from the fact that the shock – or shocks, for it is stated that there were three – were within a comparatively limited area, and included the towns of Wells, Shepton Mallet, Glastonbury, and the villages immediately adjoining these towns. The first shock was felt about 11.30 pm, accompanied by a rumbling noise, and lasted for about three seconds. People were awakened out of their sleep by the rocking of their beds and the clattering of crockery and falling articles, and some rushed into the streets in their fright. At 12.28 a second and much more severe shock was felt, but it was of shorter duration. Both shocks were felt in all of the towns named and in the surrounding villages. A third shock about four o' clock is stated to have been felt by some persons.

In Wells some of the people in St Thomas Street ran out of their houses, and the residents in Vicars' Close were greatly alarmed. In

---

89 (abridged).

some instances crockery ware was thrown from the dressers and smashed, and at the residence of Mr J N Knight, of Milton, the shock was so great that he thought his greenhouse boiler had burst, and he got up and examined the premises. In Shepton Mallet the shock was felt all up one side of Cowl Street and High Street, and at the district hospital the beds rocked like hammocks. The shocks were severely felt at Glastonbury and the village of Draycott; whilst at Coxley, people ran out of their houses, others were shaken in their beds, the furniture removed from its place, and in one instance a pillar clock was thrown down and smashed. A second but milder shock occurred at 12.15. The direction appeared to be from south to north. In all the places the effects seem to have been the same, but what was the cause, seeing the limited area? Landslips produce tremors in non-volcanic areas resembling earthquakes, and the falling-in of roofs of subterranean cavities has also been suggested as a cause, but is only likely to affect a small area.

Between 11 and 12 pm on Saturday, two distinct shocks of earthquake were felt in Baltonsborough. The oscillation came northward and travelled one mile southwards. The shocks were preceded by a dull rumbling noise. No damage was done, but fears were entertained for the chimneys, especially on the hill.

An earthquake of considerable violence was experienced in Priddy and the immediate neighbourhood about 11.20 on Saturday night, and another, less violent, about an hour later. The cause of the earthquake would appear to have been a violent subterranean explosion, as the shaking of the earth was accompanied with a dull sound, as of a huge dynamite explosion. The shakings, apparently about six or seven, were quite distinct, lasting about six seconds, and were of such violence as to shake the doors and windows, and in the smelting house of the lead works, shook the dust from the rafters. The second shock lasted only about half the time, and was not nearly so severe. In one house in the parish, through the bolted windows, the ivy was distinctly heard beating against the wall, and rustling as though rubbed violently by a passing animal; this description, that of a passing animal, is given by others. Another describes it as a huge avalanche of snow slipping from the roof. As far as one could judge, the shock seemed to be travelling in a northerly direction.

A severe shock of earthquake was felt at Wookey on Saturday night, accompanied by a loud rumbling sound. It seemed as if the earth was assuming an undulating motion, such as is observed on the waves of the sea. As nearly as possible it was about 11.20 pm. The animals round were exceedingly restless just then, and the dogs continued to bark for some time afterwards, and were very much disturbed. A second shock was felt at 12.30 on Sunday morning. This was quite different, and seemed more of a tremor than the other, causing things to rattle, pictures to sway, and windows to shake. A third shock was noticed by some about four o'clock, but it was very slight.

At Wookey Hole the shocks of earthquake were very severe under the hills. The first was preceded by what seemed a terrific explosion; persons were thrown from the chairs and from bed. The first shock occurred on the 30th at 11.20 pm; the second shock at 12.28 was not accompanied by so much noise, but was much more violent, for the houses and everything on the shelves vibrated about two seconds.[1]

Thomas Hardy could conceive the passing of the year on a cosmic scale, and in a memorably sacrilegous poem, published in January 1907 (and perhaps unthinkable a few years earlier) he had the temerity to hold a conversation with God. By this date he had lost any belief in a Christian deity.

---

1   *Somerset & Dorset Notes & Queries,* iv (1895) 45-7, quoting *Western Gazette,* 5 Jan. 1894.

New Year's Eve
Thomas Hardy

'I HAVE FINISHED ANOTHER year,' said God,
    'In grey, green, white, and brown;
I have strewn the leaf upon the sod,
Sealed up the worm within the clod,
    And let the last sun down.'

'And what's the good of it?' I said,
    'What reasons made you call
From formless void this earth we tread,
When nine-and-ninety can be read
    Why nought should be at all?

'Yea, Sire; why shaped you us, "who in
    This tabernacle groan" –
If ever a joy be found herein,
Such joy no man had wished to win
    If he had never known!'

Then he: 'My labours – logicless –
    You may explain; not I:
Sense-sealed I have wrought, without a guess
That I evolved a Consciousness
    To ask for reasons why.

'Strange that ephemeral creatures who
    By my own ordering are,
Should see the shortness of my view,

Use ethic tests I never knew,
    Or made provision for!'

He sank to raptness as of yore,
    And opening New Year's Day
Wove it by rote as theretofore,
And went on working evermore
    In his unweeting way.[1]

By contrast William Barnes, the pious, sociable clergyman whom Hardy greatly respected, celebrated New Year's Eve as a time to reaffirm friendships and family ties.

Zitten Out the Wold Year
William Barnes

 HY, RAIN OR sheen, or blow or snow,
    I zaid, if I could stand so's,
I'd come, vor all a friend or foe,
    To sheake ye by the hand, so's;
An' spend, wi' kinsvo'k near an' dear,
A happy evenen, woonce a year,
    A-zot wi' me'th
    Avore the he'th
To zee the new year in, so's.

There's Jim an' Tom, a-grown the size
    O' men, girt lusty chaps, so's,
An' Fanny wi' her sloo-black eyes,
    Her mother's very daps, so's;

1   Hardy, T, *Complete poems* (1979 ed.), no. 231.

An' little Bill, so brown's a nut,
An' Poll, a gigglen little slut,
  I hope will shoot
  Another voot
  The year that's comen in, so's.

An' there, upon his mother's knee,
  So peart do look about, so's,
The little woone ov all, to zee
  His vu'st wold year goo out, so's.
An' zoo mid God bless all o's still,
Gwain up or down along the hill,
  To meet in glee
  Agean to zee
  A happy new year in, so's

The wold clock's han' do softly steal
  Up roun' the year's last hour, so's;
Zoo let the han'-bells ring a peal,
  Lik' them a-hung in tow'r, so's.
Here, here be two vor Tom, an' two
Vor Fanny, an' a peair vor you;
  We'll meake em swing,
  An' meake em ring,
  The merry new year in so's.

Tom, mind your time there; you be wrong.
  Come, let your bells all sound, so's:
A little clwoser, Poll; ding, dong!
  There, now 'tis right all round, so's.
The clock's a-striken twelve, d'ye hear?
Ting, ting, ding, dong! Farewell, wold year!
  'Tis gone, 'tis gone! –

Goo on, goo on,
An' ring the new woone in, so's![1]

Bells are a recurring theme for writers about New Year's Eve. The practice of muffling church bells, which was referred to earlier by the Dorchester newspaper reporter, was witnessed by Hardy at St Peter's church in 1884, and he preserved an account of it in his autobiography.

Tenor's Out
Thomas Hardy

ECEMBER 31ST. To St Peter's belfry to the New-Year's-Eve ringing. The night-wind whiffed in through the louvres as the men prepared the mufflers with tar-twine and pieces of horse-cloth. Climbed over the bells to fix the mufflers. I climbed with them and looked into the tenor bell: it is worn into a bright pit where the clapper has struck so many years, and the clapper is battered with its many blows.

1   Barnes, W, *Poems* (1962 ed.), i, 178-9.

The ringers now put their coats and waistcoats and hats upon the chimes and clock and stand to. Old John is fragile, as if the bell would pull him up rather than he pull the rope down, his neck being withered and white as his white neckcloth. But his manner is severe as he says, 'Tenor out?' One of the two tenor men gently eases the bell forward – that fine old E flat, my father's admiration, unsurpassed in metal all the world over – and answers, 'Tenor's out'. Then old John tells them to 'Go!' and they start. Through long practice he rings with the least possible movement of his body, though the youngest ringers – strong, dark-haired men with ruddy faces – soon perspire with their exertions. The red, green and white sallies bolt up through the holes like rats between the huge beams overhead.[1]

Of the Dorset acquaintances of Hardy's youth, the closest male friendship he ever formed was with Horace Moule, fourth of seven sons of the vicar of Fordington, the parish between Stinsford and Dorchester. Moule had a brilliant mind and an engaging personality, and was destined for a successful academic career. There is a good deal of him in Hardy's character Stephen Knight, the hero's rival in love in A Pair of Blue Eyes. *But he had a problem with alcohol, and perhaps opium, and suffered bouts of depression. In 1873 he committed suicide.*

During Hardy's adolescence, in the 1850s, when he was articled to a Dorchester architect, Moule inspired him to read widely in literature, philosophy and the classics; and the following poem dates from this period of relative stability in both their lives. Moule's poem was published twenty years later, after his death, and was prefaced by a note explaining that it was 'suggested by a midnight walk to Grey's Bridge, on the mild and beautiful Old Year's Night of 1858'. Grey's Bridge, it will be recalled, was where Hardy in The Mayor of Casterbridge *made Henchard meditate, and close to the Ten Hatches where he contemplated suicide.*

1   Hardy, T, *The life and work of Thomas Hardy* (M. Millgate ed., 1984), 176.

The Muffled Peal
Horace Moule

 LOW GENTLY, SWEET Frome, under Grey's gleaming arches,
    Where shines the white moon on thy cold sparkling wave;
Flow gently tonight, while Time silently marches
    Fast hastening to lay the Old Year in his grave.

How tranquil the night is! the few sounds that break it
    But draw deeper silence on meadow and hill:
Dogs barking, doors shutting, are all that awake it,
    Or a hoof's distant clatter, now softer, now still.

The sands are fast ebbing; the Young Year undaunted,
    Stands ready to run as his sire ran before; –
And shall no bell be rung, or no requiem chanted,
    For the Old pilgrim dying before his son's door?

I said it half musing, when bells that, sweet sounding,
    Seemed now like a distant chime, now like a dirge,
Sadly and strange through the calm air resounding,
    Pealed from the turrets of knightly Saint George.

All muffled and mournful the tones they were ringing,
    Now booming from far and now whispering near,
Wild voices of ghosts that were muttering, singing,
    Wailing around an invisible bier.

But hark, they are still! the last echoes are sweeping
    Down the lone valley where Frome's waters run;
The slow lingering hours, half smiling, half weeping,
    Have left the dead Father to welcome the Son.

Now sounds the knell on the Tenor sonorous;
    The last hour is come and the last breath is drawn; –
One moment more, and the whole pealing chorus
    Seem changing the midnight to clamorous dawn!

So mournful before, now so joyous and cheerful,
    Twofold is the story they sang to the stars:
I caught the twin echoes, the gay and the tearful,
    And long will their music ring sweet in my ears.

Farewell, farewell, to the joy and the laughter
    We've known in the years we are leaving behind!
Ah, who can tell us the friend that comes after
    Will be like the old one, as pleasant, as kind?

Words, kisses, and smiles, in the year that is over
    Drift far, far behind us while we hurry on;
Some poor paltry remnant may Memory recover,
    The root glides away with the days that are gone.

'But say, did no sorrow embitter the pleasure?
    Was gay laughter clouded with never a tear?
Are no wants, disasters, cares, griefs without measure,
    Borne far away with the old parting year?

'Oh yes! and while Hopes, pointing upward, remind us
    The new will be old, as the old was once new,
Let not the Past with sad memories blind us –

'Welcome' be said, while we murmur 'Adieu.'

'Then go forward boldly, and fearless of danger,
　　With souls that gain vigour from –graves of old years,
With hearts firm and ready to meet the young Stranger,
　　To smile with his laughter and weep with his tears!'

The river flows on down the lone valley wending,
　　The white moon is setting, the bells they are done;
Be joy to the New Year, kind blessings attending,
　　And peace evermore be with those that are gone.[1]

For Llewelyn Powys, too, the gentle, troubled philosopher of the Dorset coast, it was the bells of the turning year that triggered the deepest contemplation.

West Bottom
Llewelyn Powys

HERE ARE OCCASIONS when religious feeling will suddenly take possession of the most obdurate spirit. It happened so with me three weeks ago as I watched out the Old Year. Suddenly the sound of bells came drifting over downs stiff and ashen white with hoar-frost. In the sound were all the romantic associations of mediaeval piety. The moon was shining and in her white, cold, beautiful light I knew that there was rising from the pastures of every English shire, far up into the wintry heavens, this wonderful crystal music familiar in the time of our fathers and in the old times before them. Every separate grass-blade, every single twig in

1　Handley, C G Moule, *Dorchester poems* (1878), 24-6.

the thorn hedges, and the top bar of each field-gate was glittering, and over the frozen plough-lands covered with flints came the tumbling rhythm of the belfry changes, now loud, now faint, as though caught upon the wind from a wedding procession taking place far away on the other side of the distant hills, where by some enchantment spring was already, with yellow daffodils and yellow primroses strewing the path of true lovers happy at last.

I knew that on that night the whole of Dorset was lying under the spell of the moon. With an influence strong enough to draw the sea high up the shelving banks of the Chesil Beach, the radiance of this mysterious dead planet was spread over the country. It was upon the stonework of Hardy's Monument; it was upon the dove-cot attic above the great nave of Sherborne Abbey; it was upon the feathered bodies of dreaming Abbotsbury swans, and upon the shining horns of the winter-coated heifers recumbent upon Batcombe Downs, their heavy breathing visibly bringing warmth to the midnight air of High Stoy.

Behind this old-world music of the Lulworth bells there was audible at regular intervals a sound as deep-throated as the respiration of a dragon. It is rumoured that the prophet Daniel once silence a Babylonian dragon with a diet of hair and pitch – but where is the thaumaturge [wonder-worker] who can bring repose to the restless sea which for millenniums beyond the computation of man has been subject to the treacherous charm of the moon?

It is not only through the sense of hearing that the imagination can be stirred to a heightened consciousness of earth existence. From time out of mind certain localities have been renowned for evoking moods of spiritual awareness. In ancient days when a cultivated Roman approached some place where the natural scenery was particularly solemn and impressive – a mountain gorge or a forest glade – it was his custom to utter in the form of a grace these words: '*Numen in est,*' 'Deity is in this place.'

Of such places of worship in Dorset I think none is more awe-inspiring than that portion of the coast known to fishermen and rabbit-catchers as West Bottom. It is the first of the Bottoms between White Nose and Lulworth walking eastward that drops away to the sheer cliff's edge. Its sloping sides are so steep and so slippery that nobody inclined to giddiness should venture down them. Far below on the very edge of the dizzy cliff is a diminutive spinney of weather-stunted alder-trees, and to the right rises the Fountain Rock, a squared column of chalk banded with flints, and of such enormous proportions that it could, I believe, without strain or displacement support the whole weight of Salisbury Cathedral. This Cyclopean pillar of native marble rises straight up from the level of the beach below to tower high above the cup of this downland valley.

Even in summer weather, when butterflies are everywhere, fritillaries and chalk-hill blues and Lulworth skippers, West Bottom remains a desolate place. Many a time have I disturbed a fox there and sent it hustling away to its inaccessible earth halfway down the precipice. Many a time, attracted by the shrill cry of the peregrine falcon, I have witnessed the death of a carrier-pigeon as, tired of wing, it was flying homewards to its familiar backyard loft in Weymouth. Two other birds, the cormorant and the raven, both of them fowls of ill omen to man from earliest times, are frequently to be seen flying in this undisturbed place. And yet if boy or girl, old man or old woman heavy of heart, and impatient of human comforters, wishes to bow before the knees of Nature, the stern mother of us all, they could do not better than to visit West Bottom.

No vexations connected with the follies of society could torment the mind of one standing alone in this awful temple not made with hands. Anxieties deriving from worldly preoccupations could not but weigh lightly here, where the facile spirit in its habitation of bones is nursed in the lap of these noble hills. "As the race of leaves so the race of man is," wrote Homer. To us the Fountain Rock appears as a foundation stone of eternity, and yet in the eyes of God it is but yesterday that its substance was cemented together out of crushed shells from the sea's floor. We are nurtured in illusions. Which of us has a soul firm enough to understand the crying of the winds or to construe the words of the waves?[1]

In his autobiography, Skin for Skin, *Llewelyn Powys recalled another nocturnal expedition on New Year's Eve, with his brother Theodore.*

The Enchanted Circle
Llewelyn Powys

T SUPPER THAT night, Theodore and I decided that we would walk over the downs to the Stone Circle. We had a fancy to see the old year out within the circumference of that heathen dolmen. It was a frosty night. As soon as the white garden-gate had clicked back on to its latch, we found that the road under our feet was no longer muddy, but was already sparkling in the star-shine., Away we went, past the old barn, past the field where the sea-gulls collect, our walking-sticks hitting on the resonant ground, and one topic of conversation following on

1   Powys, L, *Dorset essays* (1935), 106-8.

the heels of another, like baboons along an escarpment-ledge. As we came through the farmyard at West Chaldon, we paused to watch a labourer in the long, thatched stable giving fodder to his horses. The look of that warm interior, on this last day of the year, hay-smelling, harness-smelling, horse-smelling, put us in mind of the simple lives of these people, and of how the seasons pass over their heads in swift succession, from sowing-time even unto ploughing-time, and how they take it all as calmly and naturally as the old draught mare we could even now see, with outstretched neck and thick prehensile lip, nuzzling at the hay in the rack above its head.

Once on the downs, all was clear and translucent. Fold upon fold of these ancient hills lay before us in all their midnight beauty. We would come to a gate, with the rime gleaming upon its top bar, open it, and pass on to an upland, even more remote, more secluded. We passed the grey wall, near where, in the early autumn, we had one day filled our handkerchiefs with button-mushrooms, cold mushrooms so sweet that even in their raw state it was pleasant to nibble at them. We passed the holly-hedge from which we had gathered red berries to decorate our room for Christmas, the very places where we had broken off branches clearly visible in the starlight.

At last we were there. Theodore entered the ring first, the shadow of his bowed figure – he had taken his old cloak about him – appearing, as it fell across the deep-sunken stones, like the shadow of some Biblical prophet, like the shadow of the prophet Amos ! And with what curious, prophetic eyes he squinnied up at the sky during those still, frosty moments!

We were silent. There we stood, in the enchanted circle, like two fools, like two conjured haggards, looking out beyond the great square, of Pegasus, beyond the Milky Way, to the furthest, uncharted tracts of a material Universe without beginning and without end.[1]

---

1 Powys, L, *Skin for skin* (1925), 128-30.

Alfred Williams, folklore collector and reporter of the Wiltshire countryside, was also a poet – of uneven quality, it has to be admitted. These two sonnets, written on New Year's Eve 1910, are among his best.

The Passing of the Year
Alfred Williams

THE AIR HANGS dull and heavy; not a breath
    Stirs in the poplar pointing bare and high,
    No scarce-heard sound or whisper, not a sigh
Escapes, and silent is the world beneath;
Calm flows the river; in many a twining wreath
    Down from the elmtree pillar standing by
    The verdant ivy droops; leaden the sky;
All nature's buried in the gloom of death.
'Tis the year's parting sorrow, for he grieves
    And suffers inner anguish, like to one
    Viewing Time's happiness for ever gone.
But lo! as the old dweller darkly leaves,
A new inheritor the rule receives,
    And other joys come rushing endless on.

'Tis but a step to midnight; one stroke more,
    One fleeting space for sorrows and farewells,
    One last look backward where high Memory dwells,
Then in the untrodden path that lies before
We must push onward, ever to that shore
    Toward which our utmost fate draws and compels.
    Hark! from the starlit tower the merry bells
Peal as they've pealed a thousand times of yore.
All this is banished, whether good or ill;
    Our joys and sufferings, our toils and pains

Diminish, our life's star waxes and wanes.
Ere the dark wave close o'er us, deep and still,
Let us go forth, fearless in mind and will,
 And grapple with the future that remains.[1]

Thomas Hardy must have the last word. Without him, perhaps, Wessex would not have an identity, and the literature of Christmas would be greatly impoverished. The Christmases he conjured up were not always merry, and Hardy himself was more Scrooge than Santa. But the great tragedian had learnt that the buffetings of ordinary life reveal themselves with greater intensity – greater poignancy – when silhouetted against a background of joyful celebration. Burning the holly on Twelfth Night signifies the close of the Christmas season, the destruction of the pagan emblems; it also, in Hardy's hypnotic poem, bids farewell to the Christian emblems, the madonna and child.

Burning the Holly
Thomas Hardy

 YOU ARE SAD on Twelfth Night,
I notice: sad on Twelfth Night;
You are as sad on Twelfth Night
 As any that I know.

'Yes: I am sad on that night,
Doubtless I'm sad on that night:
Yes; I am sad on that night,
 For we all loved her so!'

1 Williams, A, *Poems in Wiltshire* (1911), 72-3.

Why are you sad on Twelfth Night,
Especially on Twelfth Night?
Why are you sad on Twelfth Night
     When wit and laughter flow?

– 'She'd been a famous dancer,
Much lured of men; a dancer.
She'd been a famous dancer,
     Facile in heel and toe. . .

'And we were burning the holly
On Twelfth Night; the holly,
As people do: the holly,
     Ivy, and mistletoe.

'And while it popped and crackled,
(She being our lodger), crackled;
And while it popped and crackled,
     Her face caught by the glow,

'In he walked and said to her,
In a slow voice he said to her;
Yes, walking in he said to her,
     "We sail before cock-crow."

'"Why did you not come on to me,
As promised? Yes, come on to me?
Why did you not come on to me,
     Since you had sworn to go?"

'His eyes were deep and flashing,
As flashed the holm-flames: flashing;

His eyes were deep, and flashing
    In their quick, keen upthrow.

'As if she had been ready,
Had furtively been ready;
As if she had been ready
    For his insistence – lo! –

'She clasped his arm and went with him
As his entirely: went with him.
She clasped his arm and went with him
    Into the sprinkling snow.

'We saw the prickly leaves waste
To ashes: saw the leaves waste;
The burnt-up prickly leaves waste. . .
    The pair had gone also.

–'On Twelfth Night, two years after –
Yes, Twelfth Night, two years after;
On Twelfth Night, two years after,
    We sat – our spirits low –

'Musing, when back the door swung
Without a knock. The door swung;
Thought flew to her. The door swung,
    And in she came, pale, slow;

'Against her breast a child clasped;
Close to her breast a child clasped;
She stood there with the child clasped,
    Swaying it to and fro.

'Her look alone the tale told;
Quite wordless was the tale told;
Her careworn eyes the tale told
　　　As larger they seemed to grow. . .

'One day next spring she disappeared,
The second time she disappeared.
And that time, when she'd disappeared
　　　Came back no more. Ah, no!

'But we still burn the holly
On Twelfth Night; burn the holly
As people do: the holly,
　　　Ivy, and mistletoe.'[1]

1　Hardy, T, *Complete poems* (1979 ed.), no. 878.

Index

Most people and places referred to in this book are included. Places are in the pre-1974 counties of Dorset, Somerset or Wiltshire unless otherwise stated. Subjects have been selectively indexed.

Map of Wessex